BANKING

WITHOUT

BORDERS

CHALLENGES AND OPPORTUNITIES IN THE ERA OF NORTH AMERICAN FREE TRADE AND THE EMERGING GLOBAL MARKETPLACE

HAZEL J. JOHNSON

A BankLine Publication

PROBUS
PUBLISHING

Chicago, Illinois
Cambridge, England

A BankLine Publication

ISBN 1-55738-731-1

Printed in the United States of America

BB

1 2 3 4 5 6 7 8 9 0

ETL

In Loving Memory of
Ida W. Kelly and Lucille V. Johnson

Contents

Contents

Preface

In the realm of U.S. political and economic policy, few issues have been as hotly debated as the North American Free Trade Agreement, a tri-lateral treaty between the United States, Canada, and Mexico that is intended to remove both tariff and nontariff trade barriers. Before it became effective in January 1994, the debates about NAFTA focused on the potential loss of U.S. manufacturing jobs, the likelihood of increasing U.S. exports to Mexico, control of U.S. national borders, and troubling environmental protection issues. Yet one of the most significant implications of the treaty was hardly ever mentioned in the public forum. The agreement between the three countries has fundamentally changed banking and financial services industries in North America. For the first time, banks from one country have the right to freely provide cross-border financial services in the other two countries, including the establishment of wholly owned, full-service subsidiaries.

The most attractive new opportunities are associated with the Mexican financial system. Financial institutions from the United States and Canada may invest in Mexican commercial banks, securities firms, insurance companies, leasing companies, factoring firms, and limited-scope finance companies. The degree of operational flexibility conferred by NAFTA goes far beyond the powers that U.S. banks enjoy on their own turf. This book explains these new opportunities, the relative advantages of each, the banks and other financial firms that are positioning themselves to capitalize on the opportunities, and the challenges that must be overcome.

Chapter 1, The Banking Industry and NAFTA

This chapter outlines the provisions of NAFTA that relate to financial services. In addition to permitting U.S. and Canadian banks a wide range of new powers in Mexico, the treaty also provides formal, dispute resolution mechanisms. Specific provisions of NAFTA address:

- Establishment of Financial Institutions
- Cross-Border Trade
- National Treatment
- Most-Favored-Nation Treatment
- New Financial Services and Data Processing
- Senior Management and Boards of Directors
- Transparency
- Financial Services Committee
- Dispute Settlement
- Investment Transfers
- Expropriation and Compensation
- Arbitration for Transfers and Expropriation

While NAFTA represents significant new opportunities in Mexico, most of the U.S./Canadian provisions were already in effect through the Canada-United States Free Trade Agreement of 1989.

Chapter 2, Banking Transactions without Borders

There are several important aspects of banking in a multinational, regional environment. Foreign exchange transactions in North America involve three distinctly different currencies. Changes in the value of the Canadian dollar have historically been closely linked to those of the U.S. dollar, but are now diverging because of differential monetary policies in the two countries. The Mexican peso suffered massive devaluation during the 1980s, but has been bolstered by restructuring of the country's external debt, internal fiscal and monetary reforms, and a three-way $8.7 billion currency swap facility between the United States, Canada, and Mexico.

The role of electronic networks in North America will be critical. The advanced check clearing systems of the United States and Canada must be roughly duplicated in Mexico to accommodate the increase in cross-border transactions that is likely to occur within five years of NAFTA's passage. The three Mexican clearinghouses in Mexico City, Guadalajara, and Monterrey will not be sufficient to handle this volume. Another important application of electronic networks is the facilitation of trade finance. Already, electronic systems between banks and their clients permit:

- Generation and communication of documentation

- Payment transfers

- Finalization of the bookkeeping process

Ultimately, it will be possible to use such systems to:

- Make application for trade finance

- Transfer documentation electronically

- Generate letters of credit electronically

Banks that are already offering such services are Barclays in the United Kingdom, HongKong and Shanghai Banking Corporation in the United Kingdom and in Hong Kong, and Citibank in the United States. In the North American Free Trade zone, advancements in currency trading and trade finance will cause the national boundaries of the United States, Canada, and Mexico to become less meaningful.

A number of U.S. banks are making aggressive expansions plans into the Mexican market.

- Citibank has been permitted to operate in Mexico since 1929 and is the only foreign bank with this privilege. It has seven branches in Mexico and employs 800 people.

- Chase Manhattan is planning to attract banking clientele from the corporate sector through a Mexican subsidiary, concentrating on corporate banking, securities, and currency trading.

- The subsidiary of Chemical Banking will operate with twice the staff in Monterrey that it has historically maintained. The emphasis will be on corporate banking, securities, and project finance.

- Bankers Trust plans to operate a securities firm, forgoing a banking license, and will focus on (1) securities underwriting and trading and (2) derivatives.

- J.P. Morgan plans to form a subsidiary that will concentrate on corporate banking, securities, and investment management.

- Republic New York Corp. will be engaged primarily in corporate banking and trading.

In an era in which the growth potential for U.S. commercial banks is considered to be limited by regulatory restrictions and heightened competition, banking in the North American Free Trade zone is one of the few frontiers left for the expansion of market share.

Chapter 3. The Canadian and Mexican Banking Systems

The banking systems of Canada and Mexico are distinctly different in their development and, as a result, have different strengths and weaknesses. For example, Canadian banks have been permitted to own securities subsidiaries for a number of years. Today, the six largest Canadian banks account for 51% of all revenues by securities brokers. In general, the highly concentrated Canadian banking system has always had an outward focus. The country's largest bank, the Royal Bank of Canada (RBC) hopes to capitalize on its high-technology base and its nationwide banking presence in Canada to exploit the opportunities available under the North American Free Trade Agreement. Its stated objective is to acquire a small bank in the United States and then to build on that base as the barriers to U.S. interstate banking are reduced. Royal Bank is a major trader of foreign currency in the United States, one of the largest among the foreign institutions operating in the United States.

In Mexico, the challenge is to build a competitive technology base. Banamex, Mexico's largest bank, has an alliance with the U.S. telecommunications firm MCI. The bank currently processes 1.5 million transactions per day. To the extent that these transactions can be performed via telephone and ATM terminals, Banamex will be able to reduce its unit costs and access more customers. It appears that Banamex is not concerned about the relatively low average income of Mexican citizens. The bank's logic is that producing bank services through the use of high technology will enable it to be profitable. High-tech applications make it possible to produce these services at a fraction of the costs associated with a more conventional brick-and-mortar facility.

In both the Canadian and Mexican banking systems, there are changes occurring that represent opportunities for U.S. banks. In the case of Canada, the market is more mature and the competition is perhaps more intense. In the case of Mexico, there are a number of areas in which inroads can be made by U.S. and Canadian banks. These include high-technology applications, consumer finance, corporate lending, and money management.

Chapter 4, Financial Market Opportunities under NAFTA

Market reforms in Mexico have attracted the attention of investors seeking higher returns than those which are available through fixed-income securities in the United States and Europe. In January 1992, the Mexican Bolsa Index was in the range of 1400. By June 1992, the Index had risen to more than 1900—an annual compound rate of increase of 84.2%. However, the Mexican Bolsa is extremely volatile. By October 1992, the Index had declined to the range of 1300. By mid-1993, it had rallied to approximately 1800 and continued to climb. During the three-month period from November 1993 to February 1994, the Mexican Stock Market Index increased by 36% for an annual compound rate of return of 242%! Then after interest rate hikes in the United States and political uncertainty at home the stock market slid once again losing 15% of its value over a short period of time.

For well-positioned securities firms that are able to manage this volatility, Mexico is an emerging stock market with many opportunities for profit as the largest Mexican firms reach world-class status. Currently, there are 30 firms whose stock is traded on a regular basis and six of these constitute three-fifths of Mexico's entire stock market capitalization. One issue alone, Telephonos de México (Telmex) represents fully 30% of Mexico's stock market capitalization. The high degree of concentration among a few stocks in the Mexican market contributes to the market's volatility.

High inflation in Mexico has hampered the development of a corporate bond sector. However, the government securities market is extremely active. For example, in 1992, while turnover in corporate debt was the equivalent of $29 billion, government securities turnover was $3.4 trillion. As Mexico's inflation continues to moderate, the corporate market will also grow, representing an excellent opportunity for banks and other financial firms in the North American Free Trade zone.

The situation will improve as Mexican borrowers enter into the international debt markets. The well-known Mexican issuers will continue to approach the international bond markets, including Banco Nacional de Comercio Exterior (Bancomext) and Nacional Financiera (Nafin). Bancomext is Mexico's state-owned foreign trade and project finance bank. In 1993, the bank issued debt in the Yankee (U.S.) and Matador (Spanish) bond markets. Nafin is Mexico's national development bank, providing financial and technical assistance to small- and medium-sized Mexican private-sector companies. Global bonds for such issuers are often structured as medium-term notes, Euro-peso, peso-linked, Euroyen, or Yankee bonds. There are also expected to be new entrants into the international debt markets such that up to $10 billion in debt may be issued by Mexican banks and industrial firms in 1994 alone.

Chapter 5, *Other Financial Services in Mexico*

Before NAFTA, no Mexican citizen or business could purchase insurance that was not written by a Mexican insurance company and no foreign investor could own a majority stake in a Mexican insurance company. Under NAFTA, insurance companies can be established in Mexico under one of three scenarios—a wholly owned subsidiary, a joint venture, or increasing an already existing minority ownership interest.

When the nature of the Mexican insurance industry is examined, the opportunities in this market are obvious:

- Approximately 1.5 million Mexicans have personal life insurance which represents only 1.8% of the population of 85 million people.

- Since there is no compulsory liability insurance, only 24% of Mexican automobiles are insured.

- Most Mexican doctors and lawyers do not insure their practices.

- Only 2% of Mexican homes are insured.

- When an earthquake destroyed much of Mexico City in 1985, only 15% of the buildings were insured.

- Per capita expenditure on insurance premiums in Mexico is $31 as compared to $1,929 in the United States.

- Total insurance premiums collected in Mexico in 1992 amounted to approximately $5 billion or 1.7% of GNP. The corresponding statistics for the United States were $508 billion or 8.6% of GNP.

Fund management is also a promising field in Mexico. One of the oldest funds in Mexico is the closed-end Mexico Fund, managed by José Luis Gómez Pimienta. Gómez Pimienta, then an investment banker with Bancomer, began the Mexico Fund in 1981. Only the second single-country fund to be registered in the United States, the fund shrank almost immediately from $112 million to $28 million when the Mexican debt crisis erupted in 1982 and the peso lost 85% of its value. Since the restructuring of the Mexican economy, the peso's value has more than recovered. In the five years ended 1993, the Mexico Fund has increased an average of 49% per year.

With a historical lack of finance for the corporate middle-market, factoring, leasing, and finance companies can find strong demand for their financial services in Mexico. Furthermore, the foreign ownership of these firms is even less restricted than the ownership of banks, securities firms, and insurance companies. Because of the relatively liberal constraints, these industries represent a viable route to enter Mexican financial markets with few encumbrances.

Chapter 6, The Impact of NAFTA on Industry and Finance

The opportunities for banks, securities firms, and other financial institutions in Mexico will be directly proportional to the extent of economic growth. There are several specific industries that promise significant advancement in the future and, thus, present an opportunity to provide financial services to the business community and to the individuals that work in these industries.

- The *automotive* industry is evolving from an assembly operation near the U.S./Mexican border and in Mexico City to one that is more dispersed throughout the country. It is a key element in the economic development of Mexico and government policy is geared to the establishment of a complete automotive infrastructure.

- The *oil and gas* industry continues to be dominated by Pemex, the state-owned monopoly. However, Pemex is concentrating on profits, productivity, and its core businesses. In addition, the giant oil concern is actively seeking more private sector involvement in the areas of petrochemicals, oil drilling, and ancillary services.

- Successful participants in the *consumer goods* and *retailing* areas require an understanding of the Mexican market with respect to income levels, distribution channels, and major competitors.

- *Telecommunications* will be a strong growth industry in Mexico because of the extent to which systems must be brought up-to-date. The state-owned Telmex has been privatized with the new owners promising to modernize the telephone service, including basic telephone service to all towns with 5,000 or more residents, long-distance service to all towns with 500,000 or more inhabitants, and better repair service. In addition, the cellular telephone market and the market for data communications will expand dramatically.

- The *computer* industry has already exploded and promises to continue making dramatic strides. From 1982 to 1989, minicomputer sales grew at an average rate of 9.3% per year, main frame computers at the rate of 92.9%, and microcomputers at 183.5%! Even though Mexico is the 13th largest economy in the world, it has become the 6th largest personal computer market.

- *Agriculture* is an industry that has been protected from private-sector influence almost to the same extent as the oil and gas industry. Barriers to private investment are being dismantled and gradually the private-sector investment is occurring.

Commercial banks, securities firms, and other providers of financial services must understand the businesses in which their clients are engaged. This is particularly true with respect to international operations. Rapid change is occurring in these industries—all of which offer an opportunity for market expansion to the knowledgeable financier.

Chapter 7, Beyond NAFTA

All too often, the attention of the business world is directed toward Europe and Asia because of historical trading patterns (in the first case) and high rates of economic growth (in the latter case). While, clearly, there are opportunities in both these arenas, the potential for business development in Latin America should not be overlooked. Latin American countries are embracing market reforms at an unprecedented pace and it is likely that this trend will continue.

Chile has led the way in market reforms, moving so fast that the country has chosen thus far not to participate in bilateral and regional agreements in Latin America. The economy of Chile is the most admired in the region and is studied by developing countries throughout the world. The reluctance of Chile to join Latin American trade arrangements appears to be a strategic choice that reflects its long-term objectives of being integrated with the largest economies of the world. Chile has expressed interest in being included in both APEC (Asia-Pacific Economic Cooperation Group) and NAFTA. It appears that it is only a matter of time before such membership is effected.

Other Latin American countries have seen this evolution in Chile and are following suit with similar reforms. Here too, apparent objectives are not difficult to identify. Mexico now has a free trade agreement with the United States (NAFTA), an ongoing trade relationship with nine other Latin American countries (LAIA, Latin American Integration Association), a commitment to pursue free trade with Venezuela and Colombia (Group of Three), and numerous bilateral trade agreements in Latin America. Other countries in the region are linked through one or more such arrangements. In the fall of 1993, Brazil (Latin America's largest economy) proposed a South American Free Trade Agreement, linking all countries in the region in a free-trade pact. In June 1994, the powerful Mercosur (Argentina, Brazil, Paraguay, and Uruguay) gave its official backing to the concept. Market reforms in Latin America and the Caribbean will ultimately yield the same kind of results that have been seen in Chile. As industrial capacity is strengthened, trade increases, and incomes rise, the financial services industry will expand.

Banking without Borders can help bank managers to assess the new financial services environment that has been created by NAFTA. There are numerous new opportunities to be involved in a growing international market. Whether the involvement is commercial lending to middle-market firms, facilitating cross-border payments, arranging trade finance, money management, securities underwriting, securities trading, derivatives, insurance, factoring, leasing, or project finance, there is unmet need in the Mexican market. Furthermore, the economic ties between Mexico and other countries in Latin America, can provide inroads into other lucrative markets. In essence, a banking presence in the expanding Mexican market can pay ultimate dividends that extend far beyond the North American Free Trade zone.

Hazel J. Johnson, Ph.D., C.P.A.

Acknowledgments

The author would like to sincerely thank those who have been instrumental in the completion of this book, especially Sivakumar Subrahmanyan for his tireless research efforts, Laura Ahrens for her invaluable technical support, and Baldomero Garcia for his research assistance in the initial phases of the project.

The author would also like to acknowledge the following individuals for their astute, professional insights concerning the North American Free Trade Agreement and its future ramifications.

Mr. Ross Anderson, Senior Analyst
 Canadian Bankers Association

Dr. Boris Kozolchyk, Director
 National Law Center for Inter-American Trade
 University of Arizona, Tucson

Mr. Jorge Mariscal, Vice President and Manager
 Latin American Equity Research Group
 Goldman Sachs & Co.

Dr. Rima-Burns McGown, Economist
 Financial Sector Division
 Department of Finance
 Canada

Mr. Barry Newman
 Deputy Assistant Secretary
   for International Monetary and Financial Policy
 U.S. Treasury Department

Lic. Tomas Ruiz Gonzalez
 Director General of Commercial Banking
 Hacienda y Crédito Público
 Mexico

1 The Banking Industry and NAFTA

INTRODUCTION

The North American Free Trade Agreement (NAFTA) is a tri-
lateral treaty between the United States, Canada, and Mexico
that is intended to remove both tariff and nontariff trade barriers among the three countries. In this sense, it is similar to the
European Union which creates a monetary and economic block
of twelve European countries.[1] In fact, NAFTA is the continua-
tion of a world-wide trend of regional trade agreements in Europe, Latin America, and Asia. One of the most important
aspects of NAFTA is the implication that it has for the banking
industry and other financial services. For the first time, U.S. and
Canadian banks will be permitted to conduct a full range of financial services in Mexico. Also, for the first time, there is a formal mechanism for resolving disputes under the treaty. The
combination of increased flexibility to offer financial services
and the underserved Mexican market present U.S. and Canadian banks with unprecedented opportunities for both market
expansion and profit.

NAFTA permits financial institutions of the United States and Canada to operate wholly owned subsidiaries in the fields of commercial banking, securities, insurance, leasing, factoring, and limited-scope finance companies in Mexico. In contrast, NAFTA brings fewer benefits to U.S. financial institutions operating in Canada or for Canadian institutions operating in the United States. Most of the U.S./Canadian agreements in NAFTA are contained in the previously enacted Canada/ United States Free Trade Agreement of 1989. Thus, the strongest impact of NAFTA on the financial services industry is the historic opening of the financial system of Mexico.

FINANCIAL SERVICES UNDER NAFTA

Under NAFTA, the financial services that are provided within the United States, Canada, and Mexico (the three Parties) must conform to certain standards of treatment and disclosure. Generally speaking, establishment of financial institutions within the territory of one Party by investors that reside in the territory of another Party is permitted within certain guidelines, subject to review by the three Parties. Disputes are to be settled according to predetermined procedure and any expropriation of investments must be fairly compensated.

Establishment of Financial Institutions

Exhibit 1-1 outlines the NAFTA provisions for establishment of financial institutions. Each Party must be permitted to engage in a wide range of financial services. In fact, the section that refers to establishment of financial institutions states that a financial institution must be permitted to expand geographically and not be held accountable to the normal ownership requirements for foreign financial institutions. Each Party may prohibit *direct branching* into its territory, but a financial institution that resides in the territory of one Party must be permitted to estab-

EXHIBIT 1-1
ESTABLISHMENT OF FINANCIAL INSTITUTIONS

Each Party must permit investors of another Party (engaged in the business of providing financial services) to:

- Engage in a range of financial services through separate financial institutions.
- Expand geographically.
- Be exempt from ownership requirements specific to foreign financial institutions.

Each Party may:

- Require the investors of another Party to incorporate any financial institution under the Party's law.
- Impose terms and conditions consistent with the principles of national treatment.

---

lish a presence in the territory of the other two Parties via a subsidiary.

Direct branching into Mexico and Canada is prohibited because U.S. federal law does not permit nationwide branching. However, there is a specific provision that, at such time as the United States does permit commercial banks of another Party to expand either through subsidiaries or direct branches throughout the United States, then both Mexico and Canada will review this policy and perhaps relax this particular aspect of the agreement. This part of the agreement is seen as an incentive for the United States to review its own policies with respect to nationwide branching.

Each Party (that acts as a host country for the financial institution of another Party) may require the investors of the other Party to incorporate under the host country law. The host country also has the right to impose on foreign institutions the same sorts of restrictions and regulations that it imposes on indigenous institutions.

Cross-Border Trade

The United States, Canada and Mexico have agreed formally not to restrict cross-border trade in the provision of financial services. The history of this provision is linked primarily to the nationalization of Mexican Banks in 1982, the beginning of the so-called Latin American debt crisis. At the same time that banks were nationalized, Mexican citizens were prohibited from buying financial services from financial institutions in other countries. This was done in effect to stem the flight of investment capital from Mexico. NAFTA specifically states that it will no longer be permissible for one of the three Parties to impose such restrictions.

Explicitly, no Party may adopt any measure that would restrict the free flow of financial services. Each Party must allow its own citizens to purchase financial services from cross-border financial service providers that reside either in the territory of the Party or in the territory of any other Party to the agreement. Under this provision, a U.S. financial services provider may now sell financial services to Mexican citizens whether it has an operation in Mexico, United States, or Canada. As is true in many other facets of the agreement, each Party may require a cross-border provider of financial services to register with the respective Party in the normal course of business.

EXHIBIT 1-2
CROSS-BORDER TRADE

- *No* Party may adopt any measure restricting cross-border trade in financial services by cross-border financial services providers of another Party.
- *Each* Party *shall* permit its nationals to purchase financial services from cross-border financial service providers of another Party in the territory of that Party or of another Party.
- *Each* Party *may* require registration of cross-border financial service providers of another Party and of financial instruments.

National Treatment

Language that became critical in negotiations of the European Union with respect to financial services now appears in NAFTA. (See Exhibit 1-3.) The concept of national treatment has been incorporated as one of the cornerstones of the agreement. National treatment means that each Party must accord treatment that is no less favorable than that it accords its own financial service institutions, investments, or investors. The objective is to ensure that no excessively burdensome regulations are placed on financial institutions of one Party when they establish a presence in another Party. The standard is applied to all facets of operation including establishment, acquisition, expansion, management, conduct, operation and sale, or other disposition of financial institutions and investments. This is a binding obligation of each Party whether the institution is operating

---

EXHIBIT 1-3
NATIONAL TREATMENT

Each Party shall:

- Accord treatment to investors and financial institutions of another Party that is *no less favorable* than that it accords to its own similar investors and financial institutions with respect to the establishment, acquisition, expansion, management, conduct of operations, and sale or other disposition of financial institutions and investments in financial institutions in its territory.
- Accord treatment to cross-border financial service providers of another Party *no less favorable* than that it accords to its own financial service providers.
- *Not* permit measures of a state or province to violate national treatment principles.

National treatment:

- Implies equal competitive opportunities.
- Has *not* necessarily been violated because of differences in market share, profitability, or size.

---

within the national boundaries of the Party or whether the institution is providing cross-border financial services. In addition, each federal government is obligated to ensure that no state or province imposes regulations that would violate the national treatment standard.

It should be noted that national treatment requires treatment that is no less favorable than that of indigenous institutions. However, in no way does this imply a competitive advantage to the foreign institution. Instead, the foreign institution will not be subjected to competitive disadvantage. Furthermore, nothing in the national treatment obligations requires specific outcomes. In other words, there are no guarantees with respect to size or profitability or any other outcomes of doing business. National treatment provides the opportunity, not the guarantee, of access to the markets of other Parties.

Most-Favored-Nation Treatment

Exhibit 1-4 outlines the basic premise in Most-Favored-Nation (MFN) treatment. The wording of this provision is somewhat similar to that of the national treatment provision. The difference is that the treatment is compared to that which is accorded to other nations. Under MFN, each Party must provide the financial institutions of another Party, investments by investors in financial institutions, and cross-border financial service providers of another Party, treatment that is no less favorable

---

EXHIBIT 1-4
MOST-FAVORED-NATION TREATMENT

- Each Party shall accord treatment to investors of another Party, investments of investors in financial institutions, and cross-border financial services providers of another Party that is *no less favorable* than that it accords to such investors, investments, and service providers of any other Party or of a non-Party.
- A Party may recognize prudential measures of another Party or of a non-Party.

---

than it provides to the institutions of another Party or another non-Party.

Simply stated, each Party must treat the institutions of another Party no less favorably than it treats a third Party or a non-Party. For example, Canada is not permitted under this provision to treat U.S. banks any less favorably than it treats Mexican, European, Asian, or other banks. This is conventional trade agreement language that has been brought forward into the financial services arena. There is also a provision under this area that allows a Party to recognize the regulatory structure to which another Party may be subject.

New Financial Services and Data Processing

Under New Financial Services and Data Processing (Exhibit 1-5), one Party may not prohibit the financial institution of another Party from fully participating in any sort of deregulation or expansion of powers that occurs. Each Party must allow the financial institutions of another Party to provide the same new products that are permitted to be offered by indigenous financial institutions. For example, if the United States permits commercial banks to offer a new type of product, Mexican and Canadian banks will be permitted to offer the same product. This provision essentially ensures that deregulation in each

---

EXHIBIT 1-5

NEW FINANCIAL SERVICES AND DATA PROCESSING

Each Party shall:

- Permit a financial institution of another Party to provide new financial services similar to those that the Party permits its own financial institutions to provide under its domestic law.
- Permit a financial institution of another Party to transfer information in electronic or other form, into and out of the Party's territory, for data processing where such processing is required for the ordinary course of business of such institution.

---

country will be accompanied by an upgrading in the competitive opportunities of the financial institutions of the other two Parties.

In addition, each Party must permit the transmission of necessary information cross-border so that the normal types of marketing, sales, and other record-keeping information can be maintained. The transmission of such data can have significant ramifications, particularly as financial service products themselves become increasingly oriented toward technology applications. It also means that certain economies of scale can be realized in setting up a marketing operation in one country, with all the record-keeping and back-office operations in another country. For example, it may be possible to establish a credit card operation that would be located in the United States with a primary customer base either in Canada or Mexico.

Senior Management and Boards of Directors

In many cases, restrictions in international trade are imposed with respect to the key personnel of a company or a financial institution. For example, in the United States the board of directors of an Edge Act bank (a nationally chartered bank that conducts international business) must be composed of U.S. citizens. Under NAFTA, such restrictions either do not exist or have been substantially reduced. No Party may insist that the senior management of a financial institution be of any particu-

---

EXHIBIT 1-6

SENIOR MANAGEMENT AND BOARDS OF DIRECTORS

No Party may:

- Require that senior management or other essential personnel of financial institutions of another Party be of any particular nationality.
- Require that more than a simple majority of the board of directors of a financial institution of another Party be composed of nationals of the Party, persons residing in the territory of the Party, or a combination thereof.

---

lar nationality. For example, a U.S. bank may open a subsidiary in Mexico and hire senior managers of any nationality, as it deems appropriate. Notice that this provision is not limited to senior managers from the three countries that are signatories to NAFTA, i.e., any nationality is possible. Clearly, this provides total flexibility in assembling a team of qualified professionals.

Similarly, under NAFTA a Party may not require that more than a simple majority of the board of directors be composed of nationals of the Party or persons residing in the territory of the Party. For example, the board of directors for a subsidiary in Canada can include members that do not reside in Canada. This makes it possible for Mexican or U.S. citizens to be members of the board of a Canadian financial service subsidiary.

Transparency

The concept of transparency means that decision-making process concerning permission to operate in the territory of a Party will not be cloaked in secrecy. There will be an adequate appeals process, as necessary. The general guidelines for transparency are set out in Exhibit 1-7. Before any Party may introduce a regulatory measure that will affect the operation of financial institutions, the Party *must* advise the other Parties in advance to permit them to comment on the proposed change. The requirement is that interested parties should be notified. However, this notification can be accomplished through either official publication, other written form, or any other form.

Also, with respect to application for permission to establish a financial institution or to provide financial services, each Party must make available to all interested persons the requirements of the regulatory authorities in this connection. Once an application has been completed, it is the responsibility of the regulators of each Party to make a decision about that application within 120 days. If a decision cannot be reached in 120 days, the applicant must be promptly notified of the reason for the delay and the regulators of the Party must attempt to reach

EXHIBIT 1-7
TRANSPARENCY

Each Party shall:

- Provide in advance to all interested parties any measure of general application that the Party proposes to adopt in order to allow an opportunity for
  such persons to comment on the measure, with notification through official
  publication, other written form, or other form.
- Make available to interested persons the requirements of its regulatory authorities with respect to completing applications relating to the provision of
  financial services.

The regulatory authorities of each Party shall:

- Inform the applicant of the status and any required additional information
  with respect to its application.
- Make an administrative decision on a completed application of a financial institution, an investor in a financial institution, or a cross-border financial service provider of another Party within 120 days and promptly notify applicant.
  (If it is not practicable for a decision to be reached in 120 days, the regulatory authorities shall notify the applicant without undue delay and endeavor
  to make the decision within a reasonable time thereafter.)

---

a decision as quickly as possible. In the interim, the regulatory
authorities of the Party are obligated, upon request, to inform
the applicant of the status of the application. The general principle of transparency is intended to ease the process of entry into
the financial services industry in each NAFTA country. It stan-
dardizes the circumstances, feedback, and time frame that a financial institution should expect when applying for permission
to operate in either of the three countries.

It should be noted that the general principle of transparency
does not require a Party to provide access to any information
that is related to the financial affairs and accounts of individual
customers, financial institutions, or cross-border financial service providers. Nor does the transparency principle require that

a Party provide any confidential information, the disclosure of which would impede law enforcement, be contrary to the public interest, or prejudice any legitimate commercial interest of particular enterprises. Essentially, the transparency clause is ensures a reasonable procedural framework that does not violate what might be considered in the United States the constitutional right of privacy.

Financial Services Committee

One of the most important general principles of the North American Free Trade Agreement is a formal procedure for settlement of disputes. With respect to the establishment of financial services, cross-border trade, national treatment, MFN treatment, permission to participate in new financial services, data processing, and the other issues discussed thus far, there is a mechanism for dispute review and resolution.

The group with primary responsibility in the area of financial services is the *Financial Services Committee* (FSC). Exhibit 1-8 outlines the responsibilities and composition of the FSC. The first responsibility of the Financial Services Committee is to supervise the implementation of the rules for financial services

---

EXHIBIT 1-8
FINANCIAL SERVICES COMMITTEE

The Financial Services Committee shall:

- Supervise the implementation of rules for financial services under NAFTA.
- Consider issues relating to financial services that are referred to it by a Party.
- Participate in dispute settlement procedures.
- Meet annually to assess the functioning of NAFTA with respect to financial services.
- Be composed of officials of the Department of Finance of Canada (Canada), the Secretaría de Hacienda y Crédito Público (Mexico), the Department of the Treasury (U.S. banking), and the Department of Commerce (U.S. insurance).

---

under NAFTA. In this sense, the FSC is responsible for ensuring enactment of any necessary regulations or agreements in order to implement the general principles.

Also, should one Party voice a concern and raise an issue with regard to the financial services, it should address the concern to the Committee. If a certain aspect of financial services has not been directly addressed in NAFTA or needs clarification, the FSC shall respond to the related inquiries. It is the responsibility of the committee to participate in disputes that relate to financial services. In the event that a dispute is not an interpretation of NAFTA provisions but, instead, involves a claim related to an actual investment, the committee is required to reach a decision with respect to the legitimacy of that claim.

Investment on the part of an investor (lodging a claim in the dispute process) has a number of meanings within the context of NAFTA. Among them are:

- An enterprise.

- An equity security of an enterprise.

- A debt security of an enterprise:

    (a) where the enterprise is an affiliate of the investor or

    (b) where the original maturity date of the debt security is at least three years, but

    (c) does not include a debt security (regardless of original maturity) of a state enterprise.

- A loan to an enterprise:

    (a) where the enterprise is an affiliate of the investor or

    (b) where the original maturity of the loan is at least three years, but

    (c) does not include a loan (regardless of original maturity) to a state enterprise.

- An interest in an enterprise that entitles the owner to share in income or profits of the enterprise.

- An interest in an enterprise that entitles the owner to share in the assets of that enterprise on dissolution other than a debt security of or a loan to (regardless of original maturity) a state enterprise.

- Real estate or other property, tangible or intangible, acquired in the expectation or used for the purpose of economic benefit or other business purposes.

- Interests arising from the commitment of capital or other resources in the territory of a Party to economic activity in such territory such as under:

  (a) contracts involving the presence of an investor's property in the territory of the property including turnkey or

  (b) construction contracts or concessions or contracts where remuneration depends substantially on production, revenues, or profits of an enterprise.

However, investment is *not defined* as:

- claims to money that arise solely from commercial contracts for the sale of goods or services or

- the extension of credit in connection with a commercial transaction, such as trade financing, or a loan other than the type specified above.[2]

Should a claim involve an investment as defined above, a Tribunal must be established (see the section below entitled "Arbitration for Transfers and Expropriation"). However, when the claims relate to the provision of financial services, the Tribunal must solicit and act upon the recommendation of the Financial Services Committee.

The FSC is composed of officials from the primary regulatory authorities for financial services in each of the respective countries. These are:

- Department of Finance of Canada

- Secretaría de Hacienda y Crédito Público

- United States Department of Treasury and United States Department of Commerce

The Treasury Department is the official representative of the United States with respect to any banking issues. The Commerce Department represents the United States with respect to insurance matters. It is the responsibility of the Financial Services Committee to meet on an annual basis to assess the function of NAFTA with respect to financial services.

Dispute Settlement

Exhibit 1-9 sets out the guidelines for dispute settlement. In the event that the Financial Services Committee fails to decide an issue that is brought before it within 60 days of the date of the receipt of the claim, the disputing Party may request the establishment of an Arbitral Panel. The Arbitral Panel will review the claim and submit its final report on the claim to the Financial Services Committee and the report of the Arbitral Panel will be binding on the Tribunal.

The Tribunal itself is made up of three arbiters. Each Party in NAFTA agrees to permit any disputes to be settled by the Tribunal. The three arbiters are selected in the following way:

- One by the claimant

- One by the Party against which the claim has been lodged

- One by agreement of the two disputing Parties

EXHIBIT 1-9
DISPUTE SETTLEMENT

A financial services arbitral panel shall:

- Be composed of up to 15 individuals with expertise in financial services law or practice.
- Be chosen strictly on the basis of objectivity, reliability, and sound judgment.
- Consider disputes arising in the provision in financial services.
- Determine whether a measure is inconsistent with the financial services provisions of NAFTA.
- Determine whether such inconsistent measure affects (1) only the financial services sector, (2) the financial services sector and another sector, or (3) only a sector other than the financial services sector.

The establishment of the Arbitral Panel is a secondary procedure in the event that the Financial Services Committee fails to reach a decision within 60 days of receipt of the referral from the Tribunal. The Arbitral Panel may be composed of up to 15 members. The three NAFTA Parties mutually agree upon the designation of these 15 members, who serve for terms of three years with the possibility of extension. Potential members of an Arbitral Panel must:

- Have expertise or experience in financial services law or practice, which may include the regulation of financial institutions.

- Be chosen strictly on the basis of objectivity, reliability, and sound judgment.

The Arbitral Panel has considerable power in that, once activated, its final report to the Financial Services Committee is binding on the Tribunal. There are three possible findings with respect to the report of the Tribunal and each finding will have different ramifications. If it is found that a measure is inconsistent with the obligations under NAFTA, the extent to which the inconsistency affects the financial services sector must be determined.

- If the measure affects the *financial services sector only*, then the Party that has brought the action (the claimant) may suspend benefits under NAFTA only in the financial services sector.

- If the inconsistency is found to affect the *financial services sector and any other sector*, the claimant may suspend benefits in the financial services sector that have an effect that is equivalent to the effect of the measure upon its own financial services sector. That is, disproportionate reactions are not permitted.

- If the measure is found to be inconsistent with NAFTA and affects a sector *other than financial services*, the complainant may not suspend benefits in the financial services sector.

For the first time, an agreement between the United States and other countries in the area of financial services sets out specific procedures in the event of a disagreement about the application of treaty provisions. Such features were not present in the financial services portion of the Canada-United States Free Trade Agreement (CUSFTA), which served as a model for the North American Free Trade Agreement.

Investment Transfers

NAFTA also addresses the ability of each of the three countries to allow its companies to transfer investment funds across borders. There is a particular provision provided in the chapter on investments that addresses this issue. Exhibit 1-10 outlines the specific provisions with respect to these investment transfers. Each Party must permit an investor to transfer freely and without delay cash flows that are related to the operation of a business (profits, dividends, interest, capital gains, etc.), sale or liquidation of an asset, loan transactions, and other payments.

The NAFTA agreement also forbids a Party to place restrictions on the destination of these transfers. For example, a trans-

EXHIBIT 1-10
INVESTMENT TRANSFERS

Each Party shall permit transfers related to an investment of an investor of another Party to be made freely and without delay, including:

- Profits, dividends, interest, capital gains, royalty payments, management fees, technical assistance and other fees.
- Proceeds from sale of all or part of the investment or from partial or complete liquidation.
- Payments made under contract entered into by the investor, including loan payments.
- Such transfer in a freely usable currency at the market rate of exchange prevailing on the date of transfer.

---

fer that is not made into another NAFTA country may not be penalized. Nor may one Party require that a facility or an investment that is transferred out of the host country be transferred into one of the other two Parties of NAFTA.

However, nothing in this section of the agreement prohibits a host country from preventing a transfer when it is related to other matters as long as the treatment is equitable and does not discriminate against a financial institution or an investor of one of the NAFTA countries. Examples of situations in which there may be laws affecting transfers of payments and investment are:

- Bankruptcy, insolvency, or protection of creditors' rights

- Issuing, trading, or dealing in securities.

- Criminal or penal offenses

- Reports of transfers of currencies or other monetary instruments

- Ensuring the satisfaction of judgements in judicial proceedings

Expropriation and Compensation

The rules of NAFTA extend to expropriation—the most extreme form of interference in a business operation in a foreign country. This provision is important from the standpoint of investors in Mexico. In 1982, the Mexican government nationalized its banks and, with the exception of Citibank, no foreign bank has since been permitted to operate anything other than a representative office. The section in Chapter 11 of NAFTA that refers to expropriation and compensation does not preclude nationalization. Instead, it states that any expropriation must be done in accordance with due process and must be compensated. Exhibit 1-11 explains the framework for expropriation. A Party within NAFTA may expropriate only for a public purpose, that is, only the government may expropriate. Any such takeover must be effected on a nondiscriminatory basis. This means that it must be done not only to one particular company in the industry or one particular group of companies in the industry but must be done on an industry-wide basis.

Compensation must be paid, following due process and international law with respect to fair and equitable treatment. NAFTA also addresses the issues of amount and form of compensation. Generally speaking, compensation must be in the amount of the fair market value of the expropriated investment immediately before expropriation took place.

Notably, the evaluation criteria that are used in establishing the amount of compensation must include the going-concern value, asset value including declared tax value of the tangible property, and other considerations necessary to determine fair market value. The compensation must be paid quickly and be fully realizable. In other words, it would be inconsistent with NAFTA if assets were seized and actual compensation were somehow deferred unreasonably.

Also, the previous owner of expropriated investment may not be forced to face unreasonable foreign exchange risks. If the currency in which compensation is paid devalues significantly between the time of determination of the fair market value and the actual payment of compensation, the previous owner of the investment must be compensated for this devaluation.

- If the payment is made in a *G-7 currency*, the payment must include interest at a commercially reasonable rate for that currency from the date of appropriation.[3] Since

---

EXHIBIT 1-11

EXPROPRIATION AND COMPENSATION

No party shall directly or indirectly nationalize or expropriate an investment of an investor of another Party in its territory or take a measure tantamount to nationalization or expropriation, except:

- For a public purpose.
- On a nondiscriminatory basis.
- In accordance with due process and international law with regards to fair and equitable treatment.
- On payment of compensation.

Compensation upon nationalization or expropriation shall:

- Be equivalent to the fair market value of expropriated investment immediately before expropriation took place.
- Not reflect any change in value occurring because the intended expropriation became known earlier.
- Be paid without delay and be fully realizable.
- If made in a G-7 currency, include interest at a commercially reasonable rate for that currency from date of expropriation until date of actual payment.[1]
- If made in a currency other than a G-7 currency, shall be no less than if the amount of compensation owed on the date of expropriation had been converted into a G-7 currency at the market rate prevailing on that date and interest had accrued at a commercially reasonable rate from date of expropriation until date of payment.
- Be freely transferable.

[1] G-7 is an acronym for the Group of Seven, the group of industrialized nations including the United States, Canada, Japan, Germany, France, Great Britain, and Italy.

the three countries in the NAFTA agreement are the United States, Canada, and Mexico, the two G-7 currencies that are most likely to be used are the U.S. dollar and the Canadian dollar.

- Should the payment be made in a *non-G-7 currency*, actual compensation may be no less than the equivalent amount of compensation that would have resulted if a G-7 currency had been used. This stipulation includes both the principal and interest involved.

Arbitration for Transfers and Expropriation

Exhibit 1-12 sets out the basic guidelines for arbitration in the case of either an investment transfer complaint or an expropriation issue. A claimant must wait at least six months but no more than three years before filing a claim with the Tribunal. This clock starts on the date "on which investor first acquired or should have first acquired knowledge of the alleged breach."[4] The filing of a claim amounts to submission of a claim to the arbitration process. However, notice must be given at least 90 days before the claim is actually submitted. Such notice will specify the name and address of the disputing investor, the name and address of the enterprise as applicable, provisions of NAFTA that have been breached, issues and factual matters relating to the claim, the relief sought, and the approximate amount of damages claimed.

The matter is then reviewed by a Tribunal which is established in the same way that tribunals for other financial services matters are established. One member is appointed by the claimant, a second by the Party against which the claim is brought, and one by mutual agreement of the two Parties. The third arbiter is considered to be the presiding arbiter. The Tribunal may make a final award in the case of a dispute in the form of monetary damages including interest, restoration of property, or some combination of these. Each NAFTA Party must provide for enforcement of such final awards by the Tribunal. While the Party against whom the final award is made

EXHIBIT 1-12

ARBITRATION FOR CLAIMS RELATING TO INVESTMENT TRANSFERS, EXPROPRIATION, AND COMPENSATION

- No less than six months and no more than three years may have elapsed from date on which investor first acquired, or should have first acquired, knowledge of the alleged breach and knowledge that the investor had incurred loss or damage.
- The disputing party must submit notice of its intention to submit a claim to arbitration at least 90 days prior to claim submission.
- Tribunal shall be composed of three arbitrators, one appointed by each of the disputing Parties and a third, the presiding arbitrator, appointed by agreement of the disputing Parties.
- Tribunal may award monetary damages, restitution of property, or some combination of these.

has the right to appeal (through other international channels), once the appeal process is complete, the procedures are structured so that each award will ultimately be satisfied.

The provisions of NAFTA with respect to financial services represent one general set of rules for each country that is involved in the agreement. These provisions represent negotiated policies and procedures through which each country receives some measure of benefit. However, the benefit is not the same for each country. Banks and other financial service providers in the United States, Canada, and Mexico will derive distinctly different advantages as a result of the North American Free Trade Agreement.

DIFFERENT PERSPECTIVES ON THE AGREEMENT

The U.S. Perspective

When the debate concerning NAFTA began to develop, Representative Henry B. Gonzalez, Chairman of the U.S. House of Representatives Banking Committee, spoke from the House

Floor on the motivation for such an agreement. "There is more involved than just trade agreements. Nobody knows that the greatest engine driving this is finance and banking," he said.[5] The Democrat from San Antonio, Texas, believed that NAFTA would cause big business and banks in the United States to abandon the American worker. This view was shared by U.S. Labor unions and other observers concerned about the existence of a low-cost labor pool in Mexico. Perhaps the most outspoken civilian to voice concerns about the North American Free Trade Agreement was Ross Perot, who continually alluded to the great "sucking sound" that would result from NAFTA. Of course, Perot was referring to the loss of U.S. jobs to manufacturing facilities set up in Mexico.

The logic appeared to be irresistible. What would motivate the United States to pursue an agreement that eliminated trade barriers between the United States and Mexico, in the presence of a *very* low-cost Mexican labor pool? Would this not exacerbate the already existing unemployment problems in the United States?

Some observers believed that the administration under George Bush recognized the trend of regionalized trade in Europe and in Asia and sought to preempt that process by creating a free trade zone in the Western Hemisphere. Other observers felt that the North American Free Trade Agreement was a reward to the Mexican President, Carlos Salinas de Gortari, for his continued push toward free-market reforms in Mexico. Most of the public debate in the United States centered around the issue of jobs in the United States being lost to Mexican workers and the difficult problem with environmental issues in the less-regulated Mexico. There was relatively far less discussion of financial services with respect to NAFTA. Even House Banking Chair Gonzalez elected not to elaborate fully on the impact of NAFTA for financial services in his remarks on the floor of the U.S. House of Representatives. Nevertheless, the financial services industry is perhaps the greatest U.S. beneficiary of the North American Free Trade Agreement.

While it is true that industrial companies have been able to operate in Mexico for a number of years, it is not true that U.S. banks have had the same privilege. If U.S. banks were to follow their clients and capitalize on the transactions of their U.S. customers in Mexico, Mexican laws had to change. NAFTA made this change possible. Because it has been protected, the Mexican banking market, notwithstanding U.S. companies operating in Mexico, is very attractive.

The U.S. financial services industry felt that it was extremely important to include the principles of national treatment in the North American Free Trade Agreement with respect to Mexico because U.S. institutions were highly restricted in the Mexican market. Without NAFTA, U.S. banks would not be able to tap into the Mexican market and would be less able to expand their market share in North America. With NAFTA, it is possible to do so. Without NAFTA, U.S. banks were able to operate only representative offices.[6] However, under NAFTA, U.S. banks have the right not only to operate full-service banking operations in Mexico but also to operate securities and insurance affiliates. The same holding company in Mexico may own the following types of financial institutions:

- Full-service bank

- Stock brokerage house

- Insurance company

- Funds management firm

- Bonding institution

- Factoring operation

- Leasing firm

- Warehousing firm

In Mexico, the only types of financial firms in which foreign investors may not invest are credit unions, development banks, and strictly foreign exchange firms. NAFTA did not relax these prohibitions for U.S. and Canadian institutions. The Mexican market is underbanked and Mexican banks enjoy wide profit margins and have made relatively little investment in banking technology.

On the other hand, there are relatively few inducements for U.S. banks and other financial institutions with respect to the Canadian market under the provisions of NAFTA. Any benefits that exist for the United States in Canada already have been realized under the Canada-United States Free Trade Agreement (CUSFTA), effective 1989. Restrictions with respect to maximum investment permitted by foreign banks in Canada have been eased for U.S. banks. Furthermore, U.S. banks may ask for special exclusion from the normal regulatory review of other foreign banks operating in Canada.

Before 1981, no foreign bank in Canada was permitted to operate as a full-service bank. The 1981 Banking Law and Revision Act allowed foreign banks to do so. The act defined a Schedule A (now Schedule I) bank as one that was a full-service bank before 1981. Schedule B (now Schedule II) banks were created by the 1981 legislation to allow foreign banks to operate wholly owned subsidiaries in Canada. A "10/25" rule was also initiated. No single resident or nonresident investor was permitted to own more than 10% of the capital of a Schedule I bank. All foreign investors may own, in the aggregate, no more than 25% of the total capital of a Schedule I bank. In addition, the assets of all foreign banks may not exceed 12% of the total assets of all Canadian banks. Lastly, foreign banks are required to seek permission from the Canadian Minister of Finance prior to opening additional branches in Canada. Schedule II banks may be wholly owned by a foreign investor and, as long as total capital of the Schedule II does not exceed C$750 million, the 10% rule does not apply.

Under CUSFTA in 1989, U.S. banks received exemptions from the 25% limitation imposed by the "10/25" rule, the 12% ceiling on bank assets, and the requirement to obtain Ministry approval for additional branches. U.S. banks were not given an exemption from the 10% limit on individual ownership of the capital of a Schedule I bank.

NAFTA contains the same provisions for U.S. banks as does CUSFTA. The provisions have now been extended to Mexican banks. However, under both CUSFTA and NAFTA, U.S. and Mexican banks are not permitted to branch directly into Canada but instead must establish incorporated subsidiaries. Since none of the CUSFTA provisions were changed under the North American Free Trade Agreement, NAFTA adds little incentive for U.S. banks to become involved in the Canadian market. At the same time, there are considerable inducements to become involved in the Mexican banking market.

During NAFTA negotiations, U.S. banks and banking officials recognized that the Mexican banking industry had been largely sheltered from the forces of competition, especially after the 1982 Mexican bank nationalization. Thus, the phase-in period to allow the indigenous Mexican banks to become more competitive was seen as a reasonable approach to the sensitive issue of foreign banks in Mexico. U.S. government officials and bankers felt that, as long as treatment of Mexican banks in the United States was essentially reciprocated by national treatment for U.S. banks in Mexico, the agreement would be workable. The underlying rationale was that it would be difficult for U.S. industrial firms to operate in the Mexican market with its high cost of capital without sufficient, competitive banking support. It was felt that, in the absence of reduction of the restrictions on U.S. banks in Mexico, far fewer economic benefits would accrue to U.S. industrial firms under NAFTA. For their part, many U.S. banks view NAFTA as the first real opportunity to engage in universal banking and to form holding companies that can provide the full range of services.

The Canadian Perspective

In Canada, the benefits of NAFTA include (1) the establishment of general principles of free trade and (2) formal dispute resolution mechanisms—a vast improvement over the Canada-United

States Free Trade Agreement, which provided neither. The greatest market opportunities, of course, revolve around access to the Mexican market. It should be noted that there was even less enthusiasm in Canada for the prospect of a North American Free Trade Agreement than in the United States. Canada has suffered extremely difficult recessionary conditions, many of which have been blamed on CUSFTA. Record numbers of Canadian companies are currently in bankruptcy. Ontario, Canada's industrial heartland, has been particularly hard hit, losing thousands of companies and hundreds of thousands of jobs since 1990. In many cases, businesses have been moved from Ontario to the United States where the business climate is sometimes perceived to be better.

On the other hand, the banking industry in Canada is highly concentrated, with less than ten institutions controlling virtually all bank assets in the country. Thus, from the Canadian perspective, opening up a significant market for Canadian bankers was an important priority in negotiations for the North American Free Trade Agreement.

Moreover, the Canadian government did not want to see the country isolated in North America as a result of being excluded from the NAFTA negotiations. It was felt that a bilateral trade pact between the United States and Mexico would result in isolation of the Canadian economy. In a sense, such a bilateral arrangement would have created a "hub-and-spoke" system. The United States would have become a hub, with companies locating within the United States to achieve tariff-free access to all three countries. This was seen as unacceptable by Canadian officials. Besides, Mexico offered a fast-growing market since its population is expected to increase by 10 million during the presidential term of Carlos Salinas de Gortari. Of course, Mexico also represented a source of low-cost labor for Canada.

In a very real sense, Canada has not taken advantage of the potential trade opportunities with Mexico to the same extent as has the United States. In terms of sales, Canada's trade with Mexico has generally been less than $1 billion per year. This relatively low level of sales makes Mexico Canada's 17th largest export market. Mexican exports to Canada are generally somewhat higher at just under $2 billion per year.

In contrast, the trade between the United States and Canada makes these two countries the world's largest trading partners. Annual two-way trade between the United States and Canada exceeds $190 billion. Under CUSFTA, all tariffs between the United States and Canada will be completely eliminated by 1998. However, there remain certain stumbling blocks with respect to the full realization of tariff elimination. These are agricultural quotas and price support systems; Canadian protective regulations with respect to the sale and distribution of beer; restrictions on energy products, permitted by GATT for shortages, conservation, and national security; Canadian regulations that protect creative activities such as books, magazines, newspapers, video and audio recordings, and broadcasting; and government procurement preferences that are not covered by GATT.[7]

Even with NAFTA, some of these areas continue to be difficult trade issues between the United States and Canada. Canada has agreed to eliminate import quotas on dairy, eggs, and poultry products that have protected the agricultural industry in Canada for many years. However, even as it dismantles these quotas, Canada is proposing to replace some of them with tariffs that will result in no relaxation of trade barriers. For example, the Canadian government has suggested that a 350% quota be placed on butter imported from the United States. At the same time Canada, will probably ship 2.6 million metric tons of wheat to the United States in 1994, up from slightly over 1 million metric tons in 1992. U.S. farmers charge that Canada is subsidizing its wheat, causing a loss of hundreds of millions of dollars in income each year for U.S. farmers.

There seems no resolution in sight for the great controversy over beer. In August of 1993, the United States and Canada agreed to a plan that would allow U.S. brewers greater access to the Canadian market. Even with this agreement, exports of beer from the United States to Canada fell 40% in 1993 to 6.5 million gallons, while U.S. imports of Canadian beer rose 21% to 80 million gallons.

A long-standing dispute over lumber does not appear to be close to resolution. Every year, lumber valued at $5 billion crosses the border from Canada to the United States. Since 1992, the U.S. has collected $500 million in duties on this Canadian lumber. However, if the U.S. cannot show that the lumber has been subsidized by the Canadian government, these duties must be refunded to Canada. A panel composed of representatives from the two countries has ruled that there is no proof that Canada subsidizes the lumber. However, the United States plans to challenge this finding.

Government procurement issues remain contentious as well. However, one important matter has been resolved through compromise. In March 1994, Canada and the United States reached an agreement whereby Canada agrees to stop its "preferred supplier" arrangement with Northern Telecom Ltd. Terminating this arrangement (which dates back to 1939) should help the United States export more telecommunications equipment to Canada.

With all of these issues that had erupted in connection with free trade between the United States and Canada, it is perhaps not surprising that Canadians approached the whole matter of the North American Free Trade Agreement with some caution. However, the Canadians no doubt recognized the inevitability of increased cross-border trade and, in the long run, preferred to have a place at the negotiating table rather than to be left waiting in the wings.

The Mexican Perspective

While recent changes in the Canadian-U.S. trade relationship have been minimal, the last few years have witnessed rapid developments in Mexican-U.S. trade. In the last few years, Mexico has evolved from essentially a closed economy to one that has been opened to increased influences of foreign competition and trade.

The Mexican Political Experience. To understand the current state of Mexican business and finance, it is necessary to have an appreciation for the background of the Mexican economy and its political system. Spanish explorers arrived in what is now Mexico in the early 16th century. By 1535, the territory known today as Mexico became the viceroyalty of New Spain. The Spanish conquerors exploited the mineral resources of the area and used the native residents as laborers in this exploitation. Spain expanded its rule throughout Mexico and in the southwestern region of the United States.

After an unsuccessful rebellion in New Spain that lasted from 1810 to 1815, Spain eventually accepted Mexican independence in 1821. Two years later, army officers in Mexico overthrew the empire that had been established upon independence and established a federal republic. In 1836 Texas won its independence from Mexico and in the Mexican War (1846-1848) with the United States, Mexico lost even more territory. In terms of domestic politics, the republic continued to be plagued with civil unrest. In 1855 a reform movement was launched and the dictator then in power, Antonio López de Santa Anna, was overthrown. The liberal constitution, however, did not solve the political problems of Mexico and a civil war erupted. Then in 1864, Napoleon III of France established a Mexican empire as part of the then Hapsburg Empire. When the Hapsburg Empire collapsed a dictatorship was established in Mexico by Porfirio Díaz.

Díaz was able to bring economic growth and development to Mexico and there was some degree of stability. However, in the process, the wealth of the country fell into the hands of a few important families in Mexico. Because of this inequality of income distribution, revolution began to breed once again. One of the revolutionaries was Emiliano Zapata, a native Mexican tenant farmer who tried to recover expropriated village land in 1908. His army of native Mexicans (1910–1919) fought with a goal of repossessing the land, occupying Mexico City on three occasions in 1914 and 1915. Zapata was killed as a result of these activities and is still revered by native Mexicans. Francisco

Madero was a revolutionary who was successful in deposing Díaz in 1911. However, Madero himself was killed only two years later. The revolutionary Francisco "Pancho" Villa fought vigorously for Madero. In 1916, Villa led an assault in New Mexico that resulted in a brief retaliatory strike against Mexico by the United States.

A platform for reform was established when a constitution in 1917 was put in place. In 1929 the National Revolutionary Party, later renamed the Institutional Revolutionary Party or PRI, was established. The PRI has governed Mexico since that time. During the presidency of Lázaro Cárdenas (1934-1940), there was a redistribution of land. Illiteracy was substantially reduced through educational reform, power plants were built to update the infrastructure in Mexico, and some of the industries in Mexico were nationalized.

However, most of the reforms, which benefitted middle and upper classes, continued to increase the share of wealth held by only a few families in Mexico. There remained a large segment of the Mexican population that continued to live below subsistence levels. Thus, the Mexican experience with respect to foreign trade and involvement has been one of exploitation by foreigners. Historically, the economic progress that has been achieved has occurred during periods in which the economy was closed to the rest of the world.

The Maquiladora Program. Prior to the 1980s, the concentration of Mexico's economic development was based on import substitution for the most part. This focus resulted in high import tariffs to encourage the development of indigenous Mexican firms. In addition, special licenses were put in place that also discouraged imports. Foreign participation in Mexican operations was limited to no more than 49% ownership in a Mexican enterprise. This constituted inward looking, nationalistic trade and investment policies by Mexico.

The Maquiladora Program was established in 1965 to encourage industrial development and employment along the 2,000-mile border between Mexico and the United States. In every sense, the maquiladoras (or maquilas) were treated in a different manner than other than Mexican enterprises. Production in maquiladoras is *in-bond*, that is, shipments remain under the control of U.S. Customs until all customs regulations have been satisfied. This effectively means that goods leave the United States partially assembled, arrive in maquiladoras on the Mexican side of the border, and remain under the control of U.S. Customs officials. The status of the goods is maintained in this way until the goods, fully assembled, are returned to the U.S. side of the border. Most often, maquiladoras are wholly owned subsidiaries of U.S. companies. Recently, Japanese, European, and other Asian companies have begun to utilize the maquiladora system. The clear advantage is the availability of a low-cost labor pool in close proximity to the United States.

Initially, Mexico considered the output of these facilities to be outside the Mexican economy. The special laws that created the maquiladoras along the Mexican border originally stipulated that 100% of the production was to be exported. Furthermore, there was a great deal of administrative paperwork for the foreign operators. Thus, Mexican officials initially treated the maquiladoras as a necessary evil, not a system to which they would attribute significant economic development in Mexico. This detached perspective was possible because of Mexico's economic reliance on oil production and export. The country could easily afford not to be as open to foreign trade as otherwise might have been the case. Then, in 1982, it was necessary to devalue the Mexican peso and the dependability of crude oil revenues was seriously challenged by slumping oil prices. It became clear that the low-cost labor pool of Mexico would be critical in the continued economic evolution of the country.

In 1983, a Maquiladora Decree made it possible for maquiladoras to sell up to 20% of their production on the domestic market. However, this decree was only a tentative step forward because there remained many restrictions with respect to authorization, and this permission was granted for only one year at a time. Nevertheless, the trend toward integration of the Mexican economy with the rest of the world had begun.

In 1986, Mexico became a signatory to the General Agreement on Tariffs and Trade (GATT). This involved initiating tariff reductions to bring the maximum tariff down to 20% by 1990. Previously, Mexico's maximum tariffs had been as high as 100%. Joining GATT was a clear sign that Mexico intended to completely liberalize its economic system with the modernization that is commonly required in international trade agreements. In the same year, Mexico experienced another severe economic reversal as GDP declined by 4%. It became painfully obvious that exports would be the means through which Mexico might reverse its economic declines.

President Carlos Salinas de Gortari. Carlos Salinas de Gortari is the son of a former Minister of Industry and Commerce and his economist wife. At Harvard University, he earned two masters' degrees and a doctorate in political economy and government. After completing his education in the United States, Salinas returned to Mexico in 1978 and worked through several positions in the Mexican government. Salinas served under President Miguel de la Madrid Hurtado as Minister of Budget and Planning. Under the Mexican political system each president serves only one 6-year term. Typically, the president handpicks his successor before leaving office. Carlos Salinas de Gortari was de la Madrid's hand-picked successor and became the President of Mexico in 1988.

Reforms under Salinas. While economic reforms began under President de la Madrid, President Salinas has been credited with moving the Mexican economy forward more so than any of his predecessors. The government is phasing out its import substitution economic model and is privatizing formerly state-owned enterprises. The accomplishments include:

- Trade liberalization such that between 1987 and 1990 American exports to Mexico grew at the rate of almost 32% per year, and trade between the two countries increased 23% per year over the same period. Today, Mexico ranks as the third largest market for U.S. goods.[8]

- Inflation which had plagued Mexico during the 1980s, peaking in 1987 at almost 160%, was reduced to 52% in 1988 and is today approximately 10%.

- External debt largely to commercial banks has been renegotiated such that external debt service requirements have been reduced from 6% of GDP to 2% of GDP.

- Approximately two-thirds of the almost 1,200 government enterprises in 1982 have been privatized, including the nation's 18 previously state-owned banks.

- Deregulation has occurred in the petrochemical, trucking, telecommunications, financial services, agricultural, and food distribution industries. In some areas, private and foreign ownership has been permitted for the first time.

- Restrictions on foreign investment in Mexico have been drastically reduced. The outflow of capital has been slowed. In fact, capital is now flowing into Mexico at remarkable rates. In 1990, for example, over $8 billion dollars in new capital was introduced into the Mexican economy.

- After many years of economic stagnation and decline, GDP grew at the rate of 2.9% in 1989, 4.4% in 1990, and 3.6% in 1991.

A Shift Toward North American Free Trade. While Carlos Salinas assumed the office of President of Mexico with a very decided predisposition toward economic reform, he did not enter office assuming that a free trade agreement would be necessary between Mexico and the United States. One of his earliest reforms was the 1989 Maquiladora Decree. This modification of the Maquiladora arrangement accomplished two important outcomes:

1) Maquiladoras were permitted to sell their products in a much more liberalized environment.

2) Local inputs and raw materials of Mexican origin were permitted and encouraged.

This decree is indicative of the direction that Salinas and his administration has attempted to follow. The philosophy has been to open the Mexican economy to foreign competition and to foreign goods. The objective is to increase the incentive for Mexican firms to modernize and to become more competitive in an international sense. It was clear to the officials of the Salinas administration that the maquiladora operators would welcome the opportunity to sell to the Mexican economy directly. It was also clear that the competition could potentially hurt the local suppliers that were not yet internationally competitive. The maquiladoras had essentially transplanted state-of-the-art technology and skills into the Mexican economy in an isolated context. Forcing world-class quality standards on the indigenous economy could have had disruptive effects.

However, the structure of the reform helped to create a better environment for the transition from a protected indigenous economy to a more competitive one. The 1989 decree gave powerful tax incentives to those maquiladora operators that cultivated Mexican suppliers and increased the local content of their production. In addition, maquiladoras were permitted under the 1989 decree to sell on the domestic Mexican market 50% of their prior year's exports from maquiladora sites. For example, if a maquiladora operator exported $1 million dollars in goods from the maquiladora in 1993, that operator would be permitted to sell $500,000 in goods to the domestic Mexican market in 1994. Assuming that the maquiladora operation again produced $1 million in exports in 1994, the $500,000 in permissible sales to the Mexican domestic market brings total sales to $1,500,000. In 1994, the maquiladora operator is entitled to sell one-third of its production to the domestic Mexican market.

The 1989 Maquiladora Decree and other unilateral measures were seen by the Mexican government to be sufficient to continue the forward economic momentum in Mexico. In fact, in early 1990 President Salinas was not prepared to consider a comprehensive free trade agreement with the United States. When asked by a reporter for *MaClean's* in March 1990 about his perspective on a comprehensive trade agreement, Salinas responded, "We have taken the sector-by-sector approach and we are satisfied with the results that we have been getting so far."[9] This comment was made to the Canadian reporter during a tour by Salinas to promote his economic and social reforms to the Mexican people prior to the visit of then Prime Minister Brian Mulrooney.

Later in 1990, Salinas visited several European capitals. His objective was to obtain commitments for foreign investment in Mexico. He found, however, that the European countries were more concerned about the economic reform of Eastern European countries. This appeared to be the turning point in his perspective on free trade. It became apparent to him that it would be necessary to foster free trade agreements with the United States. Not long after, Salinas made it clear to President George Bush that he wanted to pursue such an arrangement. During a summit in June of 1990, Presidents Bush and Salinas laid the groundwork for future negotiations on a "gradual and comprehensive" transition to free trade and goods and services. The objectives would be:

- Phase-out of import tariffs.

- Reduction or elimination of nontariff barriers such as import quotas, licenses, and technical barriers to trade.

- Establishment of intellectual property rights and protection thereof.

- Incorporation of meaningful and speedy dispute resolution procedures.

- Establishment of actual methods through which the flow of goods, services, and investment between the two countries would improve and expand.

In September of 1990, Canada indicated that it also wanted to be a part of the free trade discussions. This was not an aspect of the agreement that Mexico particularly wanted to pursue. Mexican officials were concerned that long-standing trade disputes between the United States and Canada would seriously delay the process of free trade negotiations between the United States and Mexico. During a summit meeting in January of 1991, Canada agreed to the basic framework for the talks and stipulated that it would not delay the process of negotiation because of outstanding issues. In February of 1991, the three countries issued a joint communique which announced that the free trade talks would be trilateral. With this announcement, the European Union trading block was surpassed in size and scope. The new North American Free Trade Zone would encompass 360 million people, 40 million more than in the European Union.

Implications for Financial Services. Just as in the case of the Maquiladora Decree of 1989, administrators of the Salinas government wanted to introduce an element of foreign competition into the Mexican financial system, thereby helping it become more competitive internationally. The administration feels that historically there has been a lack of service to certain sectors in the economy—that the small and medium-sized firms have not received the kind of financial service support that is needed to spur that segment of the economy. While the largest firms (often associated with the wealthy Mexican families) have been financially supported and even have had access to international capital markets, small- and medium-sized firms have had little access to traditional banking services. It is hoped that the small- and medium-sized Mexican banks will find their niche in a more competitive banking market.

ADVANTAGES OF NAFTA FOR FINANCIAL INSTITUTIONS

In general, foreign investment in Mexican companies has been limited to 49% or less. New rules in 1989 did liberalize some of these restrictions making 100% foreign investment possible in some cases. However, foreign ownership of financial service

EXHIBIT 1-13

LIBERALIZATION OF FINANCIAL SERVICES INVESTMENT IN MEXICO UNDER NAFTA

	U.S. and Canadian Ownership Limitations	
	Individual[1]	Aggregate[2]
Banks		
Before NAFTA	5%[3]	30%[4]
After NAFTA:		
1994	1.5	8
1999	1.5	15
After 1999	4[5]	None[6]
Securities Firms		
Before NAFTA	10%[3]	30%[4]
After NAFTA:		
1994	4	10
1999	4	20
After 1999	None	None[7]
Insurance Companies		
Before NAFTA	—	49%[4]
After NAFTA:		
1994	1.5	6
1999	1.5	12
After 1999	None	None
Factors and Leasing Companies		
Before NAFTA	—	49%[4]
After NAFTA:		
1994	None	10
1999	None	20
After 1999	None	None

EXHIBIT 1-13 LIBERALIZATION OF FINANCIAL SERVICES INVESTMENT IN MEXICO UNDER NAFTA (Cont'd.)

	U.S. and Canadian Ownership Limitations	
	Individual[1]	Aggregate[2]
Limited-Scope Finance Companies		
Before NAFTA	—	49%[4]
After NAFTA:		
1994	None	3%[8]
1999	None	3%[8]
After 1999	None	None

[1] Represents the limit of U.S. and Canadian ownership by an individual investor in a specific type of financial institution as a percentage of total applicable industry capital, unless otherwise noted.

[2] Represents the limit of foreign ownership of all Mexican institutions as a percentage of total applicable industry capital, unless otherwise noted.

[3] Represents the limit for an individual foreign investor in an individual institution as a percentage of the individual institution's total capital.

[4] Represents the limit for all foreign investors, including U.S. and Canadian investors, in an individual institution as a percentage of the individual institution's total capital.

[5] After 1999, acquisitions by U.S. and Canadian investors are subject to approval by the Mexican government and will be granted only if capital of the acquired bank and that of all other Mexican banks owned by the acquiring investor is less than 4% of all Mexican bank capital.

[6] Mexico has the one-time right to freeze, for no more than 3 years, ownership of Mexican banks by foreign investors if their aggregate investment reaches 25% or more. This option is available only until January 1, 2004.

[7] Mexico has the one-time right to freeze, for no more than 3 years, ownership of Mexican securities firms by foreign investors if their aggregate investment reaches 30% or more. This option is available only until January 1, 2004.

[8] Represents the limit of aggregate assets of limited-scope finance companies as a percentage of the aggregate assets of all commercial banks and limited scope finance companies in Mexico.

Sources: 1. "North American Free Trade Agreement," Chapter 14.
2. Sczudlo, Raymond S. "NAFTA: Opportunities Abound for U.S. and Canadian Financial Institution," *The Bankers* Magazine, July/August 1993, pp. 28-33.

firms was not liberalized by the 1989 reforms. Thus, the regulations under NAFTA represent a significant opportunity for foreign entities to participate in the Mexican financial sector.

Exhibit 1-13 outlines the basic investment provisions under NAFTA for U.S. and Canadian financial institutions. Under NAFTA, a U.S. or Canadian investor (individual or corporation) may hold a 100% stake in a Mexican financial institution. The limits for U.S. and Canadian investors are stated in terms of total industry capital within specific industries, instead of the capital of an individual institution. The five different financial services industries are:

- Banks

- Securities firms

- Insurance companies

- Factors and leasing companies

- Limited-scope finance companies

The ownership restrictions are two-tiered. The first tier is the extent to which a single foreign investor (individual or corporation) may control industry capital. The second tier is the extent to which all foreign investors may control industry capital.

In the *banking* sector before NAFTA, investment by individual foreign investors had been limited to 5% of capital of the institution in question. Aggregate investment by all foreign investors was limited to 30% of capital of the institution in question. During NAFTA's transition period from 1994 through 1999, no single investor may own more than 1.5% of banking industry capital. Beginning January 1, 2000, this ceiling is increased to 4% of Mexican banking capital. During the same transition period, the aggregate limit of the ownership of Mexican bank capital by foreign institutions begins at 8% in 1994 and increases each year to 15% in 1999. After 1999, there is no limit.

However, should the aggregate foreign share of Mexican banking capital reach 25%, Mexico has the option to freeze further foreign acquisitions for a period not to exceed three years. This option expires four years after the end of the transition period, that is, January 1, 2004. These provisions have the effect of containing (1) the extent to which an individual U.S. or Canadian firm may control the Mexican banking system and (2) the extent of foreign investment in the banking industry as a whole. This means that no individual foreign interest could represent a majority share of one of Mexico's larger banks. The aggregate restriction, at least through the year 2007, prevents foreign investors from assuming a dominating position through buying control of a large number of smaller Mexican banks.

In the *securities* sector, limits have been stipulated that are similar to those in the banking industry. Prior to NAFTA, the individual limitation for securities firm ownership by foreign investors was 10% of the capital of the securities firm in question, while aggregate foreign ownership of a Mexican securities firm was limited to 30% of the Mexican firm's capital.

Under NAFTA, during the transition period (1994 through 1999), individual U.S. and Canadian investors may control up to 4% of Mexican securities firms' capital, representing a somewhat more liberal ceiling than in the case of commercial banks. During the transition period, the aggregate limit for foreign ownership of Mexican securities firms begins at 10% and increases to 20%. After the transition period, there is no limit.

As in the banking industry, there is also an option for a one-time freeze by the Mexican government in the securities industry. Between January 1, 2000 and January 1, 2004, the Mexican government may freeze further acquisition of Mexican securities firms by foreign investors for a period not to exceed three years. Nevertheless, the limits are generally more liberal in the securities industry than in the banking industry.

In the *insurance* sector, before NAFTA, foreign investment was limited to 49% of a specific Mexican insurance company. There were no individual limits.

Under NAFTA, the two-tiered limitations apply. During the transition period, a U.S. or Canadian investor may own no more than 1.5% of the Mexican insurance company capital. During 1994, the first year of the transition period, no more than 6% of aggregate Mexican insurance company capital may be owned by foreign investors. This percentage increases to 12% by 1999. After 1999, there are no such limitations.

Factors and leasing companies have fewer ownership restrictions. Before NAFTA, each individual company was limited to 49% foreign ownership.

Under NAFTA, there are no individual limits with respect to U.S. or Canadian ownership of aggregate Mexican factoring and leasing companies, either during or after the transition period. The aggregate limit on foreign ownership during the transition period is 10% in the first year of the transition period, increasing to 20% by 1999. After 1999, there are no restrictions. In terms of ownership restrictions, factoring and leasing companies represent a greater opportunity to enter the Mexican financial system.

Limited-scope finance companies present an even greater opportunity than factoring and leasing companies with respect to entry into Mexico's financial system. Limited-scope finance companies are defined as those which offer services in consumer lending, commercial lending, mortgage lending, credit card services, or other lending services that are closely related to these. Before NAFTA, only the 49% limit on total foreign ownership of an individual company existed.

Under NAFTA, the ownership restriction are defined in a different manner vis-à-vis other financial institutions. The limitations are based on *assets* instead of *capital*. The aggregate limit is 3% throughout the transition period, with no limit thereafter. There is a distinctly different framework of ownership limitation in this sector—the 3% limit is a percentage of assets of both limited-scope finance companies and of commercial banks. Because of the extent to which the banking system dominates the Mexican financial services industry, this 3% limit on assets is a liberal ceiling for a fairly specialized form of financial institution.

The North American Free Trade Agreement represents a significant opportunity for investment in the financial structure of

Mexico. The relatively liberal restrictions with respect to the limited-scope finance companies may reflect the desire of the Mexican government to cultivate those services offered by these companies. Consumer, residential mortgage, and small- to medium-sized commercial customers have not been well served in the past. At the same time, the structure of the transition period allows Mexican banks and other financial institutions to become stronger before all foreign ownership restrictions are dropped.

The phase-in period also represents an opportunity for U.S. and Canadian banks to become established in one of the niches that is not being well served—in either the banking sector or in one of the other financial service sectors. The options are varied and interesting, particularly in light of the generally over-banked condition of the United States. Under provisions of the North American Free Trade Agreement, Mexico represents an intriguing frontier for expansion and potential profitability.

SELECTED REFERENCES

Gramm, Phil. "Mexico Needs Trade, Not Aid," *North American International Business,* April 1991, p. 73.

Javetski, Bill, Stephen Baker and Ruth Pearson. "Can Mexico Embrace the U.S.—At Arm's Length?" *Business Week,* May 20, 1991, p. 63.

Laver, Ross. "Mexico Fights Back," *MaClean's,* March 26, 1990, pp. 40-44.

Laver, Ross. "Open for Business: Mexico Seeks Foreign Investors," *MaClean's,* March 26, 1990, p. 45.

Martin, Gary. "Gonzalez Blasts Trade Pact", *San Antonio Express-News,* February 23, 1993.

Newman, Gray and Anna Szterenfeld. *Business International's Guide to Doing Business in Mexico,* New York: McGraw-Hill, 1993.

"North American Free Trade Agreement," Chapters 11 and 14 and Annex VII, Washington: U.S. Printing Office, 1993.

Sczudlo, Raymond S. "NAFTA: Opportunities Abound for U.S. and Canadian Financial Institutions," *The Bankers Magazine*, July/August 1993, pp. 28- 33.

Smith, Geri, Stephen Baker, and William Glasgall. "Mexico: Will Economic Reform Survive the Turmoil?" *Business Week*, April 11, 1994, pp. 247-27.

Smith, Geri and Wendy Zellner. "The Gringo Banks are Drooling," *Business Week*, September 13, 1993, p. 84.

Texas Consortium Report on Free Trade, Final Report, Austin, Texas: Texas Department of Commerce, 1991.

Toulin, Alan. "Making Changes to Fabric of Canada," *The Financial Post* (Toronto), January 2, 1993.

"Under Recession's Hammer: Auctioneer Clears Failed Businesses to the Wall," *The Hamilton Spectator*, January 2, 1993.

"Viva NAFTA," *The Economist*, August 21, 1993, pp. 21-22.

Wood, Nancy, "Reopening the Trade Winds," *MaClean's*, March 18, 1991, pp. 42-43.

ENDNOTES

1. Beginning with the Treaty of Rome in 1957, six European countries became the European Common Market—Belgium, France, Italy, Luxembourg, Germany, and the Netherlands. In 1973, Denmark, Ireland, and the United Kingdom joined the group. Greece became a full member in 1981 and Portugal and Spain brought the number to 12 member countries in 1986.
2. These definitions are contained in Chapter 11 of the North American Free Trade Agreement.
3. The Group of Seven or G-7 countries are the United States, Canada, the United Kingdom, Germany, France, Italy, and Japan.
4. See the North American Free Trade Agreement, Chapter 11.
5. See "Gonzalez Blasts Trade Pact" by Gary Martin.
6. A representative office is one that acts only as a point of contact for the home country bank. It is not permitted to conduct banking business of any kind.

7. GATT is the acronym for General Agreement on Tariffs and Trade, a multilateral agreement that dates back to 1948, with 80 fully participating countries and 30 others signing under special arrangements.
8. The largest export market for the United States is Canada. The second largest is Japan.
9. See "Open for Business" by Ross Laver.

2 Banking Transactions without Borders

INTRODUCTION

The U.S. dollar is a reserve currency that has circulated throughout the world for decades. In the era of North American Free Trade, the role of the dollar will continue to grow. Electronic banking and currency exchange will be a vital part of the more integrated banking systems of the United States, Mexico and Canada. This enhancement of capability will not come without cost, particularly in the case of Mexico, where there is a significant need for technological upgrading.

However, the opportunities in Mexico will be considerable. First on the list of opportunities is trade finance. Trade between the United States and Mexico has increased substantially in recent years. While the trade between Canada and Mexico at this point is a mere trickle by comparison, it should expand considerably in the future. Already, Canada and the United States are the world's largest trading partners—a long-standing trend that will not be reversed.

In addition, U.S. firms are making massive investments in Mexico. These U.S. investments will no doubt be followed by investments of Canadian firms seeking to capitalize on the advantages of the North American Free Trade Agreement. Participating in the financing of such investments will represent a significant banking opportunity.

Perhaps the greatest challenge and opportunity are in retail banking because the Mexican market is severely underbanked. This is also the area in which significant capital investment will be necessary by indigenous and cross-border banks. Despite the obvious cost involved, there are numerous banks in the United States and Canada that are anxious to be a part of banking in the North American Free Trade arena.

CURRENCY TRANSACTIONS

One of the first crucial elements in international trade is the currency in which transactions will be denominated. In the case of the North American Free Trade zone, the U.S. dollar plays a critical role, as it is the only currency that is accepted throughout the region without hesitation. In this sense, it will play an even greater role in the North American Free Trade area than the deutsche mark has played in the European Union.

The U.S. Dollar Abroad

The acceptance of the U.S. dollar (US$) outside U.S. borders is not a new phenomenon. Under the Bretton-Woods system that was inaugurated in 1944, the world's major currencies were pegged to the U.S. dollar and, in turn, the dollar was convertible into gold. This caused the U.S. dollar to become the most important reserve currency. Central banks held significant quantities of U.S. dollars so that they might intervene in the market, as necessary, to maintain their currencies' respective parities vis-à-vis the dollar.

The United States government has had involvements overseas that included military installations. As a major peace-keeping ally, the United States employed hundreds of thousands of military personnel in overseas locations. In addition, it was necessary to construct large amounts of infrastructure to house both the troops and the armaments that they controlled. Harbors were built or expanded in capacity. Runways were constructed or enlarged. Roads were paved, wells dug, sewer lines laid, and electricity generated. Food and supplies were needed to support the U.S. troops. Payments for wages of these military personnel, as well as all associated expenditures, were made in U.S. dollars.

By 1965, $100 billion were in foreign hands. This large foreign overhang of U.S. dollars raised questions about the value of the dollar. It became apparent that the United States could not support gold convertibility of the U.S. dollar when foreign holdings reached $300 billion in 1971, while holdings of gold by the U.S. government amounted to only $14 billion. In 1971, the United States suspended gold convertibility, signalling the end of the Bretton-Woods currency system that had begun in 1944.

However, in terms of its utility as a reserve currency, the value of the U.S. dollar has diminished surprisingly little. It is true, of course, that the German deutsche mark and the Japanese yen have grown significantly in terms of reserve currency holdings by central bankers and in terms of corporate treasury holdings by large, multinational firms. Nevertheless, holding U.S. dollars is still very attractive, especially in emerging markets, because the U.S. dollar is virtually the only currency that is recognized worldwide. Today, it is estimated that as much as $200 billion in U.S. currency still circulates outside the United States.

In some cases, emerging countries use the U.S. dollar to stabilize their own currencies. Panama and Liberia have made the U.S. dollar their official currencies. Hong Kong and Honduras peg their currencies to the dollar. In the shopping districts of Beijing and Shanghai, renminbi is routinely exchanged for U.S. dollars on open table tops. In spite of tight trade sanctions, it is estimated that the U.S. currency circulated in Vietnam may amount to as much as $600 million. As the current exchange rate in Vietnam is 10,000 dong to one U.S. dollar, the U.S. dollar is virtually the only currency that is feasible for large transactions, such as purchases of cars, computers, or other high-ticket items.

In Latin America, the importance of the U.S. dollar is particularly striking. In 1991, Argentina pegged its currency to its own holdings of dollars, gold, and other convertible reserves. Since that time, the inflation rate in Argentina has declined from 84% to 12%. In nearby Brazil in 1993 and early 1994, the exchange rate was 749 cruzeiros to the U.S. dollar, the inflation rate was an astronomical 3,000% per year, and short-term interest rates stood at over 10,000%! In mid-1994, a new Brazilian currency called the *real* was loosely linked to the U.S. dollar and the inflation rate dropped to less than 2% per month in August. Clearly, the U.S. dollar plays a central role in the stability of financial markets in Latin America.

The Canadian Dollar

As is true with the currencies of many other industrialized countries, the Canadian dollar (C$) has floated freely since the early 1970s. However, its strong link with the U.S. dollar has kept the two currencies highly correlated. Historically, international investors have been attracted to the Canadian dollar by the higher yields available on Canadian dollar instruments, vis-à-vis those available on U.S. dollar instruments, with relatively little incremental risk. The market in Canadian dollars is large and liquid. The Canadian dollar ranks seventh in worldwide trading volume after the U.S. dollar, the deutsche mark, the yen, the British pound, the Swiss franc, and the French franc. Currency transactions involving the Canadian dollar are estimated at US$44 billion per day. Ninety-eight percent of these transactions have the U.S. dollar on the other side.

There is an active derivatives market, particularly in Canadian dollar swaps. At the end of 1992, the equivalent of almost US$99 million in Canadian dollar interest-rate swaps were outstanding. This represented an almost 61% increase over the previous year. Also as of year-end 1992, the equivalent of US$45 million in Canadian dollar currency swaps was outstanding, representing an increase of over 42% against the previous year.

The Mexican Peso

The Mexican peso ($ or Ps or Mex$) was previously subjected to a two-tier system of exchange, a controlled rate and a free-market rate. The controlled rate was previously adjusted daily by the central bank (Banco de México). The transactions for which the controlled rate was applicable were (1) most foreign trade payments and receipts, (2) external debt servicing, and (3) the majority of foreign exchange conversions by maquiladora companies.[1] The free-market rate was available for every other type of transaction including (1) capital investments, (2) securities investments, (3) dividend remittances, (4) tourists' payments, and (5) some exports. Since November 1991, however, all such controls have been eliminated. The free-market exchange rate now applies to all transactions. There are no exchange controls in Mexico and there is no restriction on repatriation of capital.

In Mexican peso transactions, large spot transactions settle in two working days, while smaller transactions may be settled earlier. Average daily turnover in the peso exceeds the equivalent of $4 billion and the market is dominated by interbank activity. Deals between banks range from $2 million to $20 million and there are 35 large market participants. Banks account for 60% of all Mexican peso transactions, with the rest attributable to corporations and individuals. There is a limited forward market in dollars/pesos, with available maturities of usually no more than one year.[2] Previously, such forward contracts had been limited to domestic corporations, but Banco de México opened the dollar/peso forward market to foreign investors and corporations in September 1992. The forward contracts are referred to as *Cobetura* (cover) contracts. While a forward contract for one year is available, liquidity beyond six months is significantly reduced.

Exchange Rate Risk

Traditionally, the Canadian dollar has had a high correlation with the U.S. dollar. There are indications, however, that additional exchange risk may arise in the future. In 1993, the value of the Canadian dollar declined from US$.7865 to US$.7553.

The Bank of Canada, Canada's central bank, is wholly-owned by the Ministry of Finance. The policy-making arm of the Bank of Canada is the Board of Governors, whose members are selected from throughout Canada and represent a number of business sectors. The Bank of Canada is responsible for:

- Regulating credit and currency in the best interest of the economy.

- Controlling and protecting the external value of the Canadian dollar.

The primary tool that the Bank of Canada uses to implement monetary policy is the overnight or call rate which, in turn, influences the three-month Treasury-bill rate. Each week the Bank of Canada sets the overnight or call rate at 25 basis points (bp) above three-month Treasuries.

In the past two years, uncertainty in the political environment of Canada has caused international investors to have less interest in the Canadian dollar and in Canadian securities. As Canada is a major exporter of commodities, the Canadian dollar has also suffered from generally depressed commodity prices. The interest rate environment has weakened the currency as well. The Bank of Canada permitted the bank rate to fall from 7.36% to 4.11% in 1993. This led to a decline in the Euro-Canadian dollar interest rate from 6.75% to 3.75%. There are concerns that further interest rate reductions may be forthcoming. As the U.S. Federal Reserve began pursuing a policy of higher interest rates in early 1994, these dynamics suggest a decoupling of Canadian and U.S. interest rates which could lead to further volatility in the U.S./Canadian dollar exchange rate.

In Mexico, Banco de México intervenes, as necessary, to maintain the value of the peso. One of the most controversial elements of the reform program of President Carlos Salinas was a daily devaluation of the peso of 20 centavos, or 20/100s of a peso.[3] The systematic devaluation is to prevent speculative runs on the peso and speculative pressure on Mexican interest rates. This particular facet of the reform program was considered quite controversial because the devaluation of 20 centavos per day was much less than the actual inflation differential between Mexico and its major trading partners.

Beginning in 1993, the *nuevo peso* (NP) began circulating. The *nuevo peso* is worth 1,000 of the previous Mexican pesos. Also in 1993, the automatic devaluation increased by NP0.0002 per day to NP0.0004 per day, doubling the rate of implied devaluation. This increase in the automatic devaluation of the peso reduced some of the previous concern about an overvalued Mexican peso in light of the inflation differentials. The steady flow of capital entering Mexico to help offset its current account trade deficit has also helped to reduce concern about the peso.

Mexican monetary authorities appear to be committed to keeping the peso within acceptable parity limits with the U.S. dollar and to providing a stable environment for foreign investors. With the cooperation of Mexican and U.S. monetary officials in early 1994, even the civil uprising in Chiapas in the southern region of Mexico, the kidnapping of Alfredo Harp Helu (the second most influential person at Banamex—Mexico's largest bank), and the assassination of Luis Donaldo Colosio (President Salinas' hand-picked successor) did not fatally undermine the Mexican peso. In July—three months after his kidnapping—Harp was released in exchange for an undisclosed ransom (estimated to have been between $30 and $60 million). Ernesto Zedillo Ponce de Leon succeeded Colosio as the PRI candidate and won the national election in August 1994. As a Yale-educated economist, Dr. Zedillo has promised to continue the policies adopted during the Salinas administration.

The monetary and treasury authorities in the United States and Mexico orchestrated an ad-hoc, multi-billion-dollar currency swap facility in the first quarter of 1994 to stabilize the peso. In April, all three NAFTA countries created a permanent $8.7 billion swap facility to ensure future stability. Notwithstanding these coordination efforts, the possibility of foreign exchange fluctuations will impact business in the North American Free Trade zone.[4]

ELECTRONIC BANKING

With the relaxation of trade restrictions in the United States, Canada, and Mexico, it will be necessary to refine the systems of cross-border banking. One of the provisions of the North American Free Trade Agreement is the free flow of information across borders and ease of data processing that is necessary in the normal course of business.

Check Clearing

In the United States alone, the amount of funds transferred over data networks reaches $2.1 trillion per day. These transactions are associated with the settlement of checking account balances both in the United States and overseas. Each day, two billion checks are written in the United States.

Banks use the Federal Reserve System and its 12 regional offices to clear these checks. Fedwire is a high-speed electronic communications network (operated by the Federal Reserve Bank of New York) that links banks with the Federal Reserve Board of Governors, the 12 Federal Reserve District Banks and their 24 branches, the U.S. Treasury Department, and other federal agencies. Fedwire is the largest dedicated network in operation.

CHIPS (Clearinghouse Interbank Payments System), owned and operated by the New York Clearinghouse Association, transfers large amounts for interbank settlements. This computerized funds transfer system links 140 depository institutions and is used primarily for international dollar payments, accounting for 90% of the interbank payments relating to international trade.

In Canada, the check clearing function is much different. Since the system is highly concentrated, a small number of banks account for 90% of all bank assets and the vast majority of checks written.[5] Accordingly, Canadian banks have large nationwide networks. Through these networks and reciprocal agreements, consumer checks are cleared on a same-day basis, despite the fact that actual settlement occurs the next day. Writers of checks in denominations of $50,000 or more (business transactions) are assessed any float costs that might accrue.

In Mexico, there are three clearinghouses, one each in Mexico City, Guadalajara, and Monterrey. The largest banks, which account for the majority of check clearing activity in Mexico use encoded checks that can be mechanically scanned during the clearing process. However, smaller banks have not adopted this practice. The existing clearing system in Mexico promises to be a binding constraint within two to three years unless improved and/or additional clearinghouse facilities are constructed.

Electronic Payments and Interbank Networks

Electronic payments are effected through *automated clearinghouses (ACHs)* or through *wire transfers*. ACHs are computer-based clearing and settlement facilities for exchange of electronic debits and credits among financial institutions. ACH entries are often substituted for recurring payments (such as mortgage payments) or in the direct-deposit distribution of Federal and corporate benefit payments (such as Social Security payments). Increasingly, this form of payment also is being used as a payment processor for payments within the corporate sector. Federal Reserve Banks provide the data processing services for most ACHs. Funds are available for withdrawal on a next-day basis.

Wire transfers are direct, electronic payments that usually involve large dollar payments between financial institutions.

Fedwire and CHIPS provide these services. These funds are available for withdrawal on a same-day basis.

The Society for Worldwide Interbank Financial Telecommunications (SWIFT) is a nonprofit, cooperative organization that facilitates the exchange of payments messages, but not the payments, between more than 1,000 financial institutions in Europe and North America. SWIFT was developed as a more efficient alternative to telex or mail. Today, it is a widely used system for the secure transmittal of financial data. A SWIFT transaction is not a payment, but instead is an advice or instruction to transfer funds of a specified amount at another bank. The actual exchange of funds takes place on the domestic clearing system. Advices for payments by U.S. banks to their correspondent banks in Canada or Mexico are then handled by the respective domestic clearinghouses.

In August 1994, eight U.S. and Canadian banks announced the formation of Multinet International Bank, a new clearinghouse for foreign exchange transactions to be fully operational in early 1995. The eight founding members of the clearinghouse are Chase Manhattan Bank, First National Bank of Chicago, Royal Bank of Canada, Canadian Imperial Bank of Commerce, Bank of Nova Scotia, Bank of Montreal, National Bank of Canada, and Toronto Dominion Bank. The combination of the members' individual clearing functions is intended to save time and money by eliminating the need to clear each trade individually. Instead, trades will be netted and only one payment per day per currency will be necessary. The seven currencies that will be traded initially are the U.S. dollar, Canadian dollar, German deutsche mark, Japanese yen, British pound, French franc, and Swiss franc. Both spot transactions and forward contracts will be settled. Once Multinet is fully operational, other banks will also be able to join the network.

Retail Applications

Technology also affects transactions by individual customers, primarily through *automated teller machines (ATMs)* and *point-of-*

sale (POS) systems. The Cirrus Network, owned by Mastercard, allows funds to be withdrawn from an account at 80,000 ATMs in the United States. The Cirrus network is located in Denver and is connected to a number of other networks around the country:

- NYCE Automated Teller Machine Network in New York

- MAC Network in New York

- Yankee Network in New England

- STAR in California

- The National Plus Network, owned by Visa International

Electronic banking affects every facet of the banking system today in the United States. The networks in Canada are as well defined and developed as those in the United States. In fact, since the Canadian banking system is composed of relatively few banks vis-à-vis that of the United States, the Canadian ATM system complements its nationwide system of branches and is perhaps even more efficient than that in the United States. On the other hand, in Mexico 70% of the ATMs are controlled by just two banks—Banamex (30%) and Bancomer (40%).[6] The Mexican retailing banking market has not been developed to its full potential. The technological experience of U.S. and Canadian banks gives them a competitive advantage in the Mexican market in this regard.

In retail banking, POS electronic links accomplish the same outcome as wire transfers. However, while wire transfers typically involve large denominations, POS transactions are geared to the smaller denomination, high-volume retail market. Examples of such applications include grocery stores and service stations. A POS transaction is effected through the use of a debit card, which results in reduction of the payor's bank account balance (that is, a "debit" to deposit account of the payor) and a "credit" to the deposit account of the payee. After initial start-up costs for the banks involved, POS significantly reduces the cost of check processing by the participating institutions. This is still a growing area of technological applications in retail banking.

Bank Management Applications

The earliest application of computers within the banking system was the use of large mainframe computers to maintain the general ledger, loan, and deposit systems. When personal computers were introduced into the banking environment, the first uses were for office automation, spreadsheets, and word processing.

The most current application of computer technology within the bank is *client-server architecture*. This configuration allows the sharing of information and software among the many users of the system. Part of this software is now electronic mail, or E-mail. In a bank that is technologically up-to-date, as much as 70% of internal written communication is done through E-mail. The modern commercial bank must be able to change and add elements to its computer software and hardware systems.

As the profit emphasis in banking has shifted away from the interest rate spread and toward the generation of fee income, there has been increased emphasis on derivatives and derivative trading. Thus, software that enables the *pricing and valuation of derivatives* and their component parts also has become an integral part of the commercial bank computer architecture.

Systems of commercial banks must be able not only to keep track of loans and deposits but also to *track performance*. Analyses of individual client relations are best conducted with the help of systems that summarize all activity of each individual client. Each department then has a better sense of the services that are, or are not, being offered throughout the bank. Alternatively, the officer that is responsible for that client relationship is more knowledgeable and can provide better service. Even mundane tasks such as accounts payable can be incorporated into the computer system by permitting the scanning of invoices when received. In this way, the payment process is updated on a continuous basis and made far more efficient.

Expanding Scope of Applications

As the emphasis shifts toward more efficient provision of services, banks are spending increasingly larger sums on providing a *larger array of services via electronic means*. The ATM is the most important point of technological contact between banks and their customers. In the United States and Canada, ATM markets are mature, that is, the customer base is well served with adequate availability of ATMs. However, in Mexico (and other parts of Latin America) the use of ATMs is not as widespread. The ATM could conceivably provide an important inroad into the Mexican market by offering a comprehensive level of service without the necessity of building or staffing a freestanding facility. In this respect, ATMs will be a strategic part of the entry into retail banking in Mexico. They can be used in remote locations (outside the major cities of Mexico) where conventional branches are limited, but where customers need convenient access to banking services. ATM networks can be shared by a number of banks in locations with a relatively large amount of traffic, including shopping areas and other well frequented common areas.

The use of ATMs will, no doubt, develop in Mexico as it did in the United States—initially for the withdrawal of cash. As the banking habit becomes more deeply entrenched in Mexico, however, the ATM network can be used for making deposits and paying bills as well. Given the extent to which the country is severely underbanked it may also be possible to franchise ATMs to developing shopping areas. This arrangement has the advantage of permitting store owners and shopping facility owners to ensure that their customers have cash available. Sharing ATMs will benefit banks because the collaborating banks will also share the cost of ATM installation, a very capital-intensive exercise.

In the retail sector, the technology exists to construct a network of wide-ranging consumer services through an ATM configuration. Already in western countries, as much as 75-80% of all cash advances are provided through ATMs. Technology will provide an added advantage for the U.S. and Canadian banks that wish to gain a position in the Mexican market. This is especially true if the ATM system incorporates image processing and multi-media. Today deposit-taking through the ATM system is based primarily on trust. However, image processing will allow these functions to be processed more effectively. Imaging deposits and bills that will ensure a higher degree of integrity is built into the system. Although not immediately feasible, multi-media terminals can give banks the ability to have a real-time link between the customer and the bank advisor (bank employee) that may be located in a central office at a distant location.

While the initial investment is considerable, establishing such a wide-ranging ATM network can give U.S. and Canadian banks an advantage in the retail market that would be extended at such time as the telephone service in Mexico is also upgraded. Once the telephone system has been brought up to western standards, the *home banking capabilities* will be easier to implement through an existing electronic network. Clearly, such a large investment is an investment in the future and should be approached from that standpoint.

The importance of electronic networks in banking goes beyond the retail market and funds transfer between institutions and corporations. The actual facilitation of trade has begun to center on technology. Until recently, very little had changed in the way of trade finance for over 1000 years. However, now the most recent innovations in trade finance involve *electronic data interchange (EDI)*. This technology is still in its infancy but promises to be the method through which international trade and finance are conducted in the future. Typically, banks have used electronic systems in their trade finance in one of three ways:

- Generation and communication of documentation (document imaging and work flow are the newest developments)

- Payment transfers (through SWIFT or telex)

- Finalization of the bookkeeping process

However, these processes were confined to interbank transactions. The latest innovation in this field is the establishment of corresponding systems of technology in the customer's facility.

At this point, systems established on client premises are being introduced for only the largest customers. However, as is true with many technological innovations, what is now rare and unusual will become, at some point in the future, commonplace and typical. Currently, these systems enable customers to complete a number of trade transactions from their own locations:

- Make application for trade finance

- Transfer documentation electronically

- Generate letters of credit electronically

Examples of those banks that are now offering such EDI systems are Barclays in the United Kingdom (TradeManager), HongKong and Shanghai Banking Corporation in the United Kingdom and in Hong Kong (Hexagon), and Citibank in the United States (Citibanking).

Citibanking is Citibank's new system, introduced in 1993. Through a single window, Citibanking permits Citibank customers to access information about trade, cash management and securities. Citibanking customers may make inquiries about their import and export letters of credit and collections. Through EDI, they may initiate transactions, monitor the status of these transactions, receive up-to-date verification of their financial obligations, and generate various reports.

Requiring a customer to establish an electronic system that will tie into a bank's system represents a large commitment for the bank client and has several effects. It tends to:

- Commit the customer to one bank

- Form a basis for future electronic interfaces

- Greatly increase the efficiency with which trade finance can be conducted

As such systems are developed and placed in operation, some form of standardization will inevitably result. This standardization will make it easier for clients to interface with more than one bank and for a variety of purposes.

Because EDI is in its formative stages, there is a real opportunity for banks to develop the standards for these systems. That system which is most widely used will set the standards for the other systems, that is, for the entire industry. In terms of trade among the United States, Canada, and Mexico, this is an opportunity that is not limited strictly to the banks with the largest physical branch network. Instead, this opportunity presents itself to the bank with the clearest vision of the future that can transform the vision into up-to-date provision of those services that are appropriate in the North American Free Trade zone.

The Mexican banking market offers opportunities and challenges in other areas as well. Because there is no organized exchange for derivative securities, Mexican banks and other large investment institutions are developing and purchasing state-of-the-art *risk management software*. In January 1994, Banamex, Mexico's largest bank, reached an agreement with Algorithmics International, a risk management and financial software firm based in Toronto. Banamex has purchased the most recent version of RiskWatch. RiskWatch is a system that is useful in measuring and managing risk in international operations. Banamex envisions using the system across all treasury operations. A particularly interesting application will be pricing and evaluating the riskiness of derivative securities. However, its first application will be to manage foreign exchange and bond trading activity.

Banamex is part of the new holding company, Banacci, that has been formed since liberalization of the Mexican banking system. Accival, the brokerage firm owned by Banacci, is Mexico's largest brokerage firm and has considerable experience in the area of derivatives. It is expected that, in 1994, the Mexican government will authorize the establishment of a derivatives trading market—specifically, a market for listed options on equity securities. Banamex's RiskWatch system will position the bank to quickly analyze options and other derivatives as they are introduced.

The opportunities are tremendous in the area of electronic banking in the North American Free Trade zone. Technology can facilitate the development of markets that previously would have taken years to develop. With the support of existing and future technological advancements, these markets can be developed in much shorter periods of time.

Nevertheless, the fact remains that establishing a presence in Mexico is a costly endeavor. In Mexico City, the country's banking center, office space currently costs between $50 and $60 per square foot annually. This rate is twice the cost in New York City. To establish a conventional trading room, it is necessary to have fiber optics technology readily available, with reliable telephone service and satellite telecommunications capabilities. Clearly, these facilities are not readily available in Mexico at this point. While the opportunities are real, infrastructure issues cannot be ignored. Remaining mindful of both the costs and opportunities will enable U.S. and Canadian banks to realize significant increases in their current markets—specifically in the areas of trade finance, corporate finance, and retail banking.

BANKING OPPORTUNITIES IN MEXICO

Trade Finance

There are ample opportunities for trade finance in the North American Free Trade zone. Canada is the largest trading partner of the United States, sending roughly 75% of its exports to the United States and receiving 65% of its imports from the United States. Goods shipped from the United States to Canada are primarily finished products (70%). Almost 30% of these U.S. exports to Canada are motor vehicles, accessories, and parts. At approximately 20% of U.S. exports to Canada, the next largest category is machinery and mechanical appliances and parts.

Other important U.S. exports to Canada are electrical machinery; equipment and parts; plastic products; optical, photographic, and precision instruments; aircraft and parts; and fabricated iron and steel. In other categories of trade, the U.S. provides Canada with fresh fruits and vegetables, processed food products, petroleum, and petroleum products and coal. In these categories, the United States is Canada's primary foreign supplier. In terms of trading patterns, the United States dominates all other foreign trading partners of Canada. Japan, Canada's second most important trading partner, ships only 10% of the goods to Canada that are shipped by the United States.

Likewise, in Mexico the United States is the most important source of imported goods. Exports of Germany, Mexico's second largest trading partner, are slightly less than 10% of the exports of the United States to Mexico. Unlike the Canadian market, the Mexican market is not yet a mature market and there are considerable opportunities for exporting to Mexico.[7]

Recently, the volume of specific exports to Mexico was analyzed by the U.S. Department of Commerce and a Best Prospects List was generated. Exhibit 2-1 summarizes the contents of this list. For each sector, annual imports or sales by foreign companies in Mexico are indicated. The extent to which the sector is growing may be assessed by reference to the annual

EXHIBIT 2-1

BEST PROSPECTS FOR EXPORTING TO MEXICO

Category	Annual Imports[1]	Annual Import Growth	Market Competition[2]	Barriers[3]
1. Automotive Parts & Service Equipment	$905	12%	3	2
2. Apparel	750	15	3	3
3. Oil & Gas Field Machinery & Services	737	12	3	3
4. Industrial Chemicals	515	11	3	4
5. Plastics Materials & Resins	472	14	2	5
6. Chemical Production Machinery	453	13	4	4
7. Cosmetics & Toiletries	405	8	3	4
8. Computers & Peripherals	403	10	3	3
9. Machine Tools & Metalworking Equipment	278	15	3	5
10. Telecommunications Equipment	274	10	3	4
11. Medical Equipment	250	6	3	5
12. Computer Software & Services	211	10	3	5
13. Household Consumer Goods	199	7	4	5
14. Sporting Goods	184	20	2	5
15. Textile Machinery & Equipment	179	12	2	5
16. Franchising	173	15	4	4
17. Textile Fabrics	170	15	2	3
18. Electric Power Systems	153	6	2	3
19. Industrial Process Controls	151	12	4	5

EXHIBIT 2-1 BEST PROSPECTS FOR EXPORTING TO MEXICO (Cont'd.)

Category	Annual Imports[1]	Annual Import Growth	Market Competition[2]	Barriers[3]
20. Laboratory Scientific Instruments	150	15	4	5
21. Pollution Control Equipment	144	18	3	5
22. Business Equipment (non-computer)	134	6	2	3
23. Management Consulting Services	128	7	4	5
24. Plastics Production Machinery	121	12	3	5
25. Food Processing & Packaging Equipment	97	7	3	5
26. Printing and Graphic Arts Equipment	95	12	3	5
27. Agricultural Machinery & Equipment	91	12	4	5
28. Forestry & Woodworking Machinery	85	10	3	5
29. Security & Safety Equipment	81	15	3	5
30. Mining Industry Equipment	66	6	3	5
31. Building Products	67	18	3	5
32. Hotel & Restaurant Equipment	62	12	3	5
33. Construction Equipment	46	15	3	5
34. Architectural/ Engineering/ Construction Services	39	4	2	4
35. Dental Equipment	25	10	3	5
36. Electronic Components	16	10	3	5
37. Toys & Games	11	6	2	5
38. Advertising	9	7	4	3

EXHIBIT 2-1 BEST PROSPECTS FOR EXPORTING TO MEXICO (Cont'd.)

Category	Annual Imports[1]	Annual Import Growth	Market Competition[2]	Barriers[3]
39. Educational & Manpower Training Services	5	2	4	4
40. CAD/CAM Software	4	12	4	5

[1] Represents estimated annual imports or estimated sales per year by foreign-owned firms in millions of U.S. dollars.

2 Represents rating on a scale from 1 (very heavy competition) to 5 (very little competition).

3 Represents rating on a scale from 1 (very severe market barriers) to 5 (very few market barriers).

Source: Exporting to Mexico, Hong Kong: Trade Media Ltd., 1992, pp. 31-36.

import growth percentage. The Commerce Department also estimated the extent of competition in each sector, rating extremely heavy competition as 1 and very little competition as 5. Market barriers were also given values from 1 to 5, with 1 representing very severe market barriers and 5 very few market barriers.

As shown by this list, there are a number of areas in Mexico that are growing at double-digit rates and none of the 40 best prospects have competition that is classified as very heavy competition. A total of 22, or 55% of the 40 sectors, have been characterized as having average competitive circumstances, that is, a competition rating of 3. The remaining sectors are classified as either slightly more competitive than average or slightly less than competitive than average.

In terms of market barriers, it is clear that there are quite a few sectors that have very few market barriers.[8] A rating of 5 has been assigned to 25, or 62.5% of the 40 categories. Of the 40 categories, seven, or 17.5%, have been assigned a rating of 3, which can be considered an average degree of difficulty in accessing markets. Another 17.5% falls somewhere between these two rankings. None has been characterized with very severe market barriers and only one has a rating of 2, that is, has slightly greater market barriers than average.

In terms of financing trade, the U.S./Canadian exchanges are conducted through long-standing arrangements with banks in these respective countries. Within Mexico, most of the internationally accepted means of cross border financial settlement are accepted. However, there are certain preferred methods of payment, including letters of credit, open account, money orders, and telegraphic transfers.

The following sections describe a number of alternatives for trade finance. The most common method of financing trade in Mexico is through letters of credit. The letter of credit is the most popular because banks guarantee payment to either a greater or lesser extent. The letter of credit is also a good instrument for first-time exporters that do not have an established relationship with the purchaser of the goods. However, once a relationship has been established, a bill of exchange can be a more efficient and timely method of financing the trade. Forfaiting is also a common method of financing Mexican trade. Although used to a lesser extent, countertrade has also been a significant form of trade finance in Mexico and Latin America. Commercial banks should be aware of the various forms of trade finance and prepared to assist their clients by either offering a particular financing alternative or by referring the client to an appropriate third party. In addition, there are a number of government support programs in the United States, Canada, and Mexico that are supportive of all of these forms of finance.[9]

Letters of Credit. A *letter of credit (L/C)* is a document, usually issued by a bank upon instructions from the buyer of goods, that permits the seller of goods to draw a specified sum of money under specified terms. These specified terms typically specify receipt by the bank of certain documents that evidence compliance with terms of the transaction within a given period of time. When the bank accepts drafts that are drawn under a letter of credit, such acceptance assures the seller (or the seller's bank) that the claim will be satisfied.

Exhibit 2-2 lists various characteristics of letters of credit. A letter of credit is most often *irrevocable*. This means that the exporter is assured that the credit will be available. Banks should generally advise their clients not to accept letters of credit that are revocable. Such an arrangement can be canceled or altered by the drawee after it has been issued by the drawee's bank. On the other hand, before the date of expiration, an irrevocable credit cannot be canceled, revoked, or withdrawn without the consent of the party in whose favor the credit is granted.

Quite often a U.S. company will require that a letter of credit be *confirmed*. This is most often the case when an exporting company is accepting a letter of credit from a country that has a higher risk profile, that is, represents higher risk of nonpayment. Confirmation is a method of enhancing the foreign bank's credit status. The beneficiary of a letter of credit (exporter) may request a local bank to confirm the letter of credit of the foreign bank. Confirmation means that the local (confirming) bank assumes responsibility for payment of all drafts under the letter of credit. This is an added assurance for the exporting firm. In the absence of this process, the letter of credit is *unconfirmed*.

A *revolving* letter of credit describes the method in which the credit may be available. A revolving letter of credit may be either revocable, irrevocable, confirmed, or unconfirmed. A revolving credit will stipulate:

- Maximum total value available under the line of credit

- Maximum individual payments under the letter of credit

EXHIBIT 2-2
TYPES OF LETTERS OF CREDIT

- Irrevocable
- Confirmed vs. Unconfirmed
- Revolving
- Transferable
- Acceptance Credit

- Dates for which these values are relevant

- Final termination date of the letter

In a revolving credit, it is incumbent upon the importer or the user of the letter of credit to properly time all charges against the letter of credit to avoid exceeding any specified maximum stipulated in the letter of credit.

A *transferable* letter of credit is one under which a beneficiary has the right to give instructions to the accepting bank (or to any bank that is entitled to effect negotiations) to make the credit available to one or more third parties. This is a "trader" or middleman credit. Alternatively, a seller/exporter may use a transferable credit to pay a subcontractor. The beneficiary of a transferable credit has the right, within the constraints outlined in the letter of credit, to transfer the credit to suppliers anywhere. The credit essentially becomes a way for a trader to pay for goods that it sells to an ultimate buyer and obtains from an original supplier. The credit typically is set at the value equal to that which the ultimate buyer agrees to pay. The amount of credit that is transferred is the amount that the supplier of goods has agreed to accept as payment for the goods. When the supplier of goods presents documents that indicate that the goods have been satisfactorily delivered to the ultimate buyer, the suppliers invoice is paid and the trader or middleman receives the difference.

An *acceptance credit* is sometimes referred to as a "term credit" or "usance credit." The acceptance credit is perhaps the mostly widely used in that it substitutes the credit of the importer's bank for the credit of the importer itself. In this situation, the exporter (drawer) draws a draft on the accepting bank, which draft is accepted, typically, by the importer's bank (drawee). The drawee will accept the draft when all terms and conditions specified in the letter of credit have been satisfied. The process of acceptance guarantees payment to the exporter on the due date. At any time after acceptance, it is also possible for the exporter to receive payment prior to the due date by discounting the draft at the face amount less interest.

There are a number of ways in which U.S. banks can participate in the L/C market without establishing locations in Mexico or Canada. When a U.S. exporter receives a letter of credit it is typically through an "advising" bank. The process of *advising* is often no more involved than a U.S. bank placing a note with the letter of credit from a foreign bank, indicating that the letter of credit is authentic. For this service, an advising bank will receive $50 to $150.

Negotiating a letter of credit is the process of examining documents after shipment and paying according to the letter of credit. Typically, the advising bank is also the negotiating bank. In terms of timeliness and ease of communication, the interests of a U.S. exporter are best served when a U.S. bank, or at least a U.S. office of a foreign bank, negotiates a letter of credit. The typical fee for negotiating ranges from .125% to .5% of the amount of the letter of credit.

As noted earlier, *confirmation* is the process through which a local bank assumes responsibility for payment in the event that a less-well-known, more risky foreign bank does not pay according to the terms of the L/C. The typical fee for confirming is between .125% and 3.0%. However, if the foreign bank is extremely risky, a U.S. bank should be cautious about confirming its letters of credit. Also, a confirming bank will should have an open line of credit between itself and the foreign bank in question.

Bills of Exchange. A *bill of exchange* is an unconditional written order that requires one party to whom it is addressed to pay on demand, or at some future date, a sum of money to the order of a named party or bearer. The bill of exchange is the general classification in which acceptances and commercial bank drafts are classified. A bill of exchange is considered dishonored if it is not accepted by the drawee or not paid by drawee. At such time that a bill of exchange is refused, "noting" is the process of having the bill dated and initialled by a notary public. Collection of the bill then proceeds through appropriate legal channels.

The two types of bills are *sight bill* and *usance bill* of exchange. A sight bill is payable on demand, that is, at sight or on presentation. A usance bill is payable on a specified date in the future or on a determinable date in the future, for example, 180 days after sight. In order to qualify as a bill of exchange, an instrument must be specific with respect to date of payment and amount of payment. Note that bills of exchange can used in the context of a letter of credit. When a draft (bill of exchange) is drawn under a letter of credit, then subsequently accepted, it becomes a *banker's acceptance (BA)*.

Forfaiting. *Forfaiting* is the purchase, without recourse, of receivables from the export sales of goods. This is similar to factoring (the sale of receivables for immediate cash) with two important differences:

- Factoring involves credit terms that typically do not exceed 180 days; forfaiting can cover several years.

- Factoring does not protect against political risk or transfer risk; forfaiting does.

Forfaiting is a competitive financing alternative in many developing countries where hard currency is scarce and is important in Mexico, South America, Asia, and parts of Eastern Europe.

The origins of forfaiting can be traced back to periods prior to World War II (WWII). However, this form of financing did not reach high levels of acceptance or become widely used until after the war. *Aval* is the payment of a bill of exchange or promissory note that has been endorsed by the signature of a third party (usually a bank) that appears on the bill, which endorsement guarantees payment in the event of default by purchaser of goods. After WWII, many war-torn Eastern European countries needed to import grain, primarily from the United States. At the same time, there was a real scarcity of foreign exchange. Swiss bankers stepped in to finance these transactions. In the process, they bought the bills of exchange of U.S. and other suppliers *without recourse*, after they satisfied themselves that there was adequate assurance of aval. The Swiss bankers than presented the bills up for payment at the maturity date. Thus, the origin of forfaiting is as a Swiss-based method of financing grain deliveries.

Over time, the former Soviet Union and other Eastern European countries faced consistently difficult situations with respect to hard currency availability. The list of items that were financed through forfaiting expanded into a full range of commodities, products, capital goods, and large projects. Today, forfaiting activity is most heavily concentrated in London, which may be seen as the forfaiting capital of the world. Now the service is offered also by major banks, with several U.S. banks offering the service worldwide.

The instruments that are used in forfaiting are either bills of exchange or promissory notes. The bill of exchange or promissory note is inscribed with *per aval*, signed, and completed in the name of the party on whose behalf the aval is being provided. Technically, the avalist assumes the role of party that commits to make the payment. From the perspective of the forfaiter, the avalist becomes the debtor. The aval then is a simply form of guarantee for the forfaiter. This procedure is according to the old *Code Napoleon*. In international circles, there is no standardized guarantee. However, there are certain elements that must be contained in the aval. For example, the guarantee must be assignable and transferrable to permit the forfaiter to trade the debt in the secondary market, if so desired. It must indicate that the aval is unconditional. Thus, the aval and the letter of guarantee are the traditional forms of security for forfaiters.

There is also a secondary market in forfaiting circles. The paper that is generated can be sold in the secondary market to help spread the risk of the forfaiter and to increase the forfaiter's liquidity.

Countertrade. International *countertrade* is a practice in which a supplier commits contractually, as a condition of sale, to reciprocate and undertake certain specified commercial initiatives that compensate and benefit the buyer. Almost all countertrade activities are influenced by government intervention or scrutiny, either through legislation or through regulation at the ministerial level. Countertrade, or compensatory trade, is linked primarily to the inability of many developing countries to generate sufficient amounts of hard currency to purchase needed or desired imports. In some cases, countertrade is an alternative to no trade at all.

Countertrade is not appropriate for all exporters or for all types of trade transactions. Countertrade arrangements typically involve structuring deals that are tailor-made for the two sides of the transaction. This requires a large commitment of time and administrative resources. As a result, countertrade is most successful when undertaken either:

- Between countries that have an established relationship,

- By firms that have established foreign market positions, or

- By entities that have a substantial dollar value of transactions, together with substantial profit margins to absorb the administrative costs associated with countertrade.

In Latin America, the pressure to engage in countertrade has been reduced somewhat because of the reversal of previous capital flight.[10] Countertrade policies in Mexico during the 1980s crises included regulations that permitted Mexican firms to engage in countertrade activities. In 1982 and 1983, foreign exchange controls stipulated that Mexican firms had the right to reacquire, for import purposes, the foreign exchange that they had generated from exports and earlier sold to national credit institutions. Alternatively, Mexican exporters were permitted to sell or transfer their export-generated foreign exchange to Mexican importers. Thus, Mexican exporters had access to the foreign exchange that they earned from exports—either for their own import purposes or to facilitate the imports of other Mexican businesses. Countertrade transactions under these regimes require an approval by the Bank of Mexico and also a favorable opinion from the Ministry of Trade and Industry. In 1984, the country issued guidelines that outlined the rules by which hard currency export proceeds could be left abroad for future purchases.

In 1985, the Program for Integral Promotion of Exports (Profiex) endorsed the use of countertrade to boost exports. Examples of countertrade deals in Mexico included trading oil for cereals or trading parts for finished products among subsidiaries of the same firm. Through ALADI, the Latin American Integration Association, countertrade among the member countries was arranged through the respective countries' central banks.

Barter is the oldest form of countertrade and is an exchange of goods for goods. It is a one-time arrangement under a single contract. There are no financial transfers involved in barter transactions. Typically, these arrangements are made on a government-to-government basis. If the needs of one party in the transaction do not match the goods that are supplied by the other party, it may be necessary to employ a third party broker to dispose of the goods on the world commodity markets. Brokers can also swap deliveries of equivalent commodities such as, for example, petroleum, for other clients around the world to save on transportation costs.

In *buyback* or *compensation* countertrade, the original exporter accepts as full or partial payment products that are derived from the original exported product. This process can support the construction and financing of productive facilities such as, for example, the export of machine and capital products. An early example of the buyback arrangement was seen in the early 20th century in the United Kingdom, France, and especially Germany. In these cases, chemical companies purchased feed stocks from other European countries with less well developed industrial infrastructures and returned to them a specified amount of finished products such as pharmaceuticals and fertilizers. Buyback arrangements have now been used to finance turnkey plants or retrofitting and modernization of manufacturing facilities in developing countries.

Counterpurchase is an agreement through which the original exporter will accept, as full or partial payment, products that are not related to the original exported product. The items most often involved in counterpurchase arrangements have been traditional exports, such as agricultural commodities, fertilizer, bulk chemicals, and minerals. In some cases, the transactions have also included industrial and chemical goods, coffee, and textiles.

An interesting aspect of countertrade has been in oil trading. In the 1970s, OPEC had begun to agree on quotas in terms of each member country's individual oil shipments.[11] As the price of oil increased, many of these producers wanted to sell more than their quota. Exchanging oil in countertrade transactions blurred the economic effect because the oil was not sold for cash. In the early 1980s, a Boeing 747 air craft was exchanged for oil from Saudi Arabia. More recently, British Aerospace exchanged Saudi oil for Tornados. Since the mid-1980s, however, oil quotas have become less of a binding constraint and countertrade based on oil has declined in volume.

Nevertheless, countertrading continues to be applied in various ways in many countries. A firm conducting countertrade has two choices with respect to organizational approach. It can either structure an *in-house capability* to negotiate and manage the transactions or it can solicit the help of an *outside source*. If a firm elects to adopt the in-house approach, a senior countertrader must be employed, along with two or three support staff, office support for that staff, and associated expenses. The associated expenses will include primarily telephone expense and substantial outlays for travel. A company should be prepared to devote $300,000 to $400,000 per year to maintain such an in-house facility.

If the company decides to use an outside countertrade service, the providers may be banks, trading houses, and/or consultants. Major banks in New York, London and Frankfurt have large and experienced countertrade departments, generally included with their trade finance activities. Most commercial banks participate in the process by providing financial support for the countertrade and do not accept a commodity risk (either ownership or responsibility for sale of the commodity). On the other hand, trading houses will accept the actual commodities. However, it is relatively difficult to find a trading house that will accept finished manufactured goods. Consultants can be helpful in finding parties for the countertrade transactions. Typically, consultants will not accept the responsibility for the commodities or the financing.

One of the attractive features of countertrade for banks is that it is actually a two-sided transaction. The two transactions are tied to each other and the bank can provide interim financing since the two transfers of goods typically will not take place at the same time. Handling the interim financing associated with the countertrade can be a good source of interest and fee income for commercial banks.

Government Support. In Canada, new strides are being made to support the export industry. The *Export Development Corporation (EDC)* is Canada's official export credit agency. Under recent changes in its structure and bylaws, EDC will be permitted to engage in equity financing and securitization. EDC had been operating under the provisions of a legislative act that dates back to 1969. Three sectors have been opened with a recent change in the structure of the organization:

- Securitization

- Venture-capital-style equity investment

- Pre-export financing

The organization will now be permitted to securitize Canadian receivables and to provide insurance as a part of that securitization. When EDC is associated with an equity offering, the credibility of the issuing company will be significantly enhanced by the EDC affiliation. Pre-export financing will enable the Canadian agency to provide financing that previously was not available. Previously, Canadian firms were able to receive no assistance from EDC for the upfront costs of research and development, product development, or export market development. Now, some of that cost can be supported by the government agency.

In 1985, Mexico began a phase-out of credit and fiscal incentives for import substitution. In that year alone, the percentage of imports that were subject to licensing was slashed from 83% to 37%. Now most of the import substitutions incentives have been eliminated. The reform measures, however, do retain certain items that are consistent with GATT principles.[12] Foreign suppliers of equipment and material to Mexican export-oriented firms can benefit from certain advantages under these programs:

- Exemptions or rebates on tariffs for imports used in the production of exports

- Faster processing when obtaining approvals from administrative agencies

- Incentives for establishing trade companies

The Program for Temporary Imports to Produce Export Goods (PITEX) exempts Mexican firms from paying tariffs on goods that they have imported for the purpose of producing export items. There is a zero tariff assessed on such goods because they are being brought in only to be exported. In order to be eligible for the exemption, Mexican companies must export more than $500,000 per year or must export more than 10% of their total sales. Those companies that can demonstrate that their imports are being brought in for re-export will have a comparative advantage in the Mexican market.

The *Program for High-Volume Exporters (ALTEX)* helps Mexican firms to receive priority processing for applications. This priority treatment involves timeliness of authorizations, import rebate, and other elements. Firms that export 40% of sales or at least $2 million annually are eligible for the ALTEX program.

Foreign Trading Companies (ECEX) is structured to encourage the formation of trading companies in Mexico. While there are many exporting enterprises, few have evolved into sizable firms. Companies that qualify under this program receive the ALTEX treatment and financial and administrative perks. In order to be eligible, trading companies must export the equivalent of US$3 million annually and have the equivalent of US$100,000 in capital.

In the United States, the *Export-Import Bank of the United States (Eximbank)* is an independent public banking corporation that was established in 1934. The Eximbank facilitates the financing of exports, imports, and commodities exchanges between the United States and foreign countries. It will often offer direct credit to non-U.S. borrowers, as well as export guarantees, export credit insurance, and discount loans.

The Eximbank is perhaps the largest trade creditor in North America and has been primarily interested in Latin American trade from its inception in 1934. The bank has been particularly active in financing high-ticket U.S. exports such as aircraft and power generators. As of the third quarter of 1993, Latin America represented 40% of its worldwide exposure, with Mexico alone (its single largest market), accounting for 17% of its global exposure.

As trade increases among the United States, Canada, and Mexico, commercial banks have significant opportunities to participate in trade finance. There are many ways to become involved and many niche markets that can be filled. The first step for any commercial bank is identifying the market niche for which that institution is best suited.

Corporate Finance

Historically, the Mexican economy has been dominated, to a large extent, by state-owned enterprises and there was little foreign presence. However, since reforms of the Salinas administration have been introduced, investment by the private sector and by foreign investors has increased substantially. Between 1985 and 1989, aggregate foreign investment grew by over 70% from roughly $15 billion in 1985 to almost $26 billion, with most of this increase occurring after 1986 when Mexico joined GATT.

From 1987 to 1991 the investment by U.S. investors grew from $5 billion to $21.5 billion, representing 63% of all foreign investment in Mexico.

Even before the negotiations for the North American Free Trade Agreement were complete, a number of important laws and rules were introduced that opened the Mexican market to increased private investment. Among these were:

- Reform of foreign investment regulations (May 1989)

- New franchising rules (January 1990)

- New regulations transfer of technology (June 1990)

- New protection for intellectual property (June 1991)

- Several improvements in taxation of foreign businesses

Under the new rules for *foreign investment* in Mexico foreign investors are permitted to own 100% of enterprises in areas that represent more than two-thirds of the Mexican economy. Prior approval is still required by the National Foreign Investment Commission (NFIC). However, it is easier and faster to comply with the new rules. New foreign investment need not be reviewed by the NFIC if all of the following conditions are met:

- It does not involve more than $100 million in investment

- Funding is from abroad

- It is not located in Mexico City, Monterrey or Guadalajara

- A plan is presented that demonstrates the foreign exchange earnings and expenses over the first three years will be in balance

- The investment creates permanent jobs and worker training programs

- The facility will use adequate technology

Under the new *franchising* law, only a simple registration is required with minimal disclosure. Previously, every franchise agreement required individual registration with the government, even individual franchise outlets.

Under the new *technology-transfer* rules, parties are now permitted complete freedom in setting royalty payments. Many restrictions on the length of agreements have been removed, although some conditions still apply.

Before the *Law for Development and Protection of Industrial Property*, it was not illegal for anyone in Mexico simply to use a patented process or product. The new law is in line with the principles of GATT and the World Intellectual Property Organization (WIPO). Twenty-year patents are now issued for all processes and products, including those for chemicals, alloys, pharmaceuticals, foods, beverages, biotechnology, and plant varieties. Industrial and trade secrets are also protected by this law. Trademarks are registered for goods and services without any requirement of previous use in commerce and are protected for ten years. The judicial procedures surrounding the enforcement of the law have been simplified. Lastly, criminal and civil sanctions for violations of the intellectual property law have been strengthened.

All these changes have made it possible for foreign investors to more easily do business in Mexico. While impediments have not been eliminated entirely, it is a much conducive environment for corporate investment and operation. In this new environment, U.S. banks have made a significant contribution. For example, lending by U.S. banks in 1991 to private Mexican companies amounted to $3.5 billion—9.6% of lending by Mexican banks.

Retail Banking

Severely underbanked is perhaps the best phrase to describe the Mexican retail market. The population per Mexican bank branch is 19,000. In the United States, the comparable statistic is 4,000 residents per bank branch. In Mexico consumer credit is

6% of GDP, in the United States 65%. As incomes and employment opportunities improve in Mexico, the opportunities for retail banking will also increase. The opportunities relate primarily to credit cards, mortgage finance, automobile loans, and other consumer finance.

Many of the possibilities with respect to retail banking through ATMs and credit cards have been discussed above. (See the section entitled "Electronic Banking.") In addition to the consumer market in checking, savings, and credit card accounts, the *mortgage market* represents considerable promise. In the 1980s, the mortgage market in Mexico was essentially stagnant. To obtain a residential apartment, individuals were often required to pay cash. As a result, there is considerable pent-up demand for mortgage finance in Mexico. Unlike the United States, Mexico has virtually no secondary mortgage market. The Mexican government has identified mortgage-backed securities as one important element in the development of Mexican capital markets.

This is not to suggest that there are no challenges to be overcome in the development of the Mexican mortgage market. The Mexican rules will require clarification with respect to the transfer of property titles so that mortgages can be assigned easily as collateral in mortgage pools that back bond issues. In addition, it will be necessary to modify the Mexican procedure for foreclosing on defaulted mortgages. In some cases, a considerable amount of time is required to obtain title for the property that has been pledged as collateral.

If these procedures can be streamlined, however, it is apparent that there will be ample market for residential mortgages. In addition to foreign investors that may be anxious to earn the high yields available on such mortgage-backed securities, there are also domestic insurance companies, mutual funds, and pension funds that are affiliated, in many cases, with the new financial groups that have been formed in Mexico.[13]

For U.S. banks, there is a considerable incentive to become involved in the Mexican mortgage market. Most mortgages are denominated in floating interest rates and are reset each month.

Currently, the floating rate is in the neighborhood of 26%! This compares quite favorably with the 28-day rate on Mexican government securities of 14%. The third largest bank in Mexico, Banca Serfin, recently introduced fixed-rate mortgages for up to 15 years at 18%.

U.S. and Canadian banks have an opportunity to enter the mortgage finance arena and take advantage of what is currently a relatively inefficient system of credit assessment. Computerizing systems and careful monitoring of outstanding loans can make a new entrant much more efficient than other banks currently operating in the Mexican retail mortgage market. Historically, the Mexican mortgage market has been one of the best sectors in terms of low default rates. Homeowners are typically very conservative and a mortgage is one of the first obligations that is paid. In contrast, credit card loans in Mexico have a higher default rate. The retail market promises to be a strong arena for growth in the banking industry of Mexico.

There has been some hesitation on the part of non-Mexican banks to enter the Mexican retail market because of the concentration of assets among the top three—Banamex, Bancomer, and Banca Serfin. However, the fact remains that retail banking will be benefited by Mexican demographics. Roughly 50% of the Mexican population is under the age of 20 years. This suggests that, to the extent that employment opportunities are available, the relatively young population will continue to represent a large segment of the population, incomes will rise, and there will be strong demand for all forms of financial services that are customarily associated with a population of growing families.

NORTH AMERICAN BANKING

In the North American Free Trade zone, advancements in currency trading and trade finance will cause the national boundaries of the United States, Canada, and Mexico to become less meaningful. As these banking markets gradually harmonize, the availability of corporate finance and retail banking will converge within the three countries. Many of the largest U.S. and Canadian banks are poised to enter Mexico, if they have not already done so. Among these are Citibank, Chemical, Chase Manhattan, Morgan Guaranty, Bankers Trust, Bank of America, Midland, NationsBank, First Union, Bank of Montreal, Royal Bank of Canada, and the American units of the European banks, Deutsche Bank and Swiss Bank Corporation.

Citibank has been permitted to operate in Mexico since 1929 and is the only foreign bank with this privilege. It has seven branches in Mexico and employs 800 people. In the early 1990s, Citibank participated in $10 billion of fundraising by Mexican borrowers, including $3 billion of securitized receivables, $2 billion in commercial paper programs, $1.7 billion in Eurobond issues, $1 billion in Mexican bank certificates of deposit, $1 billion in medium-term notes, and $1.1 billion in a single jumbo bridge loan for CEMEX, the Mexican cement producer. Citibank is the U.S. depository bank for most American Depository Receipts (ADRs) of the stock of Mexican companies.[14] In addition, Citibank has placed a large number of the Mexican government securities issues outside of Mexico. Citibank is actively pursuing a buildup of its consumer banking network in Mexico through its Diners Club credit card franchise and the 30 new branches that it plans to open in Mexico City, Guadalajara, Monterrey, and Tijuana. Thus, Citibank plans to pursue the areas of corporate and consumer banking, securities, and leasing.

Other major U.S. banks also plan a significant presence in Mexico.

- Chase Manhattan is planning to attract banking clientele from the corporate sector through a Mexican subsidiary, concentrating on corporate banking, securities, and currency trading.

- The subsidiary of Chemical Banking will operate with twice the staff in Monterrey that it has historically maintained. The emphasis will be on corporate banking, securities, and project finance.

- Bankers Trust plans to operate a securities firm, forgoing a banking license, and will focus on (1) securities underwriting and trading and (2) derivatives.

- J.P. Morgan plans a subsidiary that will concentrate on corporate banking, securities, and investment management.

- Republic New York Corp. will be engaged primarily in corporate banking and trading.

- Fleet Financial plans to start a mortgage bank in a joint venture with Banco Mexicano.

Smaller banks also are planning to take advantage of the reduced barriers to trade and capital flow associated with NAFTA. International Bank of Commerce in Laredo Texas, with $2 billion in assets, has 27 branches and most of them are located along the Texas/Mexican border.

There are a number of different opportunities for U.S. and Canadian banks in the newly expanded market in North America. Some require a presence in Mexico or Canada, others simply require expertise in a particular area of trade finance or telecommunications. In an era when the growth potential for U.S. commercial banks is considered to be limited by regulatory restrictions and heightened competition, banking in the North American Free Trade zone is one of the few frontiers left for the expansion of market share.

SELECTED REFERENCES

"Agreement Brings Down Banking Barriers," *Euromoney* supplement, January 1993.

Carroll, Paul B. "Mexico Family to Pay Ransom for Executive," *Wall Street Journal*, August 3, 1994, p. A5.

Dunford, Campbell, editor. *The Handbook of International Trade Finance*, New York: Woodhead-Faulkner (Simon & Schuster), 1991.

"Emerging-Market Indicators," *The Economist*, March 26, 1994, p. 132.

Exporting to Canada, Hong Kong: Trade Media Ltd., 1992.

Exporting to Mexico, Hong King: Trade Media Ltd., 1992.

Gandy, Tony. "The Best of Both Worlds (Technology)," *The Banker*, November 1993, pp. 88-92.

"Guide to Currencies," *Euromoney* supplements, 1993 and 1994.

Kessler, Judd L. "How Mexican Laws Affect Foreign Business," *Export Today*, January/February 1993, pp. 42-45.

King, Paul. "New Law Enables EDC to Cultivate Fresh Assets," *Euromoney* supplement, September 1993, p. 31.

Kurtzman, Joel. *The Death of Money: How the Electronic Economy Has Destabilized the World's Markets and Created Financial Chaos*, New York: Simon & Schuster, 1993.

Leuchter, Miriam. "NY Banks Rush to Expand in Mexico," *New York Times*, July 11, 1994.

Lipin, Steven. "Eight Banks Form Clearinghouse to Cut Cost of Foreign-Exchange Transactions," *Wall Street Journal*, August 1, 1994, pp. A2 & A4.

Marray, Michael. "Mortgage-Backed Market Coming Next," *Euromoney*, November 1993, p. 22.

Messner, Stephen C. "South America: The Comeback Continent," *Export Today*, November/December 1993, pp. 40-44.

Moffett, Matt. "Mexico's New Peso May Look Like Less But It's Worth More," *Wall Street Journal*, January 8, 1993.

Newman, Gray and Anna Szterenfeld. *Business International's Guide to Doing Business in Mexico*, New York: McGraw-Hill, 1993.

Peagam, Norman. "Appetite for Latin Deals Increases," *Latin American Trade Finance, Euromoney* supplement, May 1994, pp. 144-151.

Rehberg, Virginia. "Letters of Credit: Cracking the Code," *Export Today*, September 1991, pp. 21- 23.

Rosenberg, Jerry M. *Dictionary of International Trade*, New York: John Wiley & Sons, 1994.

Talmor, Sharona. "After You (Technology)," *The Banker*, March 1994, pp. 74-76.

Talmor, Sharona. "Trade Partners Get Hooked Up (Technology)," *The Banker*, February 1994, pp. 65-67.

Talmor, Sharona. "Step-by-step (Technology)," *The Banker*, January 1994, pp. 71-75.

Ullmann, Owen, Pete Engardio, Peter Galuszka, and Bill Hinchberger. "The Global Greenback," *Business Week*, August 9, 1993, pp. 40-44.

Verzariu, Pompiliu. *International Countertrade: A Guide for Managers and Executives*, Washington, D.C.: U.S. Department of Commerce, International Trade Administration, 1992.

Verzariu, Pompiliu and Paula Mitchell. *International Countertrade: Individual Country Practices*, Washington, D.C.: U.S. Department of Commerce, International Trade Administration, 1992.

Zecher, Joshua. "Banamex Cuts the Risk Designer-Style," *Wall Street Technology*, Vol. 11, No. 11 (April 1994), pp. 46-50.

ENDNOTES

1. See Chapter 1 for a description of the maquiladora program in Mexico.
2. A forward exchange contract is an agreement between two parties to exchange one currency for another on a future date. The contracts do not involve standard amounts of currency and, unlike futures contracts, do not trade on organized exchanges.
3. See Chapter 1 for a description of the economic reforms of Mexican President Carlos Salinas.
4. It should be noted that the ultimate goal of the Mexican authorities is for the peso to have a fixed rate against the U.S. dollar.
5. See Chapter 3 for a description of the Canadian banking system.
6. See Chapter 3 for a description of the Mexican system.
7. In fact, in the first quarter of 1994, U.S. exports to Mexico totaled almost $12 billion, implying an annualized export volume of $48

billion. This would represent a 15% increase over the $41.9 billion shipped to Mexico in 1993.

8. Market barriers are classified as either government or private sector barriers.

9. It should be noted that selling on open account has a very different context in Mexico than in the United States. In the United States, an open invoice has the power of a legal document. Should the invoice not be paid, the purchaser of the goods can be sued in a court of law for nonpayment. On the other hand, in Mexico an invoice is not a legal document and this recourse is not available to the seller. Thus, more fully documented forms of finance should be recommended to bank clients that export to Mexico.

10. In Eastern Europe and the former Soviet Union, the lack of hard currency continues to exert major pressures that favor countertrade arrangements.

11. OPEC is an acronym for Organization of Petroleum Exporting Countries.

12. GATT is an acronym for General Agreement on Tariffs and Trade. The multilateral trade treaty was signed on January 1, 1948. As a result of this treaty, average worldwide tariffs have been reduced from 40% to 5%. Since Mexico joined GATT in 1986, the country has worked to develop market structures that are consistent with world standards of competitiveness and efficiency.

13. See Chapter 3 for a detailed description of the new Mexican financial groups.

14. A depository receipt allows the trading of foreign stocks within the United States on organized stock exchanges. The shares of a firm are deposited into a bank in the country in which the firm is incorporated (in this case, a Mexican bank). An American bank then issues depository receipts for the securities. In this way, the foreign ownership of the stock is registered. See Chapter 4 for a discussion of Mexican ADRs.

3 The Canadian and Mexican Banking Systems

INTRODUCTION

The United States is now linked with Canada and Mexico in an agreement that is intended to increase trade across the national boundaries of these three countries. For U.S. bankers, this represents new opportunities and new challenges, particularly in the Mexican market. While each of the three systems is based on the same basic principles of banking, in practice, the Canadian and Mexican systems differ significantly from that of the United States. Both the Canadian and Mexican banking systems are highly concentrated with a large share of banking assets held by relatively few institutions. Both bank systems have traditionally enjoyed special status in their respective countries with respect to government legislation, including protection from foreign competition—at least until recently.

THE CANADIAN BANKING SYSTEM

The Canadian banking system is a nation-wide, high-technology system of banking. Six institutions control over 90% of Canadian banking assets:

- Royal Bank of Canada

- Canadian Imperial Bank of Commerce

- Bank of Montreal

- Toronto-Dominion Bank

- Scotiabank

- National Bank of Canada

Exhibit 3-1 shows that these six banks controlled US$456 billion in assets at the end of 1992 and US$23 billion in capital. Tier 1 capital as a percentage of assets ranges from 3.98% to 6.90%.[1] Provisions for loan loss in 1992 caused negative operating results for Canadian Imperial Bank of Commerce and National Bank of Canada. The country's largest bank, Royal Bank of Canada, barely was profitable at a .05% return on assets. The Bank of Montreal, Toronto-Dominion Bank, and Scotiabank earned solid ROAs ranging from .90% to 1.23%.

The process by which the Canadian banking system became so concentrated is an interesting contrast to the experience in the United States. Because of its special relationship with government, the Canadian banking system has been permitted to evolve into a well established and protected system. At the same time, because of that special relationship and protection, it is possible for foreign banks to find and fill competitive niches in the Canadian market.

Historical Overview

The first banks in Canada prior to the 1800s were actually merchants who performed banking functions. Subsequent develop-

EXHIBIT 3-1
MAJOR CANADIAN BANKS - 1992

Bank	Tier 1 Capital	Assets	Capital Ratio	Profits	Return on Assets
Royal Bank of Canada	$5,435	$106,900	5.08%	$ 51	.05%
Canadian Imperial Bank of Commerce	4,950	99,258	4.99	-18	-.02
Bank of Montreal	4,081	85,610	4.77	855	1.00
Toronto-Dominion Bank	3,906	56,591	6.90	512	.90
Scotiabank	3,684	75,780	4.86	931	1.23
National Bank of Canada	1,255	31,536	3.98	-27	-.09

Note:
1. Amounts are in millions of U.S. dollars.
2. Capital ratio does not use risk-weighted assets.

Source:
"Top 100 by Country," *The Banker*, July 1993, pp. 145-175.

ment of a true banking system facilitated the flow of goods and services. Early trade in Canada (as was true in the United States) was concentrated in commodities and natural resources. Fur trade was a particularly important element of the Canadian economy.

During the 19th century, Britain was Canada's primary source of capital. Canada's relationship with the United States was strained in the early 19th century because of hostilities between the British in the United States and the French in Canada. In fact, tensions between the British and the French divided Canada itself for many years. Under the British North America Act of 1867 the Canadian Confederation was formed. The Dominion of Canada became self-governing with the provinces of Ontario, Quebec, New Brunswick, and Nova Scotia. These founding members of the confederation were joined by Manitoba (1870), British Columbia (1871), Prince Edward Island (1873), Alberta and Saskatchewan (1905), and Newfoundland (1949). In 1869, the Northwest Territories were purchased from the Hudson's Bay Company, a British Corporation that had been chartered to operate the fur trade monopoly in North America.[2]

Canada is an extremely large country as a result of the confederation in the 19th century. It is the world's top exporter of minerals and forest products. It is second only to the United States in grain exports. Even today, commodities represent 60% of Canadian exports. However, this huge land mass is inhabited by only 28 million residents, as compared to 255 million in the United States. Most of the industry in Canada is concentrated around the Canadian-U.S. border. The Canadian economy is more dependent on its exports than that of any other leading industrialized country. Its small home market simply is not large enough to generate the kind of economic activity necessary to maintain its relatively high standard of living. In the 1870s, Canada imposed heavy import tariffs to help develop its own industries.

The banking system has been influenced by these dynamics within Canada. The first real bank in Canada was the Bank of

Montreal, which began operations in 1817 and received its formal charter in 1822. The government influence over the Canadian banking system was reflected in this early charter. The original charter:

- Was granted for only 10 years

- Prohibited the bank from owning real estate other than bank premises

- Prohibited the bank from making loans collateralized by real estate

- Required annual reports to shareholders with specified information

- Placed a ceiling of 6% on loan interest rates

In contrast, strict U.S. government supervision of commercial banks in the United States did not begin until enactment of the National Bank Act of 1863.

In terms of regulation, the Finance Ministry of Canada implements both fiscal and monetary policy. The original Bank Act was passed in 1871 and subsequent amendments to this act have shaped the financial system of Canada. The Bank Act Amendment of 1924 established the Office of the Inspector General of Banks, Canada's primary bank examiner. The Canadian Central Bank, the Bank of Canada, was created by a 1934 amendment of the Bank Act.

Over time, government restriction of Canadian bank operations has eased. Residential mortgage loans with a 15% government guarantee have been permitted since 1936. In the mid 1940s, the government began to guarantee short- and intermediate-term bank loans to farmers and veterans. Also, the government lifted loan interest rate ceilings in 1967. This development is particularly noteworthy because it was 13 years before the major deregulatory thrust in the United States.

In the early 1980s, Canadian banks were permitted to offer discount brokerage services. In the late 1980s, Canadian banks were permitted to own securities subsidiaries, a practice that is allowed for only a few U.S. banks. In July 1994, the most recent acquisition by a Canadian bank involved the Bank of Montreal. With its purchase of Burns Fry Ltd. for C$403 million (US$293 million) and the merger of this new firm with its already existing brokerage subsidiary (Nesbitt Thomson Corp.), Bank of Montreal created Canada's largest brokerage firm in terms of equity capital (C$450 million) and number of registered brokers (1100). The new firm—Nesbitt Burns—is substantially larger than the next largest competitor, RBC Dominion Securities with equity of C$256 million and 902 brokers. This latest acquisition brings the share of Canadian brokerage revenues controlled by the six largest Canadian banks to 51%.

The heavy involvement of the government in the banking industry in Canada has not implied as much restriction of activity as has been the case in the United States. There has been a good relationship between government and the banking industry in Canada. Canadian banks have been permitted to expand their lending powers virtually as desired and have enjoyed a great deal of freedom to offer a variety of deposit instruments. This contrasts sharply with the U.S. experience in which the legislative process has been relatively slow to expand bank powers and, for the most part, deregulation has been implemented by federal and state regulators.

The equivalent of a commercial bank in Canada is a *chartered bank*. Between 1820 and 1970, only 157 charters were granted. The Canadian authorities made a conscious effort to avoid what they considered the fragmented banking system of the United States that resulted from a large number of banks. Of the 157 charters, 60 were never used, 45 banks either failed or ceased operation for some other reason, and a number of these were merged with other banks. As a result, the concentrated system in which relatively few banks hold the majority of Canadian banking assets has emerged.

Just as the industrial sectors of Canada look to export markets to realize their growth potential, Canadian banks today are expanding their scope of operation in search of market expansion. In the 1980s, Canadian banks began to concentrate more on North America. Having been permitted greater powers through deregulation they have purchased Canada's largest securities dealers, made major acquisitions in the trust industry, started insurance subsidiaries, and assumed a major role in the mutual fund industry. Canadian banks are actively looking for acquisitions in Southeast Asia and the Americas. Notably, Scotiabank has recently bought a small stake in Inverlat, the Mexican financial services group. The outward focus of Canada is reflected in the outward focus of the Canadian banking system. The North American Free Trade Agreement will facilitate international expansion by the banking system.

The Royal Bank of Canada

The Royal Bank of Canada is the largest bank in Canada with assets in excess of $100 billion. It is also Canada's largest bank credit card issuer and controls 26% of all Canadian personal deposits. The institution began operations as the Merchants Bank in 1864. Almost from the beginning, its focus has had a southern exposure, as its first operations were located in Halifax, the port city of Nova Scotia. When Merchants Bank was established, Halifax was enjoying considerable trade activity that had been stimulated by the U.S. Civil War.

The bank was incorporated as the Merchants Bank of Halifax in 1869, after which time it began opening branches in other cities of Eastern Canada. In 1882, Merchants opened a branch in Bermuda. When gold was discovered in Canada and Alaska, the bank began to establish branches in Western Canada. It then expanded into New York and Cuba in 1899. It was so successful in Cuba that it purchased two banks—Banco de Orient in 1903 and Banco del Comercio in 1904. To avoid confusion with another bank, Merchants changed its name in 1901 to Royal Bank of Canada. Then in 1907, the bank transferred its headquarters from Halifax to Montreal and continued to grow, in many cases, through acquisitions. Among the acquisitions that were added to the Royal Bank empire were:

- Union Bank of Halifax (1910)

- Traders Bank of Canada (1912)

- Bank of British Honduras (1912)

- Quebec Bank (1917)

- Northern Crown Bank (1918)

- Union Bank of Canada (1925)—its largest acquisition

After WWII, Royal Bank of Canada became an aggressive financier of the Canadian oil-and-gas and minerals industries, placing it squarely in the center of Canadian economic growth. At the same time, the bank maintained its outward focus in terms of international operations. Although it was forced to sell its Cuban banks after Fidel Castro assumed power in Cuba in 1959, it continued to expand into other offshore arenas. In the late 1970s and early 1980s, there were acquisitions in Britain, Germany, Puerto Rico, and the Bahamas. Its already existing New York subsidiary, Royal Bank and Trust Company, was further strengthened.

Deregulation in the Canadian banking system has been fully embraced by the Royal Bank of Canada. In 1987, Royal Bank required Dominion Securities after the stock market crash in October 1987 had reduced the price of acquisition by $100 million. In 1991, the U.S. Federal Reserve approved a Section 20 subsidiary for the Royal Bank in the United States, RBC Dominion.[3] This authorization gave the Royal Bank (through RBC Dominion) the power to underwrite equities securities in the United States. Also in 1991, the Royal Bank acquired the Quebec-based investment banking firm of McNeil Mantha Inc. for $22 million dollars.

Like other large Canadian banks, the Royal Bank of Canada hopes to capitalize on its high-technology base and its nationwide banking presence in Canada to exploit the opportunities available under the North American Free Trade Agreement. Its stated objective is to acquire a small bank in the United States and then to build on that base as the barriers to U.S. interstate banking are reduced.[4] Royal Bank is a major trader of foreign currency in the United States, one of the largest among the foreign banks operating in the United States.

Of course, its expansion plans have been complicated by the economic recession in Canada which has generated higher loan loss provisions and a reduction in corporate banking profits. Early in 1993, the Royal Bank closed its office in Buffalo and announced plans to eliminate as well its Pittsburgh and Atlanta offices. The bank will concentrate on its remaining U.S. offices for the time being—New York, Chicago, Houston, Los Angeles, and Miami. Despite these temporary setbacks, the Royal Bank of Canada remains committed to an eventual expansion in the United States and opportunities that are yet to unfold.

Foreign Banks in Canada

Because of the high concentration in assets held by the top six commercial banks in Canada and the close relationship that these banks have with the Canadian government, foreign bank entry into the current Canadian banking market has been somewhat difficult. Barclays Bank of the United Kingdom was the first foreign bank to open a Canadian office in Montreal in 1928. Other European banks followed, concentrating primarily on portfolio investments by European investors. Even by the 1960s, the presence of foreign banks in Canada was marginal. In 1966, 89% of the shares of all banks in Canada (both Canadian and foreign-owned institutions) were held by Canadians. This was true despite the fact that there was no limit on foreign ownership of Canadian banks until 1967.

In 1963, Mercantile Bank (a European bank in Canada) was acquired by First National City Bank of New York (now Citibank). This acquisition raised concerns about the extent to which the Canadian banking system would come to be dominated by U.S. institutions. Generally, the extent of direct investment by U.S. nonbank corporations had stimulated fear that Canada would be unable to control its own destiny. The Bank

Act of 1967 was based on the premise that Canadian control of the banking system was based on sound principles and a desirable objective. The act stipulated that no single shareholder could own more than 10% of the shares of an individual bank and that non-residents in the aggregate could own no more than 25% of the shares of an individual bank. While the act was not retroactive, further growth of a bank that did not meet these guidelines was limited. Citibank reduced its holdings in Mercantile Bank to 24.2% by 1975 and Mercantile was purchased by National Bank of Canada in 1986.

While the Bank Act of 1967 placed significant restrictions on the operation of foreign banks in Canada, it did not prevent them from operating under other nonbank federal or provincial charters. Canadian subsidiaries of foreign banks could operate as "financial institutions." As such, they were not permitted to call themselves banks or to accept deposits that were transferable by check. In the early 1970s, the Canadian market was attractive because of strong growth in the economy, strong loan demand (especially in the oil-and-gas and natural resources sectors), and a stable political environment. The target market was large corporate loans—from $2 million to $8 million. Foreign bank subsidiaries could offer a number of services that could not be provided by indigenous Canadian banks such as factoring and leasing. Since the foreign subsidiaries could not accept checkable deposits, these investments were funded through other liabilities, primarily commercial paper (often guaranteed by the parent bank). By 1976, 60 foreign banks, of which approximately half were U.S. institutions, operated more than 120 Canadian affiliates. Most of these banks concentrated on money market transactions and commercial lending. Approximately 40 other institutions operated representative offices in Canada.

The Canadian government recognized the benefit of having a competitive element introduced into the banking system and, through the Bank Act of 1980, brought these foreign operations under Canadian regulatory control. A new type of bank was introduced—the Schedule B bank (now referred to as a Schedule II bank). Under the act, a Schedule B bank:

- Must be capitalized separately from its parent bank.

- May *not* obtain a parent-company guarantee for its borrowings. (This eliminated an advantage that the foreign affiliates enjoyed vis-à-vis Canadian institutions.)

- Must pay a withholding tax on all funds borrowed from the parent.

- Must finance at least half of its Canadian-dollar assets with Canadian-dollar liabilities. (This permits better control over foreign exchange by the Canadian government.)

- May lend no more than one-half of capital to a single borrower.

- May open branches subject to the approval of the Canadian Minister of Finance.

- May own another affiliate in Canada only if the latter is engaged in those activities permissible for subsidiaries of Canadian banks.

Foreign banks were permitted to retain their nonbank affiliates provided that:

- The affiliates did not accept deposits transferrable by check.

- That the affiliates ceased offering leasing and factoring services.

The Bank Act of 1980 also designated existing Canadian banks as Schedule A banks (now referred to as Schedule I banks). Pursuant to the Bank Act of 1967, no more than 10% of the equity of a Schedule I bank may be held by one party. No more than 25% of the equity of a Schedule I bank may be held by non-Canadians.

However, as long as the capital of a Schedule II bank does not exceed C$750 million dollars, the 10/25 restrictions do not apply. Thus, the Schedule II framework is a method through which foreign institutions can enter the Canadian banking market through wholly owned subsidiaries. At such time as the equity of a Schedule II bank reaches C$750 million, the foreign bank is required to divest 35% of its equity shares to the public. If the Finance Minister considers it "appropriate," an exception to this provision may be granted, subject to any terms or conditions established by the Finance Minister.

In the aggregate, foreign banks were never permitted to represent more than 8% of the total assets of the Canadian banking system. This ceiling has since been raised to 12%. Combined, these provisions suggest that unless a foreign bank, operating as a Schedule II bank, establishes a strong presence in the Canadian market, growth in the Canadian system can be limited. Also, the withholding tax (on any monies borrowed from the parent) and the requirement for separate capitalization add to the cost of funds for foreign banks operating as Schedule II banks.

The rather sizeable hurdles that foreign banks must jump in Canada illustrate the degree to which the Canadian government attempts to protect the industry while, at the same time, introducing an element of competition to encourage innovation and upgrading of banking services. It should be noted that under the Canada-United States Free Trade Agreement, U.S. banks have been exempted from the 25% and 12% restrictions.[5] Also, U.S. banks are not required to seek approval from the Minister of Finance to open new branches once their Canadian subsidiaries have been established. These basic exemptions are incorporated also in the North American Free Trade Agreement.

With a strong presence of the six Canadian banks, the foreign banks that have been most successful in Canada have found specific niches for themselves. The National Westminster Bank of the United Kingdom has focused on the top-tier corporate market, providing such services as project finance and securitization. Barclays, also of the United Kingdom, is capitalizing on its strength in trade finance. In some circles, Barclays is considered to be the leading provider of structured trade finance.

On the other hand, Swiss banks appear to have concentrated in the off-balance-sheet financial services. Most notably, the Union Bank of Switzerland, Canada's only AAA-rated bank, is particularly strong in the market for swaps. Fully 47% of all bonds issued by Canada are held outside that country with Germans and Swiss being large buyers in both 1991 and 1992. This has opened up a significant market for the Union Bank of Switzerland. In 1993, UBS arranged a C$2.1 billion swap facility for the Canada Deposit Insurance Corporation, in connection with the takeover of a failed trust company.

The 10 Japanese banks that operate in Canada service the members of their Japanese *keiretsu*. These institutions enjoy a sound spread over the cost of funds for their Canadian-based business.[6]

With respect to U.S. banks, the Bank of Boston Canada and Republic National Bank of New York (Canada) have targeted decidedly middle-market sectors. Republic National, having recently acquired the Canadian operations of Bank Leumi Le-Israel, has successfully catered to the textiles and garment industry in Montreal with its connections to New York. Bank of Boston has found its niche in the mid-market companies in Ontario and Quebec, particularly those that do business in the New England region of the United States. BT Bank of Canada (Bankers Trust) and Morgan Bank of Canada offer advice on mergers and acquisitions and other investment banking products. These two institutions advise clients that are considering expansion into the United States as a result of NAFTA. BT and Morgan have a strong presence in the derivatives market. While Morgan continues to conduct most of its operations from its New York facilities, BT Bank of Canada has established more of a presence within Canadian borders.

Citibank employs 870 people in Canada and is a major foreign presence there. The bank has attempted to replicate its retail banking success in Australia (with financial, economic, and demographic features that are comparable to those of Canada).

However, the resistance of Canadian retail banking customers to a foreign institution forced Citibank to reduce the number of its branches from eight to four. This experience has taught Citibank to focus on more niche markets even in the retail sector. The bank has consolidated and strengthened its credit card business in the area of Visa, En Route credit card (purchased in 1992) and Diner's Club operations. In corporate banking, Citicorp has experienced significant growth in providing Canadian corporations access to the U.S. high-yield debt market, a line of business that the bank was permitted to pursue in 1990. This is an important niche for Citibank because there is no comparable high-yield market in Canada.

In terms of finding its niche, the most successful foreign bank in Canada has been the HongKong Bank of Canada because it has been able to transform itself into the equivalent of a small-scale Schedule I bank. With C$13 billion in assets, the HongKong Bank is one of the largest institutions in the tier of banks immediately below the top six chartered banks. Much of its critical mass was built when the HongKong Bank acquired the failing Bank of British Columbia in 1986. Through this acquisition, it acquired 55 branches in the western provinces of British Columbia and Alberta. Wisely, the bank permitted the retention of the old name in most locations, thereby retaining the confidence of the customers of these branches. The HongKong Bank was further strengthened in 1990 with the acquisition of the Canadian operations of Midland Bank and Lloyds Bank (British institutions). Its branches in Canada now number 109 and cover virtually every Canadian province.

The niche that the HongKong bank has successfully pursued is the Asian immigrant market. Each year, Canada receives 250,000 immigrants, with as many as 30,000 of these originating from Hong Kong. The HongKong Bank of Canada has taken advantage of its roots to capture a large part of the banking business of these Asians. The bank has grown and simultaneously maintained rigorous credit standards. Loan losses average on the order of .4% of assets, versus an industry average of 1.0%.

Thus, the Canadian banking market is one that is full of challenges for a foreign bank wishing to establish a presence. At the same time, the opportunities are also considerable. Canadian banking customers have realized benefits from the presence of foreign competition in that indigenous Canadian banks have improved their services as a result of the competition. Today, Canadian banks:

- Have worked through most of their previous loan portfolio problems (many of which have been associated with real estate speculation, as is true in the United States).

- Have streamlined their operations for increased efficiency.

- Are integrating their recently approved investment banking and corporate banking activities.

Stimulus for the outward focus of Canadian banks continues, particularly in light of the North American Free Trade Agreement. The Royal Bank of Canada has recently hired a specialist in trade finance (from Barclays) as a consultant. Scotiabank, which only recently gave minimal credit support to its trade finance area, has opened an office in Mexico and is reportedly targeting the medium-term market.

The experience of foreign banks in Canada, and particularly U.S. banks since the Canada-United States U.S. Free Trade Agreement, underscores an important lesson in this outward focus. The successful bank will first identify the right niche in expansion under the North American Free Trade Agreement.

THE MEXICAN BANKING SYSTEM

The Mexican banking system is undergoing transformations that are even more dramatic than those occurring in Canada. After being part of a highly regulated system for many years, Mexican banks are now members of rapidly diversifying financial groups. These banks are becoming more efficient and are seeking alliances with foreign banks in order to increase both the level of their efficiency and the quality of their product offerings.

Exhibit 3-2 identifies the ten largest banks in Mexico, in order of Tier 1 capital. The top-ranking institution is Bancomer, with approximately $1.3 billion in Tier 1 capital. For the year ended December 1992, its return on assets (ROA) was a staggering 3.18%.[7] This gives some indication of the attractiveness of the Mexican market for many non-Mexican banks. Margins have been wide because the banking system has been protected from a high degree of competition. Banamex is the next most strongly capitalized Mexican bank and its ROA for 1992 was 2.77%. Banca Serfin is the third of the "big three" Mexican banks. Because of provisions for loan loss during 1992, Banca Serfin's ROA was .72%, low by Mexican standards but fairly respectable by U.S. standards.

Beyond the top three, the size of Mexican banks in terms of capital and assets declines quickly. Both capital levels and profitability are quite variable. The reason for the disparity in size and performance among the top ten banks is a direct result of the history of the Mexican banking system and of its recent control by the Mexican government.

Historical Overview

Until the 1970s, the government of Mexico subscribed to the theory of economic development often referred to as *import substitution*. When a developing country pursues import substitution, it will attempt to build industries within its own national boundaries that can effectively make it independent of imports for its critical industrial sectors. The program for import substitution includes tariffs, quotas, and direct subsidies. The items that had typically been imported by Mexico included consumer goods, durable goods (such as automobiles), and nondurable luxuries (for example, certain items of clothing). Local financial systems were encouraged to develop financing vehicles to pay for items produced within the country that substituted for these

EXHIBIT 3-2
MAJOR MEXICAN BANKS

Bank (date)	Tier 1 Capital	Assets	Capital Ratio	Profits	Return on Assets
Bancomer (12/92)	$1,285	$33,161	3.88%	$1,054	3.18%
Banamex (12/92)	974	37,823	2.58	1,048	2.77
Banca Serfin (12/92)	854	20,989	4.07	152	.72
Multibanco Comermex (12/92)	461	9,858	4.68	99	1.00
Banco Internacional (12/91)	137	7,718	1.78	-94	-1.22
Banco Mercantil del Norte (12/91)	123	1,900	6.47	87	4.58
Banca Promex (12/91)	80	1,401	5.71	53	3.78
Banco del Atlantico (12/91)	59	3,434	1.72	n.a.	n.a.
Banco BCH (12/91)	n.a.	2,128	1.88	12	.56
Banca Confia (12/90)	26	1,798	1.45	47	2.61

n.a. Not available

Note:

1. Amounts are in millions of U.S. dollars.
2. Capital ratio does not use risk-weighted assets.

Source:
"Top 100 by Country (Latin American Banks)," *The Banker*, August 1993, pp. 43-48.

imports. This necessarily meant that many of the commercial banks offered primarily short-term financing. Short-term financing had the added advantage of protecting the lenders from undesirable inflation effects.

At the same time, long-term corporate financing was primarily through the retention of earnings. For the most part, private-sector financial institutions did not become involved in long-term finance. However, the government provided long-term funding through various trust funds and state-controlled credit institutions. The most notable of these government financial institutions is Nacional Financiera. Such institutions channeled public and private funds into "priority sectors" and also allocated resources from foreign lenders and investors.

Meanwhile Banco de México, Mexico's central bank, held a tight rein on the commercial banking system. From the 1940s through the 1960s, the amount of reserves (liquid assets) that were required to be held against demand and savings deposits (liabilities) ranged from 50% to 100%. In addition, banks were required to maintain a certain percentage of deposits in the form of government securities. From the 1940s through the 1960s, the percentage of deposits backed by government securities ranged from a low of 0% to a high of 75%. In addition, banks were required to invest a certain share of their deposits in the form of loans to certain private-sector industries. This requirement ensured the allocation of capital to high-priority industries.

On the other hand, nonbank financial intermediaries, especially *financieras*, had a much more flexible environment in which to operate.[8] Because of this, *financieras* really became the vehicle through which financial innovation was realized in Mexico. *Financieras* obtained financing by issuing promissory notes that were purchased by corporations and individuals. Funds raised through such note issuance were used:

- To invest in longer-term obligations.

- To finance working capital and equipment loans.

- To extend consumer loans.

In addition to the *financieras*, mortgage banks also filled a need for long-term finance. These institutions issued special mortgage bonds to finance their mortgage-lending activities.

The growth of securities markets was somewhat impeded by the fact that it was mandatory for government bonds to trade at par. The par value of government securities was maintained through trading by Banco de México and Nacional Financiera. This effectively meant that anticipated inflation could not be reflected in the securities market, as is typically the case in markets such as those in the United States. Trading in these securities was thin because the market makers were primarily the commercial banks, the *financieras*, the mortgage banks, Banco de México, and National Financiera. Furthermore, the market for long-term obligations was particularly thin. All of these factors worked together to push the cost of intermediation beyond the levels that would normally have been observed. As a result, Mexican industrial sectors did not have access to the kinds of financing that were necessary to sustain and build the industrial infrastructure.

In the 1970s, inflation became a problem that could not be ignored. Interest rate controls and high reserve requirements only made the situation for banks worse. At the same time, the minimal regulation of *financieras* meant that these institutions could offer higher interest rates on their bonds and other liabilities in this inflationary environment. The result was significant disintermediation in the Mexican financial sector, particularly Mexican commercial banks.[9] To counteract this disintermediation, new reforms were introduced in 1974 and 1975.

Restructuring within the Mexican banking system took the form of consolidating the industry and giving commercial banks powers that previously they had not enjoyed. Financial groups, or conglomerates, were constructed of different types of financial institutions—banks, brokerage houses, insurance companies, and others. In addition, banks were permitted to take equity positions in industrial firms.

The Mexican banking industry consolidated considerably as a result of the 1974 Law on Credit Institutions. This law permitted merger of different types of financial institutions. The number of banks in Mexico went from 139 in 1975 down to 60 by 1982 (when the banks were eventually nationalized).

Even with increased flexibility and reduced constraints on deposit interest rates, the problems associated with disintermediation were not completely eliminated. Market rates were still higher than the highest rates that could be paid according to government regulation. Nonbank financial institutions grew because of other developments. The Securities Market Law of 1975 created brokerage houses and reorganized the securities exchange. The oversight of the securities industry was also restructured by a reorganization of the National Securities Commission (Comisión Nacional de Valores or CNV). These changes in the securities industries encouraged the formation of brokerage houses by individual brokers and by financial conglomerates.

The securities industry was also aided by the introduction of new instruments that could be traded on primary and secondary securities markets. Perhaps the most important development in the securities market in Mexico was the introduction of government treasury notes, or *cetes*, in 1978. Before *cetes*, petrobonds (1977) had been the primary innovation in the securities markets. Petrobonds were a share in a trust at Nacional Financiera that represented rights to certain quantities of government-owned oil. As a result, the value of these bonds was linked to the price of oil. Other elements that helped spur the securities market in Mexico was the authorization by the government for the issuance of commercial paper in 1980 and the beginning of a bankers' acceptance (BA) market in 1981.

Nevertheless, the inflation that would erode confidence in the Mexican peso could not be averted. In 1976, the Mexican government devalued the peso from 12.5 pesos to the dollar to 21 pesos to the dollar. Massive capital flight ensued as investors pulled money from Mexico and reinvested it in U.S.-dollar assets. Instead of encouraging policies that would increase export activity and bring about a better balance of payments, the government elected to continue to pursue its import substitution agenda. The investments that were necessary to spur internal growth in specific industries were to be financed through increased oil exports by Mexico. In the pursuit of import substitution, the government also incurred very large budget deficits that were financed primarily by increases in external debt.

An unprecedented increase in interest rates in 1979 and the dramatic declines in oil prices in 1980 and 1981 forced Mexican authorities to admit in 1982 that external debt could not be serviced according to the original schedule. Following this announcement, there was *massive* capital flight. The government reacted with a severe peso devaluation, new foreign exchange controls, and nationalization of all but two of the country's 60 commercial banks. The two banks which escaped nationalization were Citibank and Banco Obrero, a small institution that is affiliated with the trade unions.[10]

As part of the efforts to strengthen the commercial banking system, the government reduced the number of banks from 58 to 18 through mergers, license cancellations, and the reclassification of banks. Banks were permitted to offer very high deposit rates, although the rate of inflation was sometimes greater than even these higher interest rates. The strict liquidity rules and reserve requirements effectively constrained banks from providing finance to anything other than the government sector. Few resources remained to finance private industry. Consumer finance, including home mortgages, virtually disappeared. During this period of nationalization, Mexican banks incurred high funding costs, became involved in bureaucratic red tape, were overstaffed, and did not upgrade their internal systems.

At the same time, many of the former owners of commercial banks acquired or established nonbank financial institutions. Many affiliated with brokerage firms. Others entered the insurance, leasing, or foreign exchange business. During this period, the array of nonbank financial services increased considerably. Nonbank financial institutions became the main source of financial products and services for the private sector, including commercial paper and money market mutual funds. By 1987, Mexican commercial banks held less than 50% of the assets of the country's financial institutions, the lowest percentage for any Latin American country other than Peru.

Under the administration of President Carlos Salinas de Gortari (elected in 1988), the government began to restructure and liberalize bank regulations. In the interest of bank soundness, new laws and regulations imposed stiff capital level requirements. Also, a new loan classification system was instituted that promptly recognized past-due loans and limited certain activities, such as lending to one client or lending to the bank's own affiliates. At the same time, more independent, market-oriented management was assigned to the banks. Deregulation eliminated interest rate ceilings on deposits, eliminated forced investment in government securities, and removed foreign exchange controls. In an environment of improving government finances and an active government securities market, the competition among the banks increased almost immediately. In Mexico, the equivalent of the "Big Bang" in the United Kingdom was the privatization of the 18 remaining commercial banks that had been nationalized in 1982.

Bank Privatization

The administration of President Carlos Salinas set a goal of privatizing two banks per month beginning in June 1991. At that rate, it would have required only nine months to privatize all 18 banks. While all the banks were not sold to private owners within nine months, the process was completed in an impressive 14-month period.

Exhibit 3-3 details the transactions, including the sale price (denominated in U.S. dollars at the approximate exchange rate of three new pesos to the dollar), the multiple of book value paid for each institution, and the share of total equity sold to the private sector.[11] Through this privatization the Mexican government raised more than $12 billion and realized an average price-to-book ratio just over 3. Of course, the highest prices were paid for Banamex ($3.2 billion), Bancomer ($2.9 billion), Banca Serfin ($943 million), and Multibanco Comermex ($902

EXHIBIT 3-3
MEXICAN BANK PRIVATIZATIONS

Date of Sale	Bank	Sale Price[1]	Price/BV[2]	%[3]
June 1991	Multibanco Mercantil de Mexico	$ 203.7	2.66	77.2%
June 1991	Banpais	181.7	3.02	100.0
June 1991	Banca Cremi	249.4	3.40	66.7
August 1991	Banca Confia	297.4	3.73	78.7
August 1991	Banco de Oriente (Banorie)	74.4	4.00	69.3
August 1991	Banco de Credito y Servico (Bancreser)	141.7	2.53	100.0
August 1991	Banco Nacional de Mexico (Banamex)	3,248.3	2.62	70.7
Nov. 1991	Bancomer	2,854.7	2.99	62.6
Nov. 1991	Banco BCH	292.8	2.67	100.0
Feb. 1992	Banca Serfin	942.6	2.69	51.0
Feb. 1992	Multibanco Comermex	902.0	3.73	66.5
Mar. 1992	Banco Mexicano Somex	625.5	4.15	81.6
April 1992	Banco del Atlantico	489.7	5.30	68.6
April 1992	Banca Promex	358.2	4.23	66.0
April 1992	Banoro	379.3	3.95	66.0
June 1992	Banco Mercantil del Norte (Banorte)	591.9	4.25	66.0
July 1992	Banco Internacional	495.6	2.95	51.0
July 1992	Banco del Centro (Bancen)	289.8	4.62	66.3

[1] Represents the approximate value of the sale in millions of U.S. dollars, at the exchange rate of 3 new pesos to the dollar.
[2] Represents the ratio of sales price to book value.
[3] Represents the percentage of bank equity sold to the private sector.

Source: "Booming Banks Must Stay Vigilant," *Mexico, Euromoney* supplement, January 1993, pp. 2-15.

million). The price-to-book ratios were much higher than expected and higher than those that would normally be realized
in bank sales in the United States. At the time of the sales, it was
suggested that "control" premium was justified in order to gain
a foothold in the Mexican banking market. The logic was that
there was an inherently high growth potential associated with
these institutions and that the price was reasonable to obtain
the advantage of such growth potential.

Most of the buyers were groups of local investors. Often the
buying groups were organized around a wealthy family or individual, frequently a brokerage firm.

Roberto Hernandez has been a central figure in the bank privatization effort as the new chairman of Banamex. Hernandez
originally arrived in Mexico City in the 1960s. While he attended college, he began to trade produce. In 1971, seven years
after he had earned his business degree, Hernandez and his
partner, Alfredo Harp, founded the brokerage firm of Acciones
y Valores, commonly known as Accival. This brokerage would
later become Mexico's largest securities dealer. During the 1980s
turmoil in Mexico's securities markets, Hernandez elected to remain invested in Mexico, buying up shares at rock-bottom
prices. His loyalty was well rewarded when the Mexican securities market recovered. Accival became the primary securities
trading firm and Hernandez became one of Mexico's wealthiest
individuals.

Banacci S.A. is the holding company through which Hernandez now controls both Banamex and Accival. Shortly after gaining
control of Banamex, Hernandez spearheaded an effort to make
the bank more efficient by closing some 20 offices, firing 100 outside consultants, and, in the process, saving over $100 million in
expenses. Hernandez defends the high price paid for Banamex by
explaining "it isn't every day you can buy a bank here."[12]

Banamex

Banamex was founded in 1884 and has been referred to as the
leader in large corporate business and private banking for

wealthy individuals. It is also the country's largest credit card issuer with more than nine million cardholders and half of all Mexican credit card loans outstanding. Its automated teller machine (ATM) network is the second largest and the bank operates 30% of all ATMs in Mexico. There has been a concerted effort to reduce the staffing in the bank, to improve technology applications, and to market new products. As part of its effect to improve its technology, Banamex has an agreement with BancOne (United States) for credit card processing.

The new management team is much more aggressive, with a risk-taking business philosophy that has been the watchword at Accival. The bank is active in securities trading and derives a large part of its income from these trading activities. Currently, Banamex has committed approximately 75% of its commercial loan portfolio to large corporations and companies. Its objective is to pursue new lines of business that will add value to the bottom line. This necessarily entails expanding the products that it can offer to both corporate and retail clients.

A strategic alliance with SwissBank Corporation (Switzerland) will enable the bank to offer equity derivative products. This joint venture will offer swaps, equity-linked notes, options on single stocks, and options on baskets of stocks. This alliance positions Banamex to capture significant market share in the wide range of derivatives that will likely develop after the Mexican authorities permit development of currency and interest-rate derivatives. It is anticipated that derivatives regulations will be set forth sometime in 1994.

Banamex also has an alliance with the U.S. telecommunications firm MCI. The bank processes 1.5 million transactions per day. To the extent that these transactions can be performed via telephone and ATM terminals, Banamex will be able to reduce its unit costs and access more customers. It appears that Banamex is not concerned about the relatively low average income of Mexican citizens. The logic is that producing bank services through the use of high technology will enable the bank to be profitable. High-tech applications make it possible to produce these services at a fraction of the costs associated with a more conventional brick-and-mortar facility.

Banamex also is building its mortgage base with a highly successfully *Espacios* mortgage product. Unlike most Mexican mortgages, the *Espacios* mortgage does not involve negative amortization. During the periods of high inflation, borrowers were unable to pay the full amount of monthly interest that would have been required at market rates of interest. Most of the mortgages that were made available during these periods were designed to add unpaid interest to the unpaid balance of the loan. This meant that the mortgage balance continually increased. The assumption is that the value of the real estate that secures the mortgage will also increase in value. Of course, if the value of the underlying property does not increase as fast as the unpaid balance, the lending bank is exposed to an undercollateralized loan. Banamex has structured the *Espacios* mortgage so that no negative amortization is involved and the product has been well received.

The emphasis on high-tech delivery of services and more popular mortgage products is in line with the ultimate objective of Banamex to become more balanced in terms of its retail offerings. Early in the 1990s, Banamex's loan portfolio was heavily weighted toward business loans with 70% devoted to that sector and only 30% to the retail sector. At the end of 1993, it was 55% business and 45% retail. The ultimate objective for the bank is to have its loan portfolio evenly split between commercial and retail banking.

Bancomer

Bancomer was founded in 1932 and boasts the largest branch network in Mexico. Its original mandate was to serve the retail and middle markets of Mexico. It grew during the 1970s by mergers of regional banks. Today Bancomer has Mexico's largest ATM network with 40% of the machines in operation. Bancomer is the leading bank provider of home mortgages in Mexico and has provided a large share of the country's credit card and automobile finance. As compared to Banamex, Bancomer is more conservative in that its operations are less oriented toward securities trading. Nevertheless, Bancomer competes head-to-head with Banamex.

Bancomer is looking for examples of highly efficient practices in foreign banks. Officials of Bancomer have openly admired the operations of BancOne and NationsBank (United States). Also Bancomer management appears to appreciate the approach of Barclays (United Kingdom) to the middle-market corporate sector. Structurally, Bancomer plans to operate as a group of small, very aggressive, independent banks with separate managements and profit responsibilities. The bank is organized into five autonomous units:

- Mortgage bank (providing residential and commercial mortgage products)

- Service bank (responsible for the 831-branch network)

- Consumer bank (credit cards and consumer finance)

- Institutional bank (catering to corporate clients)

- Specialized bank (brokerage and nonbanking services)

Interestingly, Bancomer appears to be less interested in derivatives-related products than Banamex. However, the bank is seeking to identify specific banks to explore particular business interests. The approach will be to form strategic alliances with banks through joint ventures in areas in which Bancomer management does not have expertise.

New Banking Groups

Under new laws and regulations in Mexico, banks have begun to form alliances with firms in other financial service industries through the holding company structure. To date, the largest degree of activity in this area has been between banks and brokerages.

Exhibit 3-4 shows the extent to which new banking groups have been formed. With the exception of Banamex, the top five banks in Mexico are now members of groups that have banking, brokerage, and insurance affiliates. It has also been reported that Banamex is actively considering and looking for an appropriate insurance affiliate for the Banacci Group.[13] All but five of the 18 privatized banks have securities affiliates. Seven of the 18 also have insurance affiliates at this point. This is an impressive pace of business formation in the few years that have elapsed since the first Mexican bank was privatized in 1991.

In addition to the new banking groups that have been formed around the 18 privatized banks in Mexico, 11 new bank licenses were granted in 1993. Banco Inbursa is part of Grupo Financiero Inbursa, currently Mexico's fourth largest financial group. This financial group is affiliated with the holding company Grupo Carso which has a market value of $9.9 billion. Both Grupo Financiero and Grupo Carso are headed by Carlos Slim, who owns 65% of the two holding companies. Taken together, the companies that Carlos Slim controls represent a full 25% of the market capitalization of the Mexican stock market.

Grupo Carso has three divisions—telecommunications, retail and restaurant service, and industrial.

- In the telecommunications division, the company manages Telmex, the largest capitalized stock in Mexico, and owns a 20.5% stake with partners Southwestern Bell and France Telecom.[14]

- In the retail division are 78 upscale department stores (Sanborns) that contain pharmacies and restaurants. This division holds the largest bookseller in Mexico and operates 35 Denny's restaurants.

- The industrial division contains companies that are involved in the manufacture of automobile parts, electrical equipment and construction activity. Condumex manufactures a wide range of products that include PVC pipe and fiber-optic cable. Mexico's largest tire maker, Euzkadi, is

EXHIBIT 3-4
MEXICO'S NEW FINANCIAL GROUPS

	Group Members		
Group	Bank	Brokerage	Insurance
Banacci	Banamex	Accival	n/a
Bancomer	Bancomer	Bancomer[1]	Seguros Monterrey[2]
Serfin	Serfin	Operadora de Bolsa (Obsa)	Seguros Serfin
Prime	Internacional	Prime	Seguros Interamericana
Inverlat[3]	Comermex	Inverlat	Seguros America[4]
Invermexico	Mexicano	Invermexico	n/a
GBM-Atlantico	Atlantico	GBM	n/a
Probursa[5]	Mercantil	Probursa	Seguros Probursa
Mexival[6]	Banpais	Mexival	Seguros Constitucion
n/a	Bancreser	n/a	n/a
Cremi	Cremi	n/a	n/a
Abaco	Confia	Abaco	Aba Seguros
BCH	BCH	n/a	n/a
Gimsa	Banorte	n/a	n/a
Finamex	Promex	Valores Finamex	n/a
Multiva	Bancen	Multivalores	n/a
n/a	Banoro	Estrategia Bursatil	n/a
Margen	Banorie	n/a	n/a

Notes:
[1] Formerly Acciones Bursatil (Absa).
[2] Indirect affiliate controlled by shareholders of the group.
[3] Scotiabank (Canada) owns a small stake.
[4] Assurance Generalli (Italy) owns a minority stake.
[5] Banco Bilbao Vizcaya (Spain) and International Finance Corporation (World Bank Group) own minority stakes.
[6] Vestcor Partners (Venezuela) owns a small stake.

n/a Not applicable.

Source: Booming Banks Must Stay Vigilant," *Mexico, Euromoney* supplement, January 1993. pp. 2-15.

fiber-optic cable. Mexico's largest tire maker, Euzkadi, is also a member of the industrial division.

With such financial clout within Grupo Carso, the affiliated Grupo Financiero Inbursa will likely exert considerable competitive pressure on both the newly privatized banks and their respective banking/financial groups. The bank affiliate, Banco Inbursa, was formed in 1993 and has already made a niche for itself by offering low-cost loans and services (such as automatic overdrafts for checking accounts) that, up to this point, have not been available in Mexico. It is clear that there will be demand for such services because after only two months of operation the bank had attracted $915 million in assets. The insurance affiliate within the group is Segumex, Mexico's largest insurance company in terms of capital and its sixth largest in terms of premiums. The Inbursa Mutual Fund, the securities affiliate of Grupo Financiero Inbursa, was formed in 1991 and has averaged a 32% average real return per year since then.

The pressure that will be exerted on banking institutions will intensify in Mexico because of the relative lack of services in the past. The new groups that are being formed around the privatized banks and the new banks that are being chartered individually are all part of a dynamic growth process in the Mexican banking system. The success of new entrants in the market suggests that there is opportunity that can be seized not only by Mexican institutions, but by U.S. and Canadian banks as well. Mexican banks are attracting international attention because of this growth potential and high levels of profitability.

Mexican Bank Profitability

Government protection and high rates of inflation in Mexico have combined to create unusually wide spreads in the Mexican banking market. The following comparison of the results of Banamex and Bancomer for 1992 helps to illustrate this point:

	ROA	ROE	Net Interest Margin
Banamex	2.3%	32.8%	7.4%
Bancomer	2.0%	27.9%	7.1%
Large U.S. Banks	0.9%	13.4%	4.5%

Even though Banamex and Bancomer are Mexico's largest banks, their ROA was more than twice the average for large U.S. banks and the same was true for ROE. This makes Mexico an attractive market for U.S. banks. While large U.S. banks in 1992 had a net interest margin of 4.5% (representing the difference between (1) interest income on loans and securities and (2) the interest expense on deposits and other borrowings), Banamex and Bancomer enjoyed spreads well over 7%. For the Mexican industry as a whole, the spread in 1992 was 9.7% and return on assets was approximately 1.5%. The rates earned on Mexican loan portfolios are high in comparison with the United States and most other industrialized countries. Even though inflation fell to 8% in 1993, Mexican business loan rates were an astronomical 25%. Consumer credit is even more pricey with mortgage or automobile loan rates of roughly 30% and credit card loan rates of 40%!

The larger Mexican companies that have the ability to do so are tapping international capital markets to lower their cost of funds. In fact, the banks themselves have begun to enter these international markets. In the last quarter of 1993, Banca Serfin offered a $365 million global offering. Also in 1993, Banamex established a NP1 billion ($320.5 million) global medium-term-note program, of which NP310 million were in the form of three-year, fixed-rate notes—the first such peso offering with a fixed coupon and the first with a maturity as long as three years. In addition, Banamex issued three-month, six-month, one-year, and two-year paper for the equivalent of $300 million. Mexican banks are boosting their capital through these international means in preparation for what will probably be 20% loan growth in Mexico for the next few years.

Because of attractive spreads, Mexican banking activity is lucrative. However, the economic recession that Mexico recently has suffered has also affected bank profitability. Many smaller enterprises that do not have access to lower-cost, international capital have been hard pressed to service high-cost bank loans and nonperforming loans have increased. As a result, the biggest challenge facing the Mexican banking system appears to be the deteriorating quality of loan portfolios. In the year ended May 1993, bank earnings rose 23% versus a year-before increase of 50%. Loan loss provisions, which had increased by 72% in the year ended May 1992, rose by 249% the following year.

However, despite increased competition in the banking sector and problematic loan portfolio conditions, growth is expected to continue in the Mexican banking sector. The fact remains that Mexico is severely underbanked and that profit margins are still wide enough to make it an attractive market for entry and expansion.

Investments and Money Management

As is true for U.S. banks, *securities* represent large share of the asset portfolios of Mexican banks. These investments have been concentrated in the government bond sector because of the historical requirement that banks invest a large share of their deposit liabilities in these instruments. The government securities that play a major role in bank portfolios are:

- *Cetes*
- *Bondes*
- *Ajustabonos*
- *Tesobonos*

Cetes (*Certificados de la Tesoreria de la Federacion*) are issued by the federal government of Mexico as bearer Treasury securities sold at a discount. Their maturities are 28 days, 91 days, 182 days, and 1 year. The minimum denomination is NP10,000.

Their rating by Standard & Poor's (S&P) is A1+. In the first half of 1993, the average yields on these four maturities were 13.6%, 14.0%, 14.3%, and 14.0%, respectively. Recently, yields on these short-term instruments have been depressed because of the strong demand for them by foreign investors. In fact, it has been estimated that as much of 60% of the *Cetes* market is controlled by foreign investors.

Longer-term government bonds, *bondes* (*Bonos de Desarrolo del Gobierno*), are registered development bonds. Their maturities are more typically one to two years in original maturity and their minimum denomination is NP100,000. These are issued twice monthly for a total issuance typically in the range of the equivalent of US$200 million. The implicit S&P rating of *bondes* (based on yields) is AA-. The rates available on *bondes* vary and are reset on a monthly basis. The rate is based on the highest of three different rates—the 28-day *cetes* rate, the 28-day promissory note rate, and the 28-day bank certificate of deposit rate. To the highest of these three rates is added a spread that is also determined by market conditions.

Ajustabonos (*Bonos Ajustables del Gobierno Federal*) are Treasury bearer bonds and their yield is linked to inflation, which for most of 1993 averaged just under 10%. A fixed interest rate is paid every 91 days on a face value that adjusts with inflation. In this way, *ajustabonos* yield a positive real rate of return. The minimum denomination of *ajustabonos* is NP100,000. There is no set schedule for issue of *ajustabonos*, but the average total issue typically amounts to the equivalent of U.S. $100 million and maturities range from three to five years. The implicit S&P rating of *ajustabonos* (based on yields) is AA-. Recently the yields have been slightly more than 5% over inflation.

Tesobonos (*Bonos de la Tesoreria de la Federacion*) are dollar-dominated Treasury bills with original maturities of 28, 91, or 182 days. These are zero-coupon, discounted securities, with a par value that is paid at maturity in pesos that are converted at the then-current exchange rate. *Tesobonos* are a relatively unimportant part of the government securities market, representing less than 1% of the total Mexican government securities.

The auction of government securities in Mexico is an interesting process. For example, in *bondes* auctions there are no restrictions on the amounts of the new issue that individual investors may obtain. The central bank, Banco de México, allocates these securities in an auction that is attended by only eight to 10 managers and brokers. These buyers purchase securities for a variety of foreign and domestic investors. Some of the buyers that represent large groups of foreign clients are Bankers Trust, Merrill Lynch, Goldman Sachs, Lehman Brothers, First Boston, and Standard Chartered. Some large mutual fund managers (such as Scudder and Fidelity) use local firms to purchase their Mexican bonds.

Interestingly, bids in government securities auctions will often cover a wide range of rates. This is indicative of the relative immaturity of the market. For example, in July 1993 the bids for *bondes* were from 110bp to 130bp over *Cetes*.[15] In addition, successful bidders often walk away with 20% to 40% of the entire issue.

The *money management* aspect of Mexican banking promises to become increasingly important as a new system of private pensions is developed in Mexico. Like other Latin American countries, Mexico experienced mounting difficulties in maintaining its state-run social security program in the 1980s because of traumatic financial market conditions. The Salinas administration seized this opportunity (or perhaps necessity) to start a private pension system that would increase savings and also help develop Mexico's capital markets.

Sistema de Harorro por el Retiro (SAR), the new Mexican retirement system, mandates that employers contribute 2% of their employees' wages to specifically earmarked retirement accounts. This is in addition to the 12.4% that employers contribute to the government social security program and the national housing fund. The program began with a first stage that simply required deposit of 2% of wages into corporate accounts at banks. In this stage, the central bank took primary responsibility for management of the funds, while, at the same time, guaranteeing a positive real rate of return. The second stage will entitle beneficiaries to transfer their funds from one retirement account to another. These accounts may be offered by banks, brokerage firms, or insurance companies. In addition, the second stage will permit employees to make voluntary contributions to their own retirement accounts.

In May 1992, the new rules went into effect and, since then, more than 11 million accounts have been opened at banks, representing almost NP4.1 billion ($1.3 billion) of pension contributions. Not surprisingly, most of these funds went to the larger banks—with Bancomer controlling 37% of the contributions and Banamex 31%. However, the banks have encountered some problems. The sheer volume of accounts has made it very difficult for the banks to manage account administration functions. As a result, the second stage of SAR has not been implemented. Nevertheless, expectations remain high. By the year 2000, it is estimated that this pool of private pension funds will amount to no less than the equivalent of US$10 billion.

NEW MARKETS, NEW NICHES

In both the Canadian and Mexican banking systems, there are changes occurring that represent opportunities for U.S. banks. In the case of Canada, the market is more mature and the competition is perhaps more intense. In the case of Mexico, there are a number of areas in which inroads can be made by U.S. and Canadian banks. These include high-technology applications, consumer finance, corporate lending, and money management.

SELECTED REFERENCES

"Banks Act to Boost Their Capital Bases (Mexico)," *Euromoney supplement*, January 1994, pp. 22-24.

"Booming Banks Must Stay Vigilant," *Mexico, Euromoney* supplement, January 1993, pp. 2-15.

Bradbury, Nicholas. "Playing Lean and Mean in Canada," *Euromoney,* November 1993, pp. 92-94.

"Calm After the Storm," *Mexico, Euromoney* supplement, January 1993, pp. 19-22.

Chai, Alan, Alta Campbell, and Patrick J. Spain, editors. *Hoover's Handbook of World Business 1993,* Austin, Texas: The Reference Press, Inc., 1993.

Fink, Ronald. "Legions of the Lost Decade," *Financial World,* July 7, 1992, pp. 52-54.

Foreign Trade Barriers, Washington, D.C.: Office of the United States Trade Representative, 1993.

Globalization of Canada's Financial Markets, Ottawa, Canada: Canadian Government Publishing Centre, 1989.

Maggs, John. "Pro-NAFTA Reception to Aim at New Members of Congress," *Journal of Commerce* (New York), February 24, 1993.

"On Their Toes (Mexico)," *The Economist,* January 29, 1994, pp. 79-80.

Robinson, Danielle. "Mexico's Big Two Fight for Dominance," *Euromoney,* March 1994, pp. 89- 96.

Shepperd, Rosie. "Deregulation to Shake Up Mexico's Fund Managers," *International Bond Investor, Euromoney* supplement, September 1993, pp. 17-21.

Smith, Geri. "Mexico's No-Frills Mogul," *Business Week,* March 7, 1994, pp. 62-64.

Smith, Geri and Wendy Zellner. "The Gringo Banks are Drooling," *Business Week,* September 13, 1993, p. 84.

"The Spreading Maple Leaf," *The Economist,* January 15, 1994, pp. 68-69.

Tugendhat, Eduardo. "The Changing Mexican Banking Scene," *Export Today,* July/August 1993, pp. 18-20.

Welch, John H. and William C. Gruben. "A Brief History of the Mexican Financial System," *Financial Industry Studies* (Federal Reserve Bank of Dallas), October 1993, pp. 1-10.

ENDNOTES

1. Since assets have not been risk-weighted, the capital ratio does not represent the Tier 1 capital ratio according to Basle guidelines.
2. The territories were transferred to the Canadian Confederation for the sum of £300,000. After this transfer Hudson's Bay Company was transformed into a large corporation with varied business interests. The Hudson's Bay Company is still in operation today in Canada.
3. A Section 20 subsidiary is a bank subsidiary that may engage in securities activities as long as these activities do not constitute more than 10% of the revenues of the subsidiary. "Section 20" refers to that section of the Glass- Steagall Act of 1933 that forbade banks from affiliating with a firm that was "principally engaged" in securities activities.
4. Its attempt to do so with Security Bancorp of Michigan in 1991 failed, but the bank has not abandoned its strategy.
5. See Chapter 1.
6. A *keiretsu* is a Japanese system of joint corporate ownership without a formal holding company. Each member of the group owns a small portion of stock in all the other members so that as much 80% of the stock of each is held by affiliated companies.
7. In contrast, Citicorp, the largest U.S. bank holding company with $7.8 billion in Tier 1 capital and $212 billion in assets at the end of 1992, realized ROA of .68% in 1992. None of the 178 U.S. banks that are included in the "Top 1000" global ranking by *The Banker* (July 1993) realized a 3% ROA.
8. *Financieras* resembled banks but had a much narrower scope of operation, often focusing on long-term loans to industry. *Financieras* are often also referred to as development banks.
9. *Disintermediation* is the withdrawal of funds from deposit accounts when other financial instruments offer more competitive rates of return.
10. Citibank opened its branch in 1928 during a particularly troublesome political episode in Mexico. Most other foreign banks withdrew from Mexico at that point, leaving only Citibank to operate in the country by 1932. In 1932, the government prohibited any foreign banks from setting up branches in Mexico. Because the law was not retroactive, Citibank remained.
11. See Chapter 2 for a discussion of the new peso.

12. See "Legions of the Lost Decade" by Ronald Fink.
13. See "Mexico's Big Two Fight for Dominance" by Danielle Robinson.
14. Telmex is an acronym for Telephonos de Mexico.
15. "Bp" is an abbreviation for basis point—one hundredth of one percent.

4 Financial Market Opportunities under NAFTA

INTRODUCTION

The North American Free Trade Agreement offers opportunities for securities firms and other financial institutions involved in securities transactions. As is the case in the banking industry, the biggest opportunities are derived from the liberalization of Mexican laws with respect to foreign investment in securities firms. In addition, stocks and bonds are being offered for public sale that were not previously available. New financial infrastructures are being built that have no precedent. Innovative financing is being pursued as a way to enhance the attractiveness of Mexican issuers on international capital markets. The potential integration of the markets is perhaps best illustrated by the rapid growth of Mexican derivative securities trading in the United States.

NAFTA PROVISIONS

Before there were any free trade agreements between the three parties of NAFTA, the U.S. and Canadian markets were fairly open to securities activities by firms in their respective countries. Mexico was completely closed with respect to the operation of foreign institutions in Mexico's securities industry. Under the administration of President Carlos Salinas de Gortari, it was possible for foreign firms to invest in a Mexican securities firm—up to a total of 30% of the target firm's capital. Individual foreign investment (by a person or a company) was limited to 10% of capital of a Mexican securities firm.

Exhibit 4-1 shows the impact of both the Canada-United States Free Trade Agreement and the North American Free Trade Agreement as they relate to securities firms. Under CUSFTA, Canadian banks were given the right to underwrite and deal in Canadian government securities within the boundaries of the United States. Before CUSFTA, only those dealers that were not affiliated with a bank were permitted to perform these functions. This restriction had been imposed because the Glass-Steagall Act gives U.S. banks permission to underwrite and deal only in U.S. Treasury securities and general obligation (G.O.) municipal bonds. Thus, a new line of securities business for Canadian banks operating in the United States was opened through the CUSFTA—underwriting and dealing in Canadian government securities.

CUSFTA did not go as far as the Canadian banking community would have liked. Beyond the powers connected with Canadian securities, there was no further relaxation of Glass-Steagall Act provisions under the agreement, despite the fact that Canadian banks had been granted the right to operate securities firms in their own country. However, under CUSFTA, the United States made a commitment to grant Canadian banks the same powers as those granted U.S. banks, in the event of any future liberalization of Glass-Steagall provisions.

Under NAFTA, the previous agreements between the United States and Canada continue. There are no new powers granted to either U.S. or Canadian banks. However, there is considerable liberalization with respect to powers in the Mexican securities market. During the phase-in period that begins in 1994 and

EXHIBIT 4-1
SECURITIES ACTIVITIES UNDER CUSFTA AND NAFTA

CUSFTA
- Canadian banks in the United States may underwrite and deal in securities of Canadian governments and their agents.
- Canadian financial institutions are provided the same treatment as that accorded to U.S. firms with respect to any amendment of the Glass-Steagall Act.

NAFTA
- No changes for U.S. and Canadian privileges in Canada, and the United States, respectively.
- Liberalization of investment opportunities in Mexican securities firms:
  a. Limit of aggregate investment by U.S. and Canadian investors set at 10% of industry capital in 1994, increasing to 20% by 1999, and no limit thereafter.
  b. Limit of individual investment by U.S. or Canadian investor set at 4% of industry capital during phase-in period (1994-1999) and no limit thereafter.
  c. Mexican government may freeze investment by U.S. and Canadian investors between 2000 and 2004 (for no more than 3 years) if aggregate investment by these investors reaches 30% of industry capital.

Legend:
CUSFTA Canada-United States Free Trade Agreement
NAFTA   North American Free Trade Agreement

ends in 1999, there is a limit on capital formation by U.S. and Canadian investors in the securities industry.

Under Mexican law, a financial group may be formed under one of three ways:

- A *bank* with leasing, factoring, foreign exchange, mutual fund management and origination, and warehousing activities

- A *brokerage firm* with leasing, factoring, foreign exchange, mutual fund management and origination, and warehousing activities

- A *holding company* with at least three of the following institutions but no more than one of each type:[1]

(1) Bank

(2) Insurance company

(3) Brokerage firm

(4) Leasing company

(5) Factoring company

(6) Bonding company

(7) Mutual funds management company

(8) Currency exchange broker

(9) Warehousing company

Clearly, the widest range of activities for a securities firm is possible through the holding company structure, rather than through a stand-alone bank or a brokerage firm.

The limit of investment by U.S. and Canadian firms in Mexican securities firms has been changed from ownership limits for an individual firm to ownership limits as a percentage of total securities industry capital. In the aggregate, U.S. and Canadian investors may hold interests in Mexican securities firms that do not exceed 10% of industry capital in the first year of NAFTA (1994). This limit increases in equal annual increments to 20% by the last year of the phase-in period (1999). Thereafter, there is no limit. In terms of individual investors, no single U.S. or Canadian investor may accumulate more than 4% of industry capital. After the phase-in period, there is no limit on an individual investment.[2] Mexico retains the right to freeze investment by U.S. and Canadian investors in Mexican securities firms for a period of no more than three years if their aggregate investment exceeds 30% of industry capital. This right expires in the year 2004. These provisions give U.S. and Canadian firms the opportunity to invest in one of the most dynamic of today's emerging capital markets.

In fact, it has been suggested that NAFTA has more impact in the area of investment than in the area of trade. Those that hold this view point to the fact that Mexico has already reduced its tariffs substantially to the 10% range, while U.S. tariffs are only in the 5% range. It is noted that the most significant issue is not the extent to which these tariffs will be further reduced under NAFTA. Instead, the most profound change is the manner in which the legal framework of Mexican financial markets has been altered and, by international treaty, will retain its new, more open structure.

THE MEXICAN STOCK MARKET

Market reforms in Mexico have attracted the attention of investors seeking higher returns than those which are available through fixed-income securities in the United States and Europe. In January 1992, the Mexican Bolsa Index was in the range of 1400. By June 1992, the Index had risen to more than 1900—an annual compound rate of increase of 84.2%.[3] However, the Mexican Bolsa is extremely volatile. By October 1992, the Index had declined to the range of 1300. By mid-1993, it had rallied to approximately 1800 and continued to climb. During the three-month period from November 1993 to February 1994, the Mexican Stock Market Index increased by 36% for an annual compound rate of return of 242%!

For well-positioned securities firms, Mexico is an emerging stock market with many opportunities for profit as the largest Mexican firms reach world-class status. Currently, there are 30 firms whose stock is traded on a regular basis and six of these constitute three-fifths of Mexico's entire stock market capitalization.[4] One issue alone, Telephonos de Mexico (Telmex) represents fully 30% of Mexico's stock market. The high degree of concentration among a few stocks in the Mexican market contributes to the market's high degree of volatility.

Also contributing to past volatility was uncertainty about the fate of NAFTA. Now that NAFTA has been approved, other factors continue to contribute to market volatility. Investors are sensitive to Mexico's trade figures and react negatively to trade deficits. As of February 1994, Mexico's cumulative 12-month trade deficit amounted to just over $14 billion. However, to the credit of the Mexican government, official reserves (as of October 1993) were $23.2 billion, up from $18.6 billion one year earlier.[5]

In addition, certain sectors of the Mexican economy have experienced slowdowns. Exhibit 4-2 summarizes rates of growth within selected sectors from 1990 through 1993 (as projected as of September 1993). From a high of 4.4%, growth in real Gross Domestic Product (GDP) had significantly slowed to a 2.3% rate per year by September 1993. (The actual GDP growth for the entire year turned out to be a disappointing 0.7% because of a de-

---

EXHIBIT 4-2
REAL GROWTH IN MEXICAN ECONOMIC SECTORS

	Annual Growth Rate			
Sector	1990	1991	1992	1993[1]
Real GDP	4.4%	3.6%	2.6%	2.3%
Agriculture	6.1	.5	<1.5>	2.4
Mining	2.8	.3	1.3	1.0
Manufacturing	5.8	3.7	1.8	1.5
Construction	7.0	2.6	7.8	6.5
Utilities	2.6	4.1	4.4	4.2
Services	3.6	4.3	2.7	2.4

[1] Represents an estimate as of September 1993.

Source: Mariscal, Jorge O. "Latin America Investment Strategy Highlights," Investment Research, Goldman Sachs, September 1993.

cline in GDP in the fourth quarter.) The agricultural sector experienced rapid growth in 1990, slowed to almost no growth in 1991, and experienced negative growth in 1992. The agricultural sector stabilized and reestablished an upward trend in 1993. The mining sector sustained similar reverses in 1991, followed by recovery in 1992 and 1993. Still, the recovery has not returned the mining sector to the 2.8% annual growth rate witnessed in 1990. In the manufacturing sector, the 1990 growth rate was 5.8% but declined to 1.5% by 1993. On the other hand, the construction industry has shown a much more robust pattern of growth in that the 7.0% rate in 1990 was surpassed by a growth rate of 7.8% in 1992, followed by a strong growth at the rate of 6.5% in 1993. The utilities sector has exhibited a relatively strong upward trend with 2.6% growth in 1990, increasing to 4.4% by 1992, and maintaining a 4.2% pace in 1993. The services sector peaked in 1991 at 4.3% and grew at the more moderate rate of 2.4% during 1993.

Among the strongest sectors, as indicated by Exhibit 4-2, are the construction and utilities sectors. This is reflective of Mexico's need to build basic infrastructure—housing, electricity, phone service, roads, and other basic infrastructure needs. The Mexican stock market is influenced by these economic trends and will reflect general economic volatility.

Major Mexican Companies

An examination of several major Mexican companies can be helpful in analyzing the country's stock market and the valuation of Mexican shares. Exhibit 4-3 provides selected highlights of some of these firms.

Telephonos de Mexico (Telmex) is the only licensed supplier of public telecommunications in Mexico. Telmex controls all public telephone exchanges, the national network of local telephone lines, and all principal public domestic and international long-distance facilities. In addition, the company provides telephone-related services such as directories (yellow and white pages), cellular telephone services, and telephone enhancement ser-

EXHIBIT 4-3
MAJOR MEXICAN FIRMS

Firm	Shares Outstanding[1]	Price 12-mo. Range	Price As of 9-10-93	EPS[2]	P/E
Telmex	382.4	$60-$41	$52.50	$5.40	9.7X
Cemex	323.0	NP65-NP27	NP58.60	NP5.67	10.3
Gemex	112.0	NP34-NP16	NP33.40	NP2.19	15.3
Grupo Televisa	382.4	$25-$13	$23.25	$0.70[3]	33.2[4]
Sear de Mexico	75.0	NP37-NP17	NP35.00	NP3.10	11.3
Kimberly-Clark de Mexico	198.0	NP42-NP19	NP40.80	NP2.70	15.1
Banacci	1,350.0	NP21-NP11	NP19.70	NP2.15	19.2

[1] Millions of shares.
[2] Represents estimate as of September 1993.
[3] Represents earnings per ADS in 1992, where each ADS equals 2 Series L shares.
[4] For 1992.

Legend:
$ U.S. dollar
NP   Nuevo Peso
EPS   Earnings per share
P/E   Price/earnings ratio

Source: Mariscal, Jorge O. "Latin America Investment Strategy Highlights," Investment Research, Goldman Sachs, September 1993.

vices (such as call waiting, call forwarding, and 800 service). In 1993, the company had over 7 million access lines in service and its cellular customers numbered over 190,000. In the United States, the annual growth rate of telephone lines is expected to be between 2.5% and 4.4% in the near future. In contrast, the growth rate in Mexico is expected to be closer to 12%.

Cementos Mexicanos (Cemex) is the largest cement producer in the Americas and the fourth largest cement producer in the world. The Monterrey-based company has 63% share of the Mexican cement market and a 72% share of the Mexican ready-mix market. Its North American operations include marine and land terminals, distribution companies, and ready-mix facilities. In recent years, it has also expanded through acquisitions in Spain—Compañia Valenciana de Cementos Portland and La Auxiliar de la Construcción. These two new subsidiaries of Cemex control 26% of the Spanish cement market. These acquisitions are intended help the company develop new technologies that will improve production techniques and reduce distribution costs.

Cemex has established itself in the Eurobond market through issues of seven-year bonds in October 1992 ($280 million) and August 1993 ($12 million). The coupon rate on the 1992 offering was 10%. The coupon rate of the 1993 offering, also a seven-year offering, was a lower 8.55%. However, the most significant issue that Cemex has brought to the Eurobond market thus far is the $1 billion issue of five-year bonds at a fixed-rate of 8.875% issued in May 1993.

Grupo Embotellador de Mexico (Gemex) is the major bottler of Pepsi-Cola products outside the United States. The territories of Gemex include Mexico City (with the world's largest population for a single city) and the states of Mexico, Guerrero, and Morelos, including 23.8 million people. In addition to Pepsi, Gemex also sells favored soft drinks and mineral water through various licensing and franchise arrangements. While the average annual growth rate of the Mexican industry was 7.4% per year over the five years ended 1993, that of Gemex was 8.8% per year over the same period. The company has new franchises that will entitle it to bottle and distribute Pepsi in the southeast region of Mexico, where few Pepsi products are sold currently. The relative youth of the Mexican domestic market (over 50% of all Mexicans are under the age of 20), the overall growth rate of the Mexican economy, and the company's present market share make Gemex one of the strongest stocks traded on the Mexican market.

Grupo Televisa is Mexico's largest media company and quickly growing into one of the largest in the Spanish-speaking world. The four Mexico City television stations that are operated by Grupo Televisa have a 90% share of the total Mexican television audience and collect 80% of all Mexican TV advertising revenues. Almost 80% of all the programming that is shown on Grupo Televisa stations is either produced by Televisa or is a part of Televisa's library. In addition, Grupo Televisa:

- Is the largest cable television operator in Mexico, with a franchise for Mexico City that includes 4 million homes.

- Operates one of the largest Mexican radio station chains.

- Controls two record company labels.

- Owns the largest Mexican feature-film production and distribution company which produces 14% of all Mexican films.

- Publishes two magazines with circulations that are among the largest in Mexico.

- Has a 37% interest in the largest outdoor advertising company.

- Owns the largest language-dubbing facility in Mexico.

- Has a 51% interest in the only nationwide paging service.

Since the 1950s, Grupo Televisa has been majority-owned and controlled by the Azcarraga, O'Farrill, and Aleman families. The company has raised capital not only in Mexico, but also in international capital markets. In 1991, Televisa sold $750 million in equity—one of the largest primary equity offerings that was not associated with a privatization effort. In October 1992, Grupo Televisa issued $200 million in international debt at 410 bp over U.S. Treasuries. However, in the secondary market, these spreads narrowed to less than 300 bp.

Grupo Televisa sells programs to 63 markets worldwide and plans to market its programming in the United States, with its large and growing market for Spanish-language television. Televisa has acquired Univision, a U.S. Spanish-language broadcaster, and has an agreement for joint production with Fox Television in the United States.

Sears de México has 35 retail stores in 26 strategically located cities in Mexico. As is true with its counterpart in the United States, Sears de México sells a wide range of clothing, household appliances, automotive equipment, and offers extensive consumer credit. Sears enjoys a high-quality image in Mexico and, in affluent areas like Mexico City, has located its upscale stores in major shopping centers with merchandise that caters to high-income residents of these areas. In more rural areas, Sears de México provides an assortment of imported appliances and household goods that are not normally available in rural stores. Sears de México derives revenues from merchandise sales, credit operations, and real estate. There are seven shopping malls in the Mexico City area. Of these, Sears de México owns one, has an equity interest in two others, and stores in five.

Kimberly-Clark de México is 43% owned by the U.S. Kimberly-Clark Corporation. The company is involved in both consumer products and in wholesale paper goods. In the consumer market, 85% of the company's sales are generated by dominant market shares in disposable diapers, personal care items, tissue products, and notebooks. The remaining sales are derived from printing and writing paper. Kimberly-Clark de México is considered a blue-chip company in Mexico and its stock is extremely liquid. Mexican demographics favor continued growth of this company. Much of the capital requirements of the firm have been satisfied through its parent in the United States. Its expansion plans will no doubt involve public offerings of debt.

Banacci is the holding company for Mexico's largest commercial bank, Banamex. Banamex holds 25% of the assets of the financial services sector in Mexico. The new holding company, Banacci, is the parent firm for both Banamex and Accival. Under the new structure, the branch network system of Banamex has been streamlined and credit controls improved. Consolidation of many of the administrative functions of Banamex and Accival has helped increase productivity within the consolidated firm. In this holding company structure, Banamex, supported by Accival, promises to offer continued leadership in mortgage finance and a wide range of other financial services.[6]

The companies described above are among the largest that are traded on the Mexican stock exchange. As Exhibit 4-3 illustrates, the prices of these shares over a 12-month period vary over a wide range of prices. For example, Telmex traded in the range from $41 to $60 per share in the 12 months ended September 1993, an approximate 50% swing. Furthermore, in September 1993, most of these stocks were trading at or near their 12-month highs. For the most part, however, the P/E ratios were not at exceptionally high levels, ranging from 9.2 to 15.3 for all but Grupo Televisa, which was selling at 33 times earnings. Based on the shares outstanding and the September 1993 price per share, total market capitalizations of these firms were [in millions of new pesos (NP) and/or dollars ($)]:

Telmex	$20,076
Cemex	NP18,927.8 ($5,735.7)
Gemex	NP3,740.8 ($1,133.6)
Grupo Televisa	$8,890.8
Sears de México	NP2,625 ($795.5)
Kimberly-Clark de México	NP8,078.4 ($2,448)
Banacci	NP26,595 ($8,059.1)

Thus, market capitalization of some of Mexico's largest firms is in the $8 billion range. Both size and market share of these firms make them attractive to international investors.

American Depository Receipts

An *American Depositary Receipt (ADR)* is a negotiable certificate issued by a U.S. bank for shares of stock issued by a foreign company. The shares are either held by the ADR-issuing bank or at an agent for the bank. ADRs are registered with the Securities and Exchange Commission (SEC) and confer the rights of stock ownership to the holder of the ADR. Exhibit 4-4 lists 42

Mexican ADRs. These firms represent a wide range of industries:

- Airline
- Beverage
- Cement
- Construction
- Drilling
- Financial services
- Food
- Glass
- Media
- Packaging
- Retail
- Shipping
- Steel
- Telecommunications
- Tourism
- Truck manufacturing

As the involvement of Mexican companies in international trade and finance continues to increase, more firms will approach the international capital markets. In fact, it has been estimated that Mexican issuers are prepared to offer as much as $5 billion in new equity in light of the approval of the North American Free Trade Agreement and the improved perception of Mexico's credit standing.[7]

EXHIBIT 4-4
MEXICAN ADRs

Issuer	Industry	Exchange
1. Aeromexico	Airline	Bolsa
2. Apasco	Cement	OTC
3. Cemex	Cement	OTC/Bolsa
4. Cifra	Retail	OTC
5. Controladora Comercial Mexicana	Retail	OTC
6. Corporacion Mexicana Aviacion	Airline	OTC
7. Desc Sociedad de Fomento Industrial	Conglomerate	OTC
8. El Puerto de Liverpool GDS	Retail	None
9. Empaques Ponderosa	Packaging	Bolsa
10. E.P.N	Drilling	OTC
11. Fomento Economico Mexicano (Femsa)	Beverages	Bolsa
12. Grupo Carso	Conglomerate	Bolsa
13. Grupo Cementos Chihuahua	Cement	OTC
14. Grupo Dina (DIN)	Truck manufacturer	NYSE
15. Grupo Embotellador de Mexico	Beverages	Bolsa
16. Grupo Financiero Mexival	Financial group	OTC
17. Grupo Financiero Bancomer	Financial group	Bolsa
18. Grupo Gigante	Retailer	Bolsa
19. Grupo Industrial Maseca	Food	OTC
20. Grupo Mexicano de Video	Media	Bolsa
21. Grupo Posadas	Tourism	Bolsa
22. Grupo Radio Centro (RC)	Radio	NYSE
23. Grupo Salinas y Rochas	Retail	OTC
24. Grupo Sidek	Steel	OTC
25. Grupo Simec (SIM)	Steel	AMEX
26. Grupo Situr	Tourism	OTC
27. Grupo Synkro	Consumer products	OTC
28. Grupo Televisa	Media/broadcasting	Bolsa
29. Grupo Video Visa	Media	Bolsa
30. ICA	Construction	NYSE
31. Industria Electrica de Mexico	Electricity	OTC
32. Interceramic	Tiles	OTC/Bolsa
33. Ponderosa Industrial	Pulp and paper	OTC

Issuer	Industry	Exchange
34. San Luis	Conglomerate	OTC
35. Sears Roebuck de Mexico	Retail	Bolsa
36. Servicios Financieros Quadrum (QDRMY)	Financial services	NASDAQ
37. TAMSA (TAM)	Steel pipe	AMEX
38. Telmex*A	Telecommunications	NASDAQ
39. Telmex*L	Telecommunications	NYSE
40. TMM*L/*A (TMM/TMMA)	Shipping	NYSE
41. Tolmex	Cement	Bolsa/OTC
42. Vitro (VTO)	Glass	NYSE

Legend: Bolsa Mexican Bolsa (Stock Exchange)
        OTC   Over-the-Counter
        NYSE   New York Stock Exchange
        AMEX   American Stock Exchange
        NASDAQ National Association of Securities Dealers Automated
                       Quotations

Source: Mariscal, Jorge O. "Latin America Investment Strategy Highlights," Investment Research, Goldman Sachs, September 1993.

THE MEXICAN BOND MARKET

Like the stock market, the bond market in Mexico has experienced considerable development since the mid-1980s. Because of previously high inflation, most debt securities have been short-term. Indeed, at the end of 1993, *government debt* outstanding was composed primarily of *Cetes* with an original maturity of one year or less (52%) and *Bondes* with maturities ranging from one to two years (25%).

The economic policies of the Salinas government, coupled with strong foreign demand for Mexican government securities, have stabilized the debt markets to a great extent. For example, in the December 1993 auction of 28-day *Cetes*, the yield was 10.85%, down from 17.78% in the February auction of the same year. The foreign interest in longer-dated paper is clearly evident in the results of the December 1993 auction:

- 182-day *Cetes* yielded 10.77%, down from 19.13% in February

- 364-day *Cetes* yielded 10.46%, down from 19.86%

Thus, 364-day *Cetes* sold at a lower yield than the 28-day Treasury bills.

Commercial banks have been the primarily issuers of private-sector debt. Corporate *commercial paper* and *bank promissory notes* are the two most important money market instruments. In 1992, commercial paper accounted for $22 billion of the $29 billion in turnover of corporate debt.

Commercial paper may be issued for up to one year, but typically maturities range from 1 to 181 days, with the most common being 28 days. These instruments can be renewed and rollovers upon maturity are common. Most commercial paper is issued at a discount in new pesos. While some commercial paper had been issued as dollar-indexed, most of this type of instrument has been replaced by dollar-denominated securities in international debt markets. *Short-term bank paper* is issued in a number of forms. Bankers' acceptances and certificates of deposit are frequently issued. However, much of the recently issued bank paper has been short-term promissory notes or *Pagares Bancarios*. Like corporate commercial paper, most bank promissory notes are discounted securities. Both *Cetes* and bank promissory notes are used as collateral for overnight repurchase agreements.[8]

In the last few years, both Mexican industrial firms and banks have financed more of their capital requirements through *longer-term debt*. Before 1977, Telmex was the main issuer of bonds with offerings of fixed-rate mortgage bonds. Then in 1977, new rules permitted firms to issue unsecured bonds. Initially, issuers experimented with variable-rate bonds with interest payments indexed to short-term rates, for example, *Cetes* rates. More recently, variable-rate bonds are indexed to the highest yield on a number of short- and long-term securities. Longer-term bank bonds have also been offered on this basis.

Floating-rate medium-term notes with maturities from one to three years are now available, as are a variety of bonds, including real estate-backed, convertible, and inflation-indexed instruments.

Nevertheless, the size and activity of the government bond market greatly overshadow the corporate debt market. For example, in 1992, while turnover in corporate debt was the equivalent of $29 billion, government securities turnover was $3.4 trillion. In the past, a major obstacle for the corporate debt market was high inflation. This is being gradually corrected as Mexican inflation moderates.

However, a second obstacle has been inadequate distribution, with many issues becoming illiquid after issuance. This situation should be helped, to some extent, by the entry of Mexican borrowers into the international debt markets. The well-known Mexican issuers will continue to approach the international bond markets, including Banco Nacional de Comercio Exterior (Bancomext) and Nacional Financiera (Nafin).[9] Bancomext is Mexico's state-owned foreign trade and project finance bank. In 1993, the bank issued debt in the Yankee (U.S.) and Matador (Spanish) bond markets. Nafin is Mexico's national development bank, providing financial and technical assistance to small- and medium-sized Mexican private-sector companies. Global bonds for such issuers are often structured as medium-term notes, Euro-peso, peso-linked, Euroyen, or Yankee bonds. There are also expected to be new entrants into the international debt markets in 1994, such that up to $10 billion in debt may be issued by Mexican banks and industrial firms.

The yields on a 1993 issue of two-year, three-year, and five-year peso-denominated banker's acceptances (BAs) by Nafin underscores the appetite for longer-dated securities:

- two-year BAs—14.50%

- three-year BAs—13.16%

- five-year BAs—12.93%

In May 1993, the Mexican government introduced reforms that will likely increase liquidity in Mexican debt markets. Financial intermediaries will be able to trade Mexican securities that have been purchased abroad and non-Mexican issuers will be permitted to issue debt in Mexico. Under provisions of the North American Free Trade Agreement, U.S. and Canadian banks will be able to take advantage of these new powers and gain considerable market share during the early stages of the development of the Mexican bond market.

INNOVATION IN AN INTERNATIONAL CONTEXT

Both the private and public sectors in Mexico's financial community have embraced internationalization of the securities industry and the Mexican economy. This is evident in the overseas expansion of services by Mexican securities firms, innovative international financing arrangements for Mexican companies, and a collaborative currency-support arrangement with the central banks of Mexico, the United States, and Canada.

Mexican Securities Firms Abroad

Operadora de Bolsa Serfin, the securities affiliate of the Serfin *grupo financiero* (or financial group, similar to a U.S. holding company), is recognized as having a strong research department that is committed to servicing institutional investors. The firm has established the largest presence of any Mexican brokerage in New York with a team of equity traders, institutional sales staff, and fixed-income sales staff. *Accival*, part of the Banacci *grupo financiero*, also has established a New York office and is recognized as a source of high-quality research on the 50 Mexican firms that it tracks.

Interacciones is a top-10 Mexican brokerage firm that elected not to bid for one of the privatized banks, but to apply for a new license. The resulting holding company is Grupo Financiero Interacciones. In March 1993, the group opened a New York office and established its clear intent to be a major Wall Street player by hiring a former Salomon Brothers director, Lee Kimmell, as Chief Executive Officer of Interacciones Global.

Valores Finamex, part of the Finamex *grupo financiero*, was the first Mexican brokerage firm to establish a representative office in Tokyo in 1992. The office is registered with the Japanese Ministry of Finance and will develop this office into a full-service investment advisory service. The New York office is a wholly owned subsidiary, Valores Finamex International. In 1993, the firm had plans to establish another office in London. The overall strategy of Finamex is to tackle the Asian market from Tokyo, the North American market from New York, and the European market from London.

Innovative Financing for Mexican Firms

In light of the relatively undeveloped debt market in Mexico, one of the most difficult problems for Mexican firms has been securing long-term finance at competitive rates of interest. This problem has been exacerbated by the fact no borrower within a country can obtain a credit rating that is higher than the country itself. This is true even if the company otherwise could qualify for a top credit rating.

With an S&P rating of BB+, bonds issued by Mexico still rate below investment grade.[10] Working with J.P. Morgan & Company, *Kimberly-Clark de Mexico* has been able to circumvent this problem. Late in 1992, Kimberly-Clark was able to place $150 million in long-term debt with institutional investors. This private placement was the first unsecured debt offering from Latin America to receive an investment-grade credit rating. The issue was in two tranches:

- $125 million of seven-year, 8.06% notes

- $25 million of 10-year, 8.65% notes

These were the longest maturities to date by any private-sector Latin American issuer.[11]

The Kimberly-Clark notes were issued at 175 bp and 190 bp over U.S. Treasuries, respectively. At the time, 5-year Mexican corporate paper was trading at 400 bps over U.S. Treasuries and Mexican sovereign bonds were trading at a 265-bp spread. Investment bank J.P. Morgan was able to achieve this pricing by appealing to the appetite of U.S. pension funds and insurance companies for longer-dated paper and by bypassing the two traditional rating agencies Standard & Poor's and Moody's Investors Service. Instead, Morgan obtained an investment-grade rating of BBB+ from *Fitch Investors Service* and a rating 2 (on a scale of 1 to 6) from *National Association of Insurance Commissioners (NAIC)*.

These ratings appear to have been justified by several factors:

- Kimberly-Clark de Mexico is one of the largest and most profitable consumer products manufacturers in Mexico.

- The firm has substantial market share.

- The demographics of Mexico favor its long-term viability.

- It is unlikely that the government would prevent Kimberly-Clark from converting Mexican pesos into U.S. dollars to service its debt. (The only time that such government intervention occurred was for a few days during the crisis in 1982.)

- Even in the event of a substantial devaluation of the Mexican peso, Kimberly-Clark de Mexico would likely have little trouble obtaining sufficient pesos to convert to dollars to service its debt. The company is under-leveraged and its selling prices and manufacturing costs (pulp, energy, water) are set on an international basis, ultimately a dollar basis. This means that, if necessary, the firm has the (balance sheet) capacity to borrow pesos for conversion into dollars. Moreover, its pricing will keep pace with changes in the value of the peso.

Even before the innovative financing for Kimberly-Clark, in 1989 *Mexicana de Cobre (Mexcobre)*, a copper producer and exporter, arranged a pre-export arrangement for $210 million over a three-year period at 11.5%. The cost of this financing was much lower than the company would have been forced to pay domestically. Banque Paribus (of France) structured this syndicated lending. The primary concerns of the syndicate members were that:

- Interest rates might rise (increasing the share of revenues that must be devoted to interest and principal payments).

- The price of copper might decline (decreasing the borrowers' revenues and making it difficult to service and repay the debt).

- Mexcobre might not have access to foreign currency (with which to service and repay the debt).

To address these concerns, Banque Paribus structured the deal with:

- A fixed interest rate
- A copper price swap
- A fixed-price export sales contract with a major European copper purchaser
- An offshore escrow account for foreign currency accessibility

The only remaining issue was the ability of Mexcobre to produce the copper necessary to sell, that is, performance risk. The syndicate members were willing to assume the performance risk. Since the original structuring, the lending has twice been refinanced.

This structured financing model has been used by investment bankers in Mexico and other Latin American countries:

- Salomon Brothers for the Comision Federal de Electricidad (Mexico), with electricity exports as collateral

- Citibank for Petroleos Mexicanos (Pemex, Mexico), oil exports

- Citibank for Sivensa (Venezuela), steel exports

- Banque Paribus for Petroleos de Venezuela (PDVSA, Venezuela), propane exports

- ING Bank (Netherlands) for Aracruz Celulose (Brazil), pulp exports

MEXICAN DERIVATIVES

Mexico is the leading Latin American market for derivatives. Since March 1993, 10 issues of equity warrants have been introduced on the Bolsa Mexicana de Valores (Bolsa).[12] The first three warrants were issued by Operadora de Bolsa, the securities affiliate of the Serfin grupo financiero. These warrants were for in-the-money, at-the-money, and out-of-the-money options on the IPC index (*Indice de Precios y Cotizaciones*), the principal price index used in Mexico.[13] Thereafter, seven warrants on individual stocks were issued:

- Grupo Industrial Alfa

- Transportacion Maritima Mexicana

- Cemex

- Cifra

- Apasco

- Telmex

- a second warrant for Cemex

In addition, the Comision Nacional de Valores (CNV—the primary stock market regulator) is working with Banco de Mexico (central bank) toward the development of a whole range of derivatives in the Mexican market, including full-scale options offerings and stock-index futures trading.

In the United States, a market for listed options on Mexican ADRs is also developing. Telmex options are consistently among the most actively traded listed options in the U.S. market. Exhibit 4-5 shows the volume of trading in Telmex options during one session in June 1994. The Chicago Board Options Exchange (CBOE) has asked the U.S. Securities and Exchange Commission (SEC) for permission to trade options on the ADRs of Transportacion Maritima Mexicana, ICA (construction firm), and Vitro (glass container manufacturer). While the SEC clears trading on the CBOE, an active over-the-counter market is being facilitated by Bankers Trust which has issued 5 million put and call options on Telmex, 500,000 calls for Apasco (cement manufacturer) and 1 million calls for ICA.[14]

Of course, the debate about Mexican derivative securities is the same as that which revolves around U.S. derivatives. Derivative markets can increase the already substantial volatility of the Mexican stock market. Currently, it is estimated that 70% to 80% of the derivatives trading on Mexican securities is intended to obtain a leveraged position in the market, rather than to hedge large positions in Mexican securities. Nevertheless, it is likely that Mexican derivative markets will continue to develop at a brisk pace, facilitating the further integration of financial markets in the North American Free Trade zone.

EXHIBIT 4-5

TELMEX OPTIONS

		Call Options		Put Options	
Strike Price	Expiration Date	Volume	Last Price	Volume	Last Price
Regular Options					
50	Aug	—	—	52	5/16
50	Nov	—	—	87	1 1/8
55	Jun	958	8 3/8	1575	1/16
55	Jul	50	8 1/4	10	3/8
55	Aug	136	8 3/4	124	3/4
55	Nov	—	—	311	2 1/8
60	Jun	3538	3 1/4	3676	7/16
60	Jul	1612	4 1/4	92	1 3/8
60	Aug	758	5 1/8	727	2 5/16
60	Nov	16	7 3/8	30	3 7/8
65	Jun	2368	1/2	519	2 7/8
65	Jul	1318	1 5/8	4	3 3/4
65	Aug	1284	2 3/4	35	4 1/2
65	Nov	289	4 3/4	—	—
70	Aug	2137	1 1/4	—	—
70	Nov	248	2 15/16	—	—
75	Aug	721	1/2	—	—
80	Aug	200	3/16	—	—
LEAPS					
35	Jan 95	28	28 3/8	—	—
45	Jan 96	31	22 1/4	—	—
50	Jan 95	40	15 1/8	5	1 1/2
55	Jan 95	20	11 1/2	22	2 11/16
60	Jan 95	694	8 3/8	10	4 5/8
65	Jan 95	19	5 3/4	—	—
65	Jan 95	345	5 7/8	—	—
65	Jan 96	—	—	30	9 3/4
65	Jan 96	14	10 5/8	30	9 5/8
70	Jan 95	63	3 3/4	—	—

EXHIBIT 4-5

EXHIBIT 4-5 (continued)

Note:
1. Activity shown is for Monday, June 6, 1994.
2. For the June 6 session, Telmex stock closed at 63 1/8.
3. Volume is in number of contracts, with one contract representing 100 shares of the underlying security.
4. LEAPS are Long-Term Equity Anticipation Securities, or long-term options.

Source: Wall Street Journal, June 7, 1994, p. C11.

SELECTED REFERENCES

"Debt and Equity Boom Brews as Mexico Awaits an Upgrade," *Mexico, Euromoney* supplement, January 1994, pp. 2-6.

Dyer, Geoff. "Foreigners' Vote of Confidence in Mexican Bonds," *Euromoney*, September 1993, pp. 299-305.

Emerging Markets Borrowers Guide, Euromoney supplement, September 1993.

Fitch, Thomas. *Dictionary of Banking Terms*, New York: Barron's, 1990.

Mariscal, Jorge O. "Latin America Investment Strategy Highlights," Investment Research, Goldman Sachs, September 1993.

Marray, Michael. "The Best Brokers for Latin America," *Euromoney*, December 1993, pp. 93-100.

Marray, Michael. "Mexico Battles to Build Derivatives," *Euromoney*, July 1993, pp. 87-88.

"Mexico," *Guide to Domestic Bond Markets, Euromoney* supplement, 1993, pp. 73-76.

"Mexico's Finamex Planning to Draw Investment in Japan," *Tokyo Business Today*, January/February 1993, pp. 50-51.

Peagram, Norman. "Appetite for Latin Deals Increases," *Latin American Trade Finance, Euromoney* supplement, May 1994, pp. 144-151.

Peagram, Norman. "Kimberly-Clark Creates a First for Mexico," *Euromoney*, March 1993, pp. 151-152.

ENDNOTES

1. See Chapter 3 for the holding companies that have been formed in connection with the 18 recently privatized Mexican commercial banks.
2. This contrasts with the banking industry, in which a 4% individual limit remains after the phase-in period.
3. $(1900/1400)^2 -1 = .8418$
4. Stock market capitalization is, for the stock of all publicly traded companies, the sum of outstanding shares multiplied by price per share.
5. Official reserves are gold, foreign currency, and Special Drawing Rights (at the International Monetary Fund) held by national governments.
6. See also Chapter 3 for a discussion of Banamex.
7. See "Debt and Equity Boom Brews as Mexico Awaits an Upgrade."
8. A repurchase agreement is a contract to sell and subsequently repurchase securities at a specified date and price.
9. See Chapter 3 for a discussion of Nafin.
10. Investment grade ratings are AAA, AA, A, and BBB.
11. There have been 10-year issues by the United States of Mexico—a Yankee bond in 1992 and private placements in 1990 and 1991.
12. An equity warrant is a certificate that gives the owner the right to buy equity securities at a stated price for a stated period or at any time in the future.
13. An in-the-money option is one that entitles the option owner to purchase a security at a strike price below market price. For an out-of-the-money option, the strike price is above the market price. For an at-the-money option, the strike price equals the market price.
14. A call option is the right to buy the underlying security. A put option is the right to sell the underlying security.

5 Other Financial Services in Mexico

INTRODUCTION

The North American Free Trade Agreement gave significant powers to U.S. and Canadian investors to become involved in financial services other than banking and securities firms. In fact, as compared to the limits imposed on banks and securities firms, the limits on ownership are much more liberal for:

- Insurance Companies
- Factoring Companies
- Leasing Companies
- Limited-Scope Finance Companies

There are considerable opportunities to provide financial services through these organizational structures. The Mexican insurance market has tremendous growth potential, in both life and non-life coverage, including fund management and export insurance. The lack of financial services for small- and medium-sized businesses suggests the need for factoring and leasing operations. Limited-scope finance companies can fill specific voids in consumer, as well as, commercial lending.

THE MEXICAN INSURANCE MARKET

NAFTA Provisions

Before NAFTA, no Mexican citizen or business could purchase insurance that was not written by a Mexican insurance company and no foreign investor could own a majority stake in a Mexican insurance company. Under the provisions of NAFTA, Mexicans may purchase certain insurance from cross-border financial service providers in the United States and Canada, as long as (1) the insurance premiums and benefits are not denominated in Mexican pesos and (2) the cross-border providers do not solicit (advertise or promote) in Mexico. Specifically, residents of Mexico are not restricted from purchasing from cross-border insurance providers of another Party (the United States or Canada):

- Tourist insurance (including travel accident and motor vehicle insurance for non-resident tourists, but not insurance for risks of liability to third parties) for individuals, purchased without solicitation via physical mobility of such individuals.

- Cargo insurance to and from each Party, purchased without solicitation, for goods in international transit from point of origin to final destination.

- Insurance purchased without solicitation for a vehicle during the period of its use in transportation of cargo (other than insurance of risks of liabilities to third parties), provided such vehicle is licensed and registered outside Mexico (including vehicles in maritime shipping, commercial aviation, space launching and freight (including satellites)).

- Intermediary services incidental to the above, purchased without solicitation.

Thus, U.S. and Canadian insurers have some limited ability to sell tourist, cargo, and automobile insurance without actually establishing a presence in Mexico. The rationale for such limited cross-border access is that permitting a greater latitude would probably result in a significant loss of premium income for the Mexican economy with no investment or creation of employment in Mexico.

The greater opportunities for U.S. and Canadian insurers are in the new capabilities to own insurance companies in Mexico. Exhibit 5-1 shows that insurance companies can be established in Mexico under one of three scenarios—a wholly owned subsidiary, a joint venture, or increasing an already existing minority ownership interest.

A wholly owned subsidiary may be established with specific limitations on individual investments and aggregate investment, similar to the restrictions that apply to commercial banks and securities firms. However, the limitations are less restrictive.

A single U.S. or Canadian investor can accumulate no more than 1.5% of banking capital during the transition period from 1994 through 1999, with a 4% limit thereafter. The individual investor limit for a securities firm is 4% during the transition period with no limit thereafter. However, the individual limit in the insurance industry is 1.5% during the transition period with no limit thereafter.

In terms of the maximum amount of aggregate capital that may be controlled by all foreign institutions during the transition period, the range is from 8% to 15% for foreign banks and from 10% to 20% for securities firms. Furthermore, until 2004, the Mexican government may impose a freeze on new U.S. and Canadian investments (for a period not to exceed 3 years) if such aggregate investment reaches 25% in the banking industry or 30% in the securities industry. In contrast, in the insurance industry, the range for aggregate investment during the transition

EXHIBIT 5-1

INSURANCE INVESTMENT IN MEXICO UNDER NAFTA

Liberalization of investment opportunities in Mexican insurance companies— both (1) life and health and (2) property and casualty:

Wholly owned subsidiaries

a. Limit of individual investment by U.S. or Canadian investor set at 1.5% of industry capital during phase-in period (1994- 1999) and no limit thereafter.
b. Limit of aggregate investment by U.S. and Canadian investors (as a percentage of total industry capital) increases from 6% to 12% between 1994 and 1999 as follows, with no limit thereafter.

Date	Percentage
January 1, 1994	6%
January 1, 1995	8%
January 1, 1996	9%
January 1, 1997	10%
January 1, 1998	11%
January 1, 1999	12%

c. Both individual and aggregate limits will be calculated separately for (1) life and health and (2) property and casualty.

Joint Ventures

a. Under certain circumstances, U.S. and Canadian equity interest in a Mexican insurance company is exempt from the individual and aggregate limits noted above.

b. In order to qualify for this treatment, percentage of Mexican insurance company's common stock that is owned by Mexican persons may not be less than the following levels for one-year periods that begin on the following dates:

Date	Percentage
January 1, 1994	70%
January 1, 1995	65%
January 1, 1996	60%

Date	Percentage
January 1, 1997	55%
January 1, 1998	49%
January 1, 1999	25%

c. After January 1, 2000, the percentages above will no longer apply.

Already Existing Equity Stakes

a. U.S. and Canadian investors that have an equity stake in a Mexican insurance company of at least 10% as of July 1, 1992 may accelerate acquisition of a Mexican insurance company.
b. An investor that qualifies with such a 10% stake in a Mexican insurance company (or more) may exercise any contract right or option in existence as of July 1, 1992 with respect to ownership interests in that Mexican insurance company.
c. An investor that qualifies with such a 10% stake in a Mexican insurance company (or more) may acquire a controlling interest in that Mexican insurance company up to 100%, effective January 1, 1996.

---

is from 6% to 12%, with no limit thereafter. Thus, the restrictions on the insurance industry are less binding.

A *joint venture* insurance enterprise may be established that is exempt from the individual and aggregate limits noted above. In the first year of the transition period, the Mexican partner in the joint venture may own no less than 70%. As shown in Exhibit 5-1, this percentage declines to 25% in 1999. Starting in 2000, these percentages no longer apply.

If a U.S. or Canadian insurance company has an *already existing equity stake* in a Mexican insurance company, any agreement between the two parties with respect to ownership interests that was in force on July 1, 1992 may be exercised. This provision, of course, is in recognition of the fact that Mexican law permits total foreign investment in an insurance company to be as high as 49%, regardless of nationality of the foreign investor(s). Moreover, NAFTA stipulates that if a U.S. or Canadian investor held at least 10% of the equity of a Mexican insurance company on July 1, 1992, that investor may acquire up to 100% of the Mexican company as soon as January 1, 1996.

The Attraction for Foreign Insurers

As Exhibit 5-2 illustrates, the Mexican insurance market has attracted considerable international attention from Germany (Allianz), Switzerland (Zurich), the United Kingdom (Commercial), Italy (Generali), Spain (Banco Santander), and the United States (AIG [American International Group], Aetna, Cigna, Chubb, and Metropolitan Life). The stakes that these companies hold in Mexican insurance companies range from 26% to 49%. Notably, the Spanish bank, Banco Santander, joined with the U.S. insurer, Metropolitan Life, to assume a 49% stake in Seguros Iberomexicana. This is a strategic alliance that indicates the future trend of increased emphasis on diversification of financial services in the Mexican market—combinations of commercial banking, investment banking, fund management, and insurance.

EXHIBIT 5-2
FOREIGN INSURANCE COMPANIES WITH INVESTMENTS IN MEXICO

Foreign Insurance Company	Mexican Insurance Company	Foreign Ownership
Generali	America	26%
Commercial Union	La Republica	44
Mapfre	Tepeyac	49
AIG	Interamericana-Indep.	49
Allianz	Cuauhtemoc	40
Aetna	Seguros Monterrey	10
Cigna	Progresso	49
Chubb	Equitativa	30
Banco Santander/ Metropolitan Life	Iberomexicana	49
Zurich	Chapultepec	30
Reliance	Proteccion Mutua	30

Source: "Investing in Mexico," Export Today, June 1993, p. 22.

When the nature of the Mexican insurance industry is examined, the reason for such interest becomes clear. Mexican firms and individuals are "underinsured" by almost any standard.

- Approximately 1.5 million Mexicans have personal life insurance, which represents 1.8% of the population of 85 million people.

- Since there is no compulsory liability insurance, only 24% of Mexican automobiles are insured.

- Most Mexican doctors and lawyers do not insure their practices.

- Only 2% of Mexican homes are insured.

- When an earthquake destroyed much of Mexico City in 1985, only 15% of the buildings were insured.

- Per capita expenditure on insurance premiums in Mexico is $31 as compared to $1,929 in the United States.

- Total insurance premiums collected in Mexico in 1992 amounted to approximately $5 billion or 1.7% of GNP. The corresponding statistics for the United States were $508 billion or 8.6% of GNP.

- The 42 existing Mexican insurance companies collected 1992 premiums that averaged $119 million ($5 billion/42 firms), while the U.S. average was lower at $85 million ($508 billion/6,000 firms).

The U.S. insurance market is mature and highly price-competitive. The Mexican market holds tremendous potential because personal incomes are rising, the small Mexican middle-class is growing, and the increasing number of corporations doing business in Mexico need insurance coverage. In addition, the formation of private retirement plans presents U.S. insurers an emerging opportunity for pension fund management.[1]

Exhibit 5-3 indicates the pace at which the Mexican insurance industry is expanding. In 1986, life and non-life insurance premiums totalled $1.4 billion. At an average rate of increase of 23.6%, 1992 premiums grew to $4.9 billion. At this rate, it has been projected that annual premiums may reach $50 billion by 2004.

Fund Management in Mexico

In Mexico, the stock and bond markets are not fully developed and Mexican officials are anxious to attract capital. Because the per capita income is low relative to that of the United States, individuals as yet do not have a major impact on the amount of funds available in capital markets. In 1992, the per capita GNP of Mexico was $3,470, while that in the United States was $23,120. With the introduction of new pension plans, together with rising incomes, this will change. More investable funds will be generated by the savings of the household sector, includ-

---

EXHIBIT 5-3
GROWTH IN MEXICAN INSURANCE PREMIUMS

Year	Life and Non-Life Premiums[1]	Growth Rate
1986	$1,358	
1987	1,456	7.2%
1988	1,992	36.8
1989	2,495	25.3
1990	2,815	12.8
1991	3,596	27.7
1992	4,850	34.9

[1] In millions of U.S. dollars.

Note: Average annual compound growth rate for the six-year period is 23.6%.

Source: Author's calculations based on data from:
"Investing in Mexico," Export Today, June 1993, p. 22.

---

ing the mandatory pension plans. Already international fund managers are an important part of the Mexican economy.

One of the oldest funds in Mexico is the closed-end Mexico Fund, managed by José Luis Gómez Pimienta.[2] Gómez Pimienta, then an investment banker with Bancomer, began the Mexico Fund in 1981. Only the second single-country fund to be registered in the United States, the fund shrank almost immediately from $112 million to $28 million when the Mexican debt crisis erupted in 1982 and the peso lost 85% of its value.

When Miguel de la Madrid took over the presidency of Mexico in late 1982, a slow recovery began. President Carlos Salinas de Gortari, elected in 1988, continued this progress and negotiated the North American Free Trade Agreement.[3] The Mexico Fund has prospered along with the Mexican economy. In the five years ended 1993, the fund has increased an average of 49% per year. The top 12 stocks that Gómez Pimienta has placed in the fund are:

Company	Industry
Apasco	Building materials
Bufete	Engineering and construction
Cifra	Retail
Comercial Mexicana	Retail
Kimberly-Clark de México	Consumer products
Jugos del Valle	Fruit juices
Grupo Bancomer	Financial services
Grupo Banacci	Financial services
Televisa	Media and entertainment
Telmex	Telecommunications
Tribasa	Construction
Gemex	Beverages

In contrast to the past few years when the entire stock market did well, Gómez Pimienta believes that specific stock selection will be the key to profitable investment in the Mexican market.[4]

Cifra and Controladora Comercial Mexicana are investing in inventory controls and personnel training. Cifra has reduced its operating expenses from 23% of sales to 16%, close the Wal-Mart benchmark. Both companies are involved in joint ventures to open warehouse stores: Cifra with Wal-Mart and Comercial Mexicana with Price/Costco.

Bufete Industrial, a construction firm in which Dallas-based Dresser Industries has a 22% stake, is the leading firm in energy construction. This segment of the company's business should benefit from the projected increases in oil refining and power-plant development. Furthermore, Bufete is diversifying into the construction of factories, building a megahotel and resort in Uruguay, and participating in the modernization of the Mexican water system.

While the consumer products market in Mexico is highly competitive, Kimberly-Clark de México has invested heavily in new plants and technology. The company has maintained its lead in consumer products through product innovation and aggressive marketing.

Jugos del Valle has a strong market share in Mexico. While Coca-Cola, Pepsi, and other soft drink companies are competing aggressively, the Valle brand continues to dominate the market.

When the Mexico Fund was introduced, the per share value was $12, but dropped to a low of $3 in the early 1980s. With the recovery of the Mexican economy and investments such as those noted above, the per share value on the New York Stock Exchange has increased to approximately $28.

It also should be noted that fund managers play an important role in providing capital to industry—a role that is recognized by the Mexican government. In some ways, mutual funds have taken over the functions of commercial banks and multilateral financial institutions such as the International Monetary Fund. For example, the peso came under pressure early in 1994 because of the political uncertainty that was stimulated by the Chiapas uprising in January, the kidnapping of prominent business leaders, and the assassination of Luis Donaldo Colosio (Salinas' hand-picked successor) in March. In response to this pressure, a group of fund managers gave the Mexican government certain policy suggestions that were geared to slow the decline of the peso. The Weston Forum consisted of representatives from Weston Group (New York investment bank that brokered $5 billion in peso-denominated securities in 1993); Fidelity; Trust Co. of the West; Scudder, Stevens & Clark; Oppenheimer; Putnam Funds Management; Soros Fund Management; Salomon Brothers, Inc.; and Nomura Securities International, Inc. While the government does not take instruction from mutual fund managers, it is clear that Treasury officials, the central bank, and major political figures listen carefully to the managers' concerns. For example, Ernesto Zedillo, the PRI candidate that was designated after the assassination of Colosio and elected to the office of president later in 1994, met with 30 large investors in April—only weeks after his selection.

Thus, while the Mexican securities markets are volatile, the government has created an environment that is conducive to foreign investment. In the long run, this will enhance stability of the markets while, at the same time, making it possible to realize healthy returns as the economy develops. Fund management is now, and will continue to be, a strong growth industry in Mexico.

Export Insurance

Another area with strong potential for insurance companies is export insurance. As noted in Chapter 2, Mexico is a growing market that represents the third largest export market for the United States.[5] Exhibit 5-4 shows that the top exports to Mexico include electronic equipment, industrial machinery, transportation equipment, chemicals, metal products, agricultural goods, rubber and plastics, petroleum products, apparel, and furniture and fixtures. The $33.3 billion in exports to Mexico in 1992 represented 7.9% of total U.S. exports.

The geographic distribution of these exports is concentrated in a few states. As indicated in Exhibit 5-5, Texas was the largest exporter to Mexico in 1991 with $15.5 billion (46.5% of the total).

EXHIBIT 5-4

TOP 15 U.S. EXPORTS TO MEXICO IN 1991

Rank	Category	Exports[1]
1.	Electric & Electronic Equipment	$5,970,832
2.	Industrial Machinery & Computers	4,786,045
3.	Transportation Equipment	4,465,519
4.	Chemical Products	2,565,267
5.	Primary Metals	2,446,266
6.	Food Products	1,721,682
7.	Fabricated Metal Products	1,500,821
8.	Scientific & Measuring Instruments	1,268,885
9.	Agriculture—crops	1,216,028
10.	Rubber and Plastic Products	1,115,784
11.	Paper Products	1,080,576
12.	Refined Petroluem Products	755,212
13.	Apparel	728,247
14.	Furniture & Fixtures	578,932
15.	Miscellaneous Manufactures	515,480
	Other categories	2,560,104
	U.S. EXPORTS TO MEXICO	$33,275,780
	U.S. EXPORTS TO WORLD	$421,853,247
	MEXICAN SHARE OF EXPORTS TO WORLD	7.9%

[1] In thousands of U.S. dollars.

Source: *U.S. Exports to Mexico: A State-by-State Overview 1987-1991*, U.S. Department of Commerce, 1992. p. 11.

California was the second largest exporter with $5.5 billion (16.6%). Also among the major exporters were Michigan ($1.6 billion, 4.9%), Illinois ($1.1 billion, 3.3%), Arizona ($1.0 billion, 3.0%), New York ($0.9 billion, 2.7%), Pennsylvania ($0.7 billion, 2.1%), Louisiana ($0.6 billion, 1.9%), Ohio ($0.58 billion, 1.7%) and Florida ($0.58 billion, 1.7%). Together, these ten states constituted 84.4% of all U.S. shipments. Exhibit 5-6 outlines the top five exports for each of these states.

Export insurance is a potentially profitable line of business because of the dominance of trade-related activity in the Mexican economy. Political risk insurance (which protects against expropriation and civil unrest) is available from government agencies, such as the U.S. Overseas Private Investment Corporation (OPIC). In addition, there are various forms of private-sector protection that can be provided, including:

- Marine insurance

- Payment risk coverage

- Performance guarantees

- Construction and engineering risk coverage

- Traveling executives insurance

Marine insurance is classified as either (1) "blue water" or ocean shipping or (2) "brown water" or inland shipping in the United States. When an ocean cargo policy covers truck, rail, air, ship, and temporary storage, the seller who is at risk knows that payment will be forthcoming and that it will not be necessary to try to collect from a stevedore or inland carrier in a foreign country. Exporters are generally advised to obtain contingent coverage even when the importer is covered. Contingent coverage fills the "holes" that may be left by the primary coverage.

Payment risk coverage is necessary to avoid the situation of a bank paying a letter of credit issued on behalf of the importer even if the letter was designed to guarantee performance and was wrongfully drawn upon (because of nonperformance). Likewise, if a piece of equipment is custom-made and requires an extended period of time to construct, payment risk coverage will pay the exporter should an embargo prevent shipment for political reasons. Private-sector insurance of this kind is necessary when the local content of the merchandise is not sufficient to qualify it for government insurance of the same type.

Performance guarantees typically do not cover damage to the equipment, but instead insures against the inability of the

EXHIBIT 5-5

STATE RANKINGS IN 1991 EXPORTS TO MEXICO

Rank	State	Exports[1]
1.	Texas	$15,485,379
2.	California	5,526,877
3.	Michigan	1,628,409
4.	Illinois	1,087,100
5.	Arizona	990,787
6.	New York	886,835
7.	Pennsylvania	693,727
8.	Louisiana	618,114
9.	Ohio	581,783
10.	Florida	578,730
11.	New Jersey	452,365
12.	Georgia	376,741
13.	North Carolina	330,540
14.	Tennessee	290,875
15.	Washington	290,573
16.	Missouri	288,245
17.	Connecticut	259,395
18.	Indiana	259,377
19.	Kansas	258,266
20.	Wisconsin	249,911
21.	Massachusetts	229,829
22.	Minnesota	216,964
23.	Kentucky	163,489
24.	Alabama	152,628
25.	Virginia	146,028
26.	Delaware	127,383
27.	Iowa	108,261
28.	Mississippi	100,639
29.	Arkansas	95,929
30.	South Carolina	94,191
31.	Colorado	90,148
32.	Oklahoma	80,354
33.	Nebraska	64,401
34.	Oregon	55,401
35.	Maryland	50,728

Rank	State	Exports[1]
36.	Utah	39,340
37.	New Hampshire	37,834
38.	Idaho	32,925
39.	West Virginia	32,504
40.	Rhode Island	24,096
41.	New Mexico	18,219
42.	Vermont	17,968
43.	Maine	14,398
44.	Nevada	11,304
45.	Montana	9,716
46.	Hawaii	6,535
47.	Wyoming	6,224
48.	South Dakota	6,105
49.	Alaska	6,045
50.	District of Columbia	4,103
51.	North Dakota	3,570
	Puerto Rico	78,943
	Virgin Islands	15,548
	U.S. TOTAL	$33,275,780

[1] In thousands of U.S. dollars.

Source: *U.S. Exports to Mexico: A State-by-State Overview 1987-1991*, U.S. Department of Commerce, 1992. p. 17.

equipment to function as promised. A related form of coverage is machinery breakdown/loss of profits insurance. This second type of policy insures against physical loss or damage attributable to a sudden event when operating, for example, pulp and paper plants, electric utilities, petrochemical facilities, metal smelting, or mining facilities.

Construction and engineering risk coverage are forms of insurance for construction projects. Construction risk coverage applies to civil engineering projects such as hydroelectric projects, roads, and transportation infrastructure. Engineering risk coverage is appropriate for risks that involve installation exposure. These policies cover physical damage to the product being installed from fire, flood, earthquake, design problems, and

EXHIBIT 5-6

TOP 10 STATES EXPORTING TO MEXICO

State	*Major Exports to Mexico*
Texas	Electric & electronic equipment, transportation equipment, industrial machinery and equipment, primary metal industries, chemical products.
California	Electric & electronic equipment, industrial machinery and computers, rubber & plastic products, fabricated metal products.
Michigan	Transportation equipment, industrial machinery & computers, fabricated metal products, electric and electronic equipment.
Illinois	Industrial machinery and computers, transportation equipment, electric and electronic equipment, primary metal industries, chemical products.
Arizona	Electric & electronic equipment, industrial machinery & computers, apparel, transportation equipment, food products.
New York	Scientific & measuring instruments, transportation equipment, industrial machinery & computers, chemical products, food products.
Pennsylvania	Primary metal industries, electric & electronic equipment, industrial machinery & computers, chemical products, food products.
Louisiana	Agriculture—crops, chemical products, food products, refined petroleum products, industrial machinery & computers.
Ohio	Industrial machinery & computers, chemical products, rubber & plastic products, electric & electronic equipment, transportation equipment.
Florida	Industrial machinery & computers, chemical products, electric & electronic equipment, transportation equipment, paper products.

Note: Industries noted are the five that generated the highest level of exports to Mexico in 1991.

Source: *U.S. Exports to Mexico: A State-by-State Overview 1987-1991*, U.S. Department of Commerce, 1992.

human error. This coverage insures all parties that are at risk—the principal for whom the project is constructed, the manufacturer of the components, and the contractor who is the manufacturer of the project itself.

Traveling executives insurance covers key personnel when they operate outside the home country. Coverage includes automobile insurance for rented or purchased automobiles, cost of transporting a sick or injured executive to a location where adequate medical attention can be obtained, medical cost for endemic diseases (such as malaria which, once contracted, recurs), and expenses associated with kidnap and ransom.

Export insurance is specialized with respect to the risks that are underwritten. Both the current level of trade and the pace at which trade is increasing suggest that export insurance is a solid niche market within the North American Free Trade zone. Furthermore, because of the low level of insurance coverage in Mexico to date, there are generally significant opportunities for market expansion in the insurance industry.

OTHER FINANCIAL SERVICES

NAFTA Provisions

Before NAFTA, foreign investors were permitted to hold no more than 49% of the equity of a factoring, leasing, or finance company in Mexico. As shown in Exhibit 5-7, under the provisions of NAFTA, there are no individual foreign investment limits for these firms either in terms of the equity of a specific company or in terms of total industry capital. The aggregate capital limit for all foreign investors in factoring and leasing firms begins at 10% of industry capital in 1994 and increases annually in equal increments to 20% in 1999. In the case of limited-scope finance companies, the aggregate capital limit is 3% of the sum of aggregate assets of limited-scope finance companies and aggregate assets of commercial banks. After 1999, no limits apply for factoring, leasing, and limited-scope finance companies. Because of relatively liberal constraints, these industries

EXHIBIT 5-7
INVESTMENT IN OTHER FINANCIAL INSTITUTIONS UNDER NAFTA

Factoring Companies

- There are no individual limits to ownership by U.S. and Canadian investors during or after the phase-in period from 1994 through 1999.
- Limit of aggregate investment by U.S. and Canadian investors (as a percentage of total industry capital) increases from 10% to 20% between 1994 and 1999 in equal increments, with no limit thereafter.

Leasing Companies

- There are no individual limits to ownership by U.S. and Canadian investors during or after the phase-in period from 1994 through 1999.
- Limit of aggregate investment by U.S. and Canadian investors (as a percentage of total industry capital) increases from 10% to 20% between 1994 and 1999 in equal increments, with no limit thereafter.

Limited-Scope Finance Companies

- There are no individual limits to ownership by U.S. and Canadian investors during or after the phase-in period from 1994 through 1999.
- Limit of aggregate investment by U.S. and Canadian investors is 3% during the transition period, with no limit thereafter.
- Aggregate limit is based on the sum of (1) *aggregate assets* of all types of limited-scope finance companies in Mexico and (2) *aggregate assets* of all commercial banks in Mexico.
- Limited-scope finance companies may not accept deposits, but may raise funds in the securities markets for operations subject to normal terms and conditions.
- Non-bank investors may establish limited-scope finance companies to provide separately consumer lending, commercial lending, mortgage lending, or credit card services. In addition, Mexico may authorize lending services closely related to the authorized business.

represent a viable route to enter Mexican financial markets with fewer encumbrances than exist in the banking or securities industries.

In both types of firms, credit information will be a critical element in successful operations. Historically, Mexico has been considered less than transparent in terms of the creditworthiness of firms. Companies were typically family-owned and resistent to disclosing financial information. Publicly available accounting information has not always been useful because of the practice of commingling personal and company assets.

However, now Standard & Poor's Rating Group (S&P) and Dun & Bradstreet Corp. are establishing or expanding their operations in Mexico to be able to provide better financial data. Recently, S&P purchased a credit rating company and Dun & Bradstreet increased its staff. It should be easier now for both firms to gather data than has historically been the case because more Mexican firms are attempting to raise funds in securities markets. Also, dozens of Mexican firms have been privatized and *must* be able to raise funds on the open market. Adequate financial disclosure is necessary in order to be able to appeal to the financial markets. In the consumer market, TRW, Inc. and Trans Union Corp. are establishing credit bureaus, to provide information for evaluating individual credit risk.

Factoring Services

Factoring is essentially the sale of a client's accounts receivable to a third party, the factor. Operationally, factoring is a portfolio of financial services in which the financial service provider helps its client assess customer credit, extends credit protection guarantees to its client, helps its client collect accounts receivable, operates the client's sales ledger, and provides short-term finance. In the context of the North American Free Trade Zone, all of these services can be very useful for a client company that is becoming involved in trade for the first time.

Since a factor receives the payments that are associated with accounts receivable, the factor is in an excellent position to as-

sess credit quality. This information is supplemented by a wide range of reference material from published financial statements, other lending institutions, and credit rating agencies.

A factor can *extend credit protection* to a client as a result of this credit assessment capability and also because factors typically have a bank line of credit. For the client, this credit protection means that the sale is complete after goods have been delivered. There is no further uncertainty with respect to payment.

Sales on open account create a need for *collections activities.* From the perspective of the client, collections activity that is too aggressive may jeopardize future sales. From the perspective of the customer that is obligated to pay the client, delay of payments can be related to administrative inefficiency, a dispute as to the shipment, or a deliberate attempt to postpone payment to receive more credit that originally agreed upon. The most difficult delay of payment, of course, is related to the customer's inability to pay. A factor can maintain a consistent level of collection activity even during peak selling seasons to free the client from the necessity of doing so. In fact, the client may even "blame the factor" for aggressive collections with which the client would not be comfortable.

When a factor performs *sales ledger administration,* the work is backed by a strong network of computer systems with dedicated personnel. The factor provides a complete sales ledger package:

- Accurate records are kept as to amounts collected.

- Customer accounts are promptly credited.

- On-line computer access is provided so that clients can track the collections activities.

- Monthly statements are provided to customers.

- Multi-currency ledgers are maintained in the case of international transactions.

Perhaps the single most important service of a factor is *providing short-term finance*. When a client sells on credit, it needs cash to replenish inventory and to pay for labor expenses. Rarely does the period during which the client may defer payment exactly match the credit period offered to the client's customer. Furthermore, for a growing concern the need to purchase new inventory will outpace the cash made available through the collection of current accounts receivable. Through a factor, the financing available to the client will depend on the extent to which the client continues to sell to creditworthy customers. As long as that creditworthiness is maintained, the client can receive immediate cash upon sale of probably no less than 80% of invoice amounts, with the balance paid upon collection. Once the sales are verified, no further security is required and no ownership interest in the client firm need be relinquished to obtain this additional financial support.

Factoring services are suited for businesses producing goods or services that are complete at the point of invoicing. Good examples include furniture manufacture, manufacture of printed circuit boards, printing, or distribution of garments. Goods or services for which further performance is required present a security risk for a factor. The factor is best positioned when the only dispute that could arise relates to ability of the customer to pay, rather than to the ability of the client to perform. In this way, a factor can offer non-recourse financing arrangements to the client in which the factor assumes the full credit risk.

The fees charged by a factor are composed of the *administrative charge* and the *discounting charge*. The administrative charge is generally a percentage of factored sales which is mutually agreed upon and reviewed on an annual basis. This fee covers the main service components of credit assessment, credit protection, collections, and sales ledger administration. The discounting charge is often a floating interest rate based on client creditworthiness and volume of discounted invoices. The discounting charge is usually calculated once per month, based on the daily average value of discounted invoices.

Export Factoring

Export factoring is a growing field because more and more creditworthy purchasers of goods in an international context are requiring that they be given credit terms on open account to avoid the inconvenience and expense of letters of credit or bills of exchange.[6] International factoring accomplishes this objective. International factors that provide an export service either have offices in other countries or are part of a network of independent factoring organizations. The largest such network is Factors Chain International (FCI). FCI was founded in 1968, consists of over 90 member companies in 35 of the world's primary commercial centers.

From the client's perspective, international factoring is no different than domestic factoring. The client continues to work with the same local factor. The client first provides information with respect to the international customer. The local factor then selects the best overseas factor for the client's sales in the country to which the goods will be shipped. The overseas factor assesses the overseas customer and offers up to 100% protection within mutually agreed credit limits.

When goods are shipped to the overseas customer, the client creates an invoice, sending a copy to the local factor which updates the client's sales ledger and makes the corresponding funds available to the client. In addition, the sales ledger maintained by the overseas factor is also updated. When the invoice is due, the overseas factor makes the collection. Funds are typically wired to the local factor via SWIFT.[7]

The majority of factored sales are in Europe (61%), with the Americas (28%) and Asia (9%) accounting for significant shares of the activity. The practice of factoring is growing rapidly. In 1983, worldwide turnover in factoring volume was $63.3 billion. By 1989, the total domestic factoring amounted to $179.2 billion, representing an annual compound rate of growth of 18.9%. International factoring is exhibiting strong growth. Over the same period, international factoring volume grew even faster at the average compound rate of 19.5% from $3.7 billion to $10.8 bil lion. Notably, Bancomer recently established a factoring venture with NationsBank.

A factoring operation with offices in the United States, Canada, and Mexico could capitalize on the strong upward trend in trade in the North American region. Such an operation would also help fill the void for financing of small- and medium-sized firms in Mexico.

Project Finance

Project finance is geared to providing funds for specific projects. In the context of the Mexican market, a limited-scope finance company specializing in commercial lending can structure relatively large financing packages based on the cash flow expectations of the project, rather than on the creditworthiness of the company undertaking the project. Project finance typically has a maturity of 10 to 15 years. Since limited-scope finance companies may not fund themselves with deposits (see Exhibit 5-7), the companies can raise longer-term debt and equity funds in the capital markets and reinvest these in relatively long-term commercial projects.[8]

Project finance became popular in the United States after the 1978 enactment of the Public Utility Regulatory Policy Act (PURPA). Under PURPA, local utilities were required to purchase all the output of qualified independent power producers under long-term contracts, at a price equal to the marginal cost of generating electricity. This law laid the foundation for contractual obligations that could be financed with non-recourse lending. The construction of a number of hydroelectric and geothermal projects followed. Once one of these facilities was completed, the "robot" plant needed no fuel and represented low operating cost.

One particularly illustrative example is the $40 million project to refurbish the hydroelectric power dam on the Penobscot River in Maine and to install automated generating equipment. Once completed, the project had an expected useful life of 50 years and would sell electricity to Central Maine Power Company under a long-term contract that covered half its useful life. The plant required no fuel and only one full-time caretaker. As a result, operating costs were a fraction of revenues. This project is a virtual "cash cow." In the unlikely event that Central Maine Power Company were to fail, the plant was structured as a supplier to the power company, not an asset of company. The plant would simply supply electricity to the utility company's successor. The financial backers of this project were thus assured that their invested capital would be returned with almost complete certainty.

This concept of finance is now being extended to manufacturing facilities. For example, in 1988, GE Capital arranged a $72 million in non-recourse project loans to build the Bev-Pac beverage container plant. This plant makes aluminum beverage cans with a capacity of 1.2 billion cans annually. Unlike most beverage can manufacturing facilities, however, the Bev-Pac plant is owned and operated independently of any single beverage maker. Independent ownership enables the plant to enter into agreements with a number of beverage makers to ensure a profitable level of output. The beverage makers themselves (1) realize the economies of not being required to manufacture a smaller, "in-house" facility that is less efficient and (2) need not depend on another beverage maker. The credit rating of the plant is likely to be better than any one of its customers because a loss of market share by one will be compensated by an increase in market share by its competitor.

The amounts involved in project finance have become increasingly large. In Malaysia, a steel plant that is due to begin operation in 1995 involves 2.4 billion Malaysian ringgits ($940 million). Accordingly, corporations that are involved in construction of major projects would prefer to commit as little of their own capital as possible and, at the same time, take advantage of the leverage benefits available with project finance.

In the context of Mexico, the project finance model can serve to assure lenders of the return of capital and provide somewhat lesser credits with the ability to obtain much needed intermediate- and long-term finance.

FINANCE IN NORTH AMERICA

There is now a wide variety of functional forms available to financial institutions in the North America Free Trade zone. While banks and securities firms will likely continue to dominate in terms of the volume of funds under management, the insurance industry in Mexico may represent the market with the greatest growth potential. Because of more lenient ownership restrictions, the establishment of factoring, leasing, and limited-scope finance companies may represent the most unencumbered route through which to enter Mexican financial markets.

SELECTED REFERENCES

Blanden, Michael. "Make Them Pay (Project Finance)," *The Banker*, January 1994, pp. 66-68.

Dunford, Campbell, editor. *The Handbook of International Trade Finance* New York: Woodhead-Faulkner/Simon & Schuster, 1991.

Johnson, Hazel. *Financial Institutions and Markets: A Global Perspective*, New York: McGraw-Hill, 1993.

Kensinger, John W. and John D. Martin. "Project Finance: Raising Money the Old-Fashioned Way," *New Developments in Commercial Banking*, Donald Chew, editor, Cambridge, Massachusetts: Blackwell Finance, 1991.

Palmeri, Christopher. "Best of Times, Worst of Times," *Forbes*, June 20, 1994, pp. 198-199.

Sauvé, Pierre and Brenda González-Hermosillo. "Implications of the NAFTA for Canadian Financial Institutions," *C.D. Howe Institute Commentary*, April 1993, pp. 1-21.

Smith, Geri, Suzanne Woolley, and Chris Roush. "Why Insurers Are Splashing Across the Rio Grande," *Business Week*, August 9, 1993, p. 68.

"Texas Consortium Report on Free Trade: Final Report," Texas Department of Commerce, Business Development Division, October 1991.

Torres, Craig and Thomas T. Vogel, Jr. "Some Mutual Funds Wield Growing Clout in Developing Countries," *Wall Street Journal,* June 14, 1994, pp. A1 and A4.

U.S. Exports to Mexico: A State-by-State Overview 1987-1991, U.S. Department of Commerce, 1992.

World Bank Atlas 1994, Washington, D.C.: The World Bank, 1994.

Young, Leah R. "What Insurance Do You Need?" *Export Today,* February 1994, pp. 12- 16.

ENDNOTES

1. See Chapter 3 for a description of *Sistema de Harorro por el Retiro (SAR),* the new Mexican retirement system that requires employers to contribute 2% of their employees' wages to specifically earmarked retirement accounts.
2. A *closed-end* fund is an investment company that issues a fixed number of ownership claims, or shares. After these shares have been sold initially, investors who wish to purchase the shares must buy them from other investors who own them. This is in contrast to a *mutual* fund, or open-end fund, in which (1) new shares are issued whenever investors wish to buy them and (2) the fund redeems shares whenever investors wish to sell them. (See Johnson, Hazel. *Financial Institutions and Markets: A Global Perspective.)*
3. See Chapter 1.
4. See Christopher Palmeri, "Best of Times, Worst of Times."
5. The largest export market is Canada, with U.S. shipments totalling $90 billion in 1992. Japan was second with U.S. shipments of $48 billion.
6. See Chapter 2 for a discussion of letters of credit and bills of exchange.
7. SWIFT is an acronym for Society for Worldwide Inter-Bank Financial Telecommunications. See Chapter 2 for a discussion of electronic banking.
8. The same funding is also feasible for consumer mortgage finance, another activity permitted in Mexico for limited-scope finance companies.

6 The Impact of NAFTA on Industry and Finance

INTRODUCTION

The opportunities for banks, securities firms, and other financial institutions in Mexico will be directly proportional to the extent of economic growth. There are several specific industries that promise significant advancement in the future and, thus, present the opportunity to provide financial services to the business community and to the individuals that work in these industries.

The *automotive* industry is evolving from an assembly operation near the U.S./Mexican border and in Mexico City to one that is more dispersed throughout the country. It is a key element in the economic development of Mexico and government policy is geared to the establishment of a complete automotive infrastructure. The *oil and gas* industry continues to be dominated by Pemex, the state-owned monopoly. However, Pemex is concentrating on profits, productivity, and its core businesses. In addition, the giant oil concern is actively seeking more private sector involvement in the areas of petrochemicals, oil drilling, and ancillary services. Successful participants in the *consumer goods* and *retailing* areas require an understanding of the Mexican market with respect to income levels, distribution channels, and major competitors.

Telecommunications will be a strong growth industry in Mexico because of the extent to which systems must be brought up-to-date. The state-owned Telmex has been privatized with the new owners promising to modernize the telephone service, including basic telephone service to all towns with 5,000 or more residents, long-distance service to all towns with 500,000 or more inhabitants, and better repair service. In addition, the cellular telephone market and the market for data communications will expand dramatically.

The *computer* industry has already exploded and promises to continue dramatic strides. From 1982 to 1989, minicomputer sales grew at an average rate of 9.3% per year, microcomputers at the rate of 92.9%, and microcomputers at 183.5%! Even though Mexico is the 13th largest economy in the world, it has become the 6th largest personal computer market.

Agriculture is an industry that has been protected from private-sector influence almost to the same extent as the oil and gas industry. Barriers to private investment are being dismantled and gradually the private-sector investment is occurring.

AUTOMOBILE INDUSTRY

The automobile industry is a key element in the economic viability of Mexico. The government policy concerning this industry has varied from one of import substitution to export orientation. Now, a complete infrastructure for automobile manufacturer is being constructed in Mexico.

The Automotive Decree of 1962

In 1962, the first decree relating to the automobile industry was crafted by Raúl Salinas Lozano, the father of President Carlos Salinas de Gortari. In 1962, 10 companies produced 67,000 vehicles per year—an average of 6,700 units each. Another seven companies imported autos that were manufactured in other countries. Barely 15% to 20% of the parts used in auto assembly in Mexico were local content, that is, manufactured in Mexico. The auto industry consistently represented a trade deficit. Without higher volume, Mexican automobile manufacturers could not realize economies of scale and could not operate profitably. The 1962 decree stipulated that:

- Parts used for assembly must be at least 60% local content.

- All motors and other critical parts must be manufactured in Mexico.

- Completely knocked-down or semi-knocked-down kits used for auto manufacturing were prohibited (because local content was rarely in excess of 20%).

- Importation of fully assembled autos was prohibited.

- Government price controls and production quotas would be established.

The government regulators established further guidelines that prevented vertical integration of foreign auto manufacturers. Thus, auto parts were to be obtained from Mexican-owned suppliers. Furthermore, decrees in 1972 and 1977 set the maximum foreign participation in an auto parts supplier at 40%.

During the years immediately following the Decree of 1962, the automobile industry became profitable. The government maintained controls over prices and production, including restrictions on the number of assembly lines that could be operated by a single manufacturer.

The Automotive Decree of 1983

The external debt crisis in 1982 severely reduced the domestic demand for automobiles. Sales in 1983 barely reached 50% of the 1981 level. President Miguel de la Madrid restructured the automobile industry in order to stimulate export activity. The 1983 Automobile Decree stipulated:

- Local content was redefined as cost of parts instead of total direct costs.

- Under the new local content calculation, the minimum was set at 50% for cars, to rise to 60% in 1987.

- Car manufacturers were permitted to offer three lines in 1984, but could produce only one line in 1986 and 1987.

- If an automobile manufacturer exported at least 80% of their production, the local content minimum for autos produced and exported in 1987 was 30% and an additional line (for export) was granted.

The 1983 Decree was intended to spur investment for the export market. At the time, Mexico was producing only 300,000 units per year. With this modest level of production, it was clear that the industry would have to grow substantially before it could realize world-class economies of scale.

One of the U.S. Big Three automakers, Ford Motor Company, stepped forward to produce a line of subcompact cars for export to the United States and Canada. The Mercury Tracer was designed by Ford's joint venture partner, Mazda of Japan. Early in 1984, Ford announced that it would invest $500 million in a new plant in Hermosillo, Sonora with a 130,000-unit annual capacity. The capacity of the plant was expanded to 170,000 units in 1989.

Nissan (Japan) and Volkswagen (Germany) soon followed suit. In this way, Mexico became a major platform for the manufacture of compact cars for the North American market. The automotive sector had represented a $2.3 billion trade deficit in 1981. By 1989, the sector generated a $1.7 billion trade surplus—an improvement of $4 billion. During this period, the automobile industry became Mexico's leading source of foreign exchange in the manufacturing sector.

The Automotive Decree of 1989

By 1989, 83% of the vehicles exported from Mexico were bound for the United States. Mexican employment in the auto sector doubled from 1983 to 1989. The Mexican government responded to the need for more openness between the economics of Mexico and the United States with the Automotive Decree of 1989. The new law stipulated that:

- Automobile manufacturers could import cars and trucks.

- Manufacturers could produce as many lines as they wished.

- Manufacturers could freely select their suppliers.

- Auto parts suppliers would no longer be restricted to 40% foreign ownership.

- Local content was redefined to national value added, that is, total domestic and foreign sales, net of imports.

- Minimum local content was set at 36%.

- For each manufacturer, the number of vehicles imported could not exceed 15% of domestic Mexican sales during 1991 and 1992 model years, 20% during 1993 and 1994.

- Each manufacturer must export 2.5 times the value of new cars imported in 1991 model year, 2.0 times in 1992 and 1993, and 1.75 times in 1994.

- Import privileges were contingent on an overall positive trade balance for each manufacturer operating in Mexico.

In 1990, immediately after the 1989 Decree and seven years after the 1983 Decree, domestic sales and exports exceed 600,000 units, up from 300,000 in 1983.

The Automotive Industry Today

NAFTA phases out the Automotive Decree over a period of ten years, including export performance requirements and import and investment restrictions. At the same time, the rules of origin have been tightened to prevent Mexico from becoming a staging platform for final assembly by auto manufacturers from outside the North American Free Trade zone. Automobiles must have 62.5% North American content in order to qualify for tariff cuts.[1] Auto makers are investing heavily in Mexico. Annual sales of cars made in Mexico are expected to reach 1 million units by the year 2000.

This level of activity is creating new centers of auto manufacturing activity. For example, the desert town of Saltillo (near Monterrey) is the site of major construction in the auto industry. A few years ago, the city manufactured only appliances and sinks, but no automobiles. In December 1993, General Motors installed the first two robots in its Ramos Arizpe plant. By the end of 1995, 16 more robots will have been installed and the Ramos Arizpe plant will manufacture the Mexican version of the Corsa, GM's European-designed subcompact. A stamping line is also planned so that the plant will make body panels for the first time. In the same town, Chrysler is building a new assembly plant that will paint 110,000 trucks a year for the U.S. and Canadian markets and redesigning its existing engine plant to make a new 4-cylinder engine.

Primarily because of this automotive activity, the population of Saltillo has grown from 400,000 to 600,000 in 15 years. While the town had a good reputation as a manufacturing site, it did not grow dramatically until the auto industry began to invest there. Labor is now in short supply and the new activities will draw workers from the neighboring state of Zacatecas (about 100 miles to the south). To accommodate the workers, Saltillo is expanding its water supply and improving its road system.

In addition to Saltillo, similar construction and upgrading is occurring in Hermosillo (state of Sonora), Silao (Guanajuato), Querétaro (Querétaro), and Aquascalientes (Aquascalientes).

The buildup of manufacturing capital is also accompanied by the establishment of auto parts suppliers nearby. Together, these factors promise to raise the living standards of Mexican auto workers who earn approximately $14,000 per year, as compared with $8,500 for the average manufacturing worker in Mexico. The automobile industry is helping to create a substantial middle-class in Mexico.

THE OIL AND GAS INDUSTRY

Mexico is estimated to be the world's fifth largest crude oil producer and the 15th largest petrochemical producer, with 3% of petrochemical production capacity. Crude oil reserves are approximately 65 billion barrels. The state-owned oil monopoly Petróleos Mexicanos (Pemex):

- Is Mexico's largest company.

- Has sales that exceed the total sales of the next 15 largest companies in Mexico (including General Motors, Telephonos de Mexico, Ford Motor, Volkswagen, Mexicana de Aviacíon, Celanese Mexicana, Nestlé, IBM, and American Express)—$29 billion in 1993.

- Represents 30% of Mexico's GNP.

- Represents 35% of Mexico's tax revenues, paying $18 billion in taxes in 1993.

Pemex

Pemex was created in 1938, when Mexico took control of the oil and gas industry after U.S. and British companies discovered the large Mexican reserves. The Mexican constitution forbade production-sharing with foreign investors, that is, forbade sharing profits with foreigners from the wells that they find through exploratory drilling. The oil industry was (and remains) the property of the state of Mexico. The primary concern was that the enterprise be an employment safety net for the country. The number of Pemex workers eventually exceeded 200,000.

Only Pemex is permitted to produce basic petrochemicals, which are defined as those that are derived from the first processing of crude oil. Its production of these basic petrochemicals is insufficient to meet domestic demand, however. To meet the shortfall, Pemex imports some basic chemicals and gasoline. Secondary petrochemicals may be produced by private firms with no more than 40% foreign equity ownership. Tertiary petrochemicals may be produced by private firms with as much as 100% foreign ownership.

This mammoth company has been beset by management and labor problems, with corruption being a long-standing problem. With 90% of its profits being turned over to the government, needed reinvestment did not occur. (In the early 1990s, it was projected that, without estimated $6 billion in needed capital investment, Pemex would be importing crude oil by the year 1997.) At the same time, the Petroleum Workers Union forced Pemex to hire tens of thousands of unneeded workers, while amassing a huge fortune from its 2% share of all oil contracts.

Restructuring the Industry

One month after President Carlos Salinas de Gortari took office in December 1988, there was a violent encounter between oil union members and the police. Joaquín Hernández Galícia, the head of the union for 28 years, was ousted and jailed with a 35-year sentence. He was replaced by Sebastián Guzmán Cabrera, a union leader that was more sympathetic to the goals of the government. Also in 1989, the Salinas administration negotiated a labor contract that was estimated to save the company $1 billion per year as it eliminated 30,000 jobs in the following year. The company was decentralized into divisions with specialized activities:

- International marketing (Mexicanos Comercial Internacional)

- Regional joint ventures (Mexpetrol)

- Exploration and development

- Refining operations

Job cuts have continued so that Pemex employment rolls have been trimmed to 110,000 and are still falling.

In 1992, explosions in Guadalajara killed 200 and were blamed on leaky gasoline pipelines that spilled into sewer lines. Residents had complained for days of smelling the leaking fuel, but Pemex officials did not respond. The tragedy was an added catalyst to restructuring the mammoth organization. There are now four profit centers, essentially four autonomous companies, that operate the main businesses:

- Oil exploration and production

- Refining

- Natural gas and basic petrochemicals (where the state maintains a monopoly)

- Secondary petrochemicals

Also in 1992, the government announced a significant reclassification of petrochemicals, reducing the number of basic chemicals from 19 to 8 and the number of secondary chemicals from 66 to 13. In 1993, legislation was passed to permit private ownership of and operation of electric generating plants.

The four new divisions of Pemex act as independent units, buying and selling gas and oil to each other at market prices. The emphasis has been placed on profits, productivity, and the core businesses. There is also more interaction with the private sector. Pemex contracts outsiders for ancillary services and even pays private firms to drill for its oil. Some of the most notable ventures with the private sector:

- In 1992, Pemex bought a 50% stake in the Deer Park refinery in Texas (owned by Royal Dutch Shell) for $1 billion. The refinery now processes the Mexican firm's Maya crude oil.

- Pemex permitted Valero Energy Corporation of Texas to win a $350 million contract to build a gasoline-additives facility in Veracruz, the first such private-sector arrangement.

- Amoco has contracts to conduct geophysical studies for Pemex.

- Texaco is engineering a fuel desulfurization plant for Pemex.

- Ten Mexican and foreign contractors have contracts to drill 36 offshore wells in the Bay of Campeche (near the Gulf of Mexico).

- Diamond Shamrock (based in Dallas, Texas) was permitted to open its first Corner Store franchise in Monterrey in June 1993—one of the 200 service stations that will be operated by Mexican citizens—bypassing the law against foreign ownership of service stations.

- In the largest project in more than a decade, Pemex plans to accept private-sector bids for the $1.4 billion construction of a refinery at Salina Cruz in Southern Mexico (Pacific Ocean coast).

At least partially because of the efforts of the private sector contractors in the Bay of Campeche, Pemex now finds more oil than it extracts.

Under provisions of NAFTA, investment restrictions are lifted on most of the basic and all of the secondary petrochemicals. Import and export licenses are required on the remaining basic petrochemicals, allowing free trade on the others. Furthermore, NAFTA enables U.S. and Canadian sell to the four divisions of Pemex under open and competitive bidding rules.

Opportunities in the Mexican petrochemical industry are open to companies that supply the petrochemicals that Pemex cannot deliver in sufficient quantities. Mexico continues to purchase natural gas in large quantities because it has not allocated adequate capital to exploring for natural gas deposits that are not associated with crude oil deposits. Also, drilling companies and those firms that can supply the ancillary services in Mexico have opportunities for expansion.

CONSUMER GOODS AND RETAILING

Demographics of the Mexican Market

The consumer market in Mexico consists of 84 million people. However, 75% of the purchasing power is held by 25% of the population. Adding to this general problem of low purchasing power is the more than 50% decline in the average real purchasing power of Mexican citizens in the last 10 years because of high inflation and wage controls. These factors have created very cost-conscious consumers in Mexico. Nevertheless, as personal incomes rise in the future (because of increased trade and investment in Mexico) and the population grows (at the projected rate of as much as 2% per year), retailing will benefit from these demographic changes.

Mexico City has the greatest concentration of population with 15 million residents. The cities of Monterrey (state of Nuevo Leon), Guadalajara (Jalisco), Puebla (Puebla), and the border cities in the north are the other important markets for consumer goods. The concentration of consumers plays an important role in the location of successful retailers in Mexico.

Distribution, Pricing, and the Competitive Climate

Distribution channels for consumer goods in Mexico are not well developed at this point. Most distribution is through wholesalers or (unstable) representative relationships. Even in Mexico City, there are large areas that are not serviced by supermarkets or department stores. The existence of small street markets and small grocers helps to explains the lack of supermarkets. Successful retailers must overcome the inherent lack of a distribution network in Mexico.

Cifra is the largest retailer in Mexico with 237 locations including supermarkets, department stores, and restaurants. Cifra is perhaps best well known for its joint venture with Wal-Mart and the Mexican version of Sam's Club (Club Aurrera).[2] In the past, the company has also waged aggressive price wars against competitors in Mexico's already price-sensitive consumer market. While the price wars have abated, Cifra continues to offer more than 2,000 products with permanently low price points. This is possible because Cifra is the low- cost producer in Mexican retailing, having:

- Introduced state-of-the-art technology.

- Maintained a high employee retention rate by offering attractive stock options and pension plans.

- Negotiated lower wholesale costs with suppliers.

Approximately 70% of Cifra's locations and 100% of its discount retailers and supermarkets are in and around Mexico City. In an environment of slim margins on sales, the store plans to compensate through geographic expansion to increase the sheer volume of sales. Projected expansion will be focused on central Mexico and the growing regions in north Mexico. With low debt levels, Cifra should be able to easily finance this expansion.

In contrast, Gigante, another major Mexican retailer, defied the distribution challenges of the country and built a large network of stores outside Mexico City, largely with borrowed funds. Between 1962 to 1979, Angel Losada Gomez, company founder, built Gigante into a 21-store chain with 13 stores in Mexico City and 8 Hermuda stores in Guadalajara. Losada continued to add to the network, including 27 locations acquired from retailer Astra, 8 stores from Sardinero, and 89 supermarkets from Blanco. Gigante is highly leveraged, having taken on $30 million in debt for the Blanco acquisition alone. Also, while Cifra has concentrated on Mexico City, Gigante's stores are in more than 20 different cities and most of these stores are in Mexico's poorest regions. Furthermore, Gigante' national expansion was complicated by the poor road and rail systems in Mexico. Internally, Gigante lacks a modern computer system with which to track inventory and sales. In 1992, while Cifra sales and profits increased by 17% and 30%, respectively, Gigante's declined.

Indeed, the cost of ignoring the realities of the Mexican consumer market can be high. The Chicago-based firm of BRK Electronics learned this lesson through trial-and-error. Their attempts to market smoke detectors in Mexico met with no success because the consuming public does not place a high value on safety-oriented products. On the other hand, BRK's rechargeable and replaceable flash lights and nightlights have sold exceedingly well because Mexican consumers are cost-conscious.

The Mexican infrastructure also influences consumer preferences. Mexico's lack of clean drinking water has spurred the bottled water industry to annual sales of $750 million with future growth estimated to be 20% per year. Because the roads in Mexico are often rough with numerous potholes, consumers require automobile tires that are stronger than their U.S. counterparts.

Even retail giants such as Wal-Mart and K-Mart have had to make adjustments to the Mexican market. In the case of Wal-Mart, early crowds in its first store in Mexico City in the fall of 1993 promised unparalleled success for the new venture. However, by mid-1994, the store's management was forced to close 51 cash registers on a Saturday—typically the peak selling day of the week. The experience of the Wal-Mart supercenter (general merchandise and groceries) in Monterrey has been much the same. A number of issues seem to have contributed to this situation.

- Prices are as much as 15% to 20% higher than in Wal-Mart stores in border cities of the United States. This price difference is attributable primarily to transportation costs to the Mexican interior and to inefficiencies in the Mexican distribution system.

- In some cases, the allure of goods made in the United States has faded. There is concern by Mexican consumers that U.S. products contain an excessive amount of preservatives and other chemicals.

- Mexican shopping patterns are different. Consumers do not buy groceries in the same place as general merchandise. To purchase the freshest possible food, Mexican consumers buy groceries at neighborhood butcher shops, bakeries, *tortillerias*, fruit stands, and egg shops.

- Mexican consumers typically have small refrigerators, making storage of a week's supply of groceries very difficult.

- Most Mexican do not own automobiles. This limits a store's geographic reach.

- Wal-Mart has done little advertising and there remains confusion about the need for a membership to shop at a Wal-Mart store (as in the case of Sam's Club).

K-Mart has apparently learned some valuable lessons from Wal-Mart's experiences.

- While Wal-Mart hired an American to manage its Mexico City store, K-Mart hired the former director of store development for El Puerto de Liverpool SA, Mexico's oldest department store chain.

- In K-Mart's meat department, very little is prepackaged in contrast to Wal-Mart's. Instead, there is a walk-in refrigerator with large sides of beef from which individual selections may be cut. Even hot dogs are packaged in the presence of the customer to give the impression of freshness.

- There are few frozen food selections.

- There is no gardening section since most Mexican consumers buy these items at large outdoor plant markets.

- K-Mart offers a bank branch on the premises.

The two approaches to retailing in Mexico are good examples of the importance of market research.

Market Research

Much of the market research information that is critical for retailers and manufacturers of consumer goods is not available from public (or even readily accessible private) sources. The successful business must investigate the market through consultation with users, retailers, distributors, and industry experts. However, if this is done intelligently, the rewards can more than outweigh the costs. With more than 50% of the Mexican population under the age of 21, the Mexican consumer market is large and growing.

TELECOMMUNICATIONS

The telecommunications industry in Mexico is changing rapidly. Telephonos de Mexico (Telmex), the national telephone company, was privatized in 1990. Until Mexico joined GATT in 1986 and undertook market liberalization measures in the late 1980s, no telecommunications equipments had been imported. L.M. Ericsson (Sweden) and Indetel (a subsidiary of U.S. ITT) agreed to produce within Mexico in exchange for special permission to import. Even though firms from other countries operated in Mexico, such as NEC (Japan) and NV Philips (the Netherlands), Ericsson and Indetel formed vertically integrated organizations that supplied virtually every need for Telmex. There was little incentive to upgrade service.

Privatization of Telmex

In September 1989, the Salinas administration announced that it planned to sell a majority stake in Telmex. The sale was contingent on the winning bidder(s) making commitments to modernize the telephone service, with the government retaining the right to regulate the industry. In 1990, a group of investors led by Carlos Slim, Southwestern Bell (United States), and France Telecom purchased a 20.5% controlling share of Telmex for $1.76 billion.[3] Also in 1990, another $2.1 billion in Telmex shares were sold in Mexico, the United States, and Europe.

Under terms of the purchase agreement, the new owners of Telmex are obligated to invest an estimated $10 billion (over the first five years of ownership) to:

- Provide basic telephone service to all towns with 5,000 or more residents.

- Provide long-distance service to all towns with 500,000 or more inhabitants.

- Make repair service more prompt.

- Increase the number of public telephones.

- Increase the number of telephone lines per 100 people from five in 1990 to 20 by 2000.

- Install four million new terminal lines during the first five years of ownership.

- Substitute obsolete switching systems in urban areas with digital technology.

- Double network capacity over the first five years through digitalization of 8,500 km of microwave network, installation of 3,000 km of fiber optic cable, and installation of 14 master stations for satellite service.

Providers of telecommunications equipment that can compete successfully with Ericsson and Indetel have a significant opportunity to expand market share in this modernization effort.

Long-Distance Competition

In mid-1994, the Mexican government announced that it would permit other telephone companies to compete with Telmex. When Telmex's monopoly on long-distance service expires in 1997, there will be no limit to the number of long-distance carriers that will be permitted to compete.

One of the emerging competitors in Mexican long- distance service is Grupo Domos SA, a Monterrey-based holding company that was established in 1989 by members of the wealthy Garza family of Monterrey. In 1994, Javier Garza Calderon, head of Grupo Domos, announced that the group would pay $1.5 billion for 49% of Cuba's telephone company, Empresas de Telecommunicaciones de Cuba. Garza Calderon also announced the formation of a $1 billion trust fund for this purpose. The fund is held by Grupo Financiero Serfin, where Garza Calderon is a board member, and foreign investment is being encouraged. By the year 2000, Domos plans to have invested $6 billion in telecommunications in Mexico and Cuba, including a national fiber-optic network in Mexico.[4] The Cuban involvement not only diversifies Grupo Domos' investment in an international sense, but also gives the company certain technical expertise to compete vigorously in Mexico.

Others that are likely to take an interest in competing with Telmex in long-distance service in Mexico are:

- Grupo Financiero Banamex-Accival SA (Banacci) and its U.S. partner MCI.

- Grupo Iusacell SA and its U.S. partner Bell Atlantic Corp.

- Grupo Protexa and its potential U.S. partner Sprint Corp.

- Grupo Financiero Bancomer and its potential Mexican partner Grupo Alfa SA.

Other Telecommunications Industries

The cellular telephone market also holds considerable promise. Grupo Domos already has a strategic alliance with BellSouth to sell wireless telephone service in Mexico. Also, Grupo Protexa and Motorola have formed a joint venture to provide half of northern Mexico with cellular service. The four principal regions for this service are Central (Mexico City and surrounding areas), North (Monterrey to the U.S. border), West (Guadalajara to the Pacific Coast) and Baja California. By 1995, the number of cellular subscribers may reach 400,000.

The fastest growing telecommunications area may be data communications services. In 1989, there were over 1,000 private systems in service with 37,000 terminals. Bypass telecommunications systems have been especially popular among the financial institutions and maquiladoras. Mexican banks have had few means to transfer funds automatically and have generally had to rely on motorcycle messengers carrying checks. Grupo Financiero Banamex-Accival (Banacci) is building such a large private network that it recently brought in MCI Communications (United States) which will pay $450 million in exchange for a 45% stake. Banamex and other banks are working together to invest jointly in an electronic clearinghouse.

NAFTA eliminates almost all investment and cross- border service restrictions in enhanced or value-added telecommunications services and private communications networks. The primary remaining restriction to U.S. and Canada involvement in Mexican telecommunications is the limitation to a 49% equity position for foreign investors in basic telecommunications services, which are excluded from the provisions of NAFTA.

Telecommunications will be one of the fastest growing industries in Mexico. Firms that participate through the manufacture of components, the provision of long-distance service, or the build-up of cellular or private networks will benefit from this growth.

THE COMPUTER INDUSTRY

Until 1990, computer production was controlled by the government, whose objective was to stimulate the domestic industry. Before the Computer Decree of 1981, all computers were imported. To encourage the development of a computer production capability, the decree required all sellers of computers in Mexico to set up production facilities within Mexico. The new computer firms were required to have majority Mexican ownership, that is, the foreign firm(s) could own no more than 49% of the equity. Furthermore, each firm was required to negotiate with the government the guidelines for local content, investment, and operations. There were no uniform foreign investment standards. This resulted in inconsistent decisions and confusing standards.

The Computer Decree of 1987 stipulated a local content of 30% for components. However, these levels could not be achieved because Mexican suppliers were not yet able to produce the high-quality components that international computer manufacturers required. In light of this situation, the government returned to the local content guidelines of the 1981 Computer Decree.

Despite this confusion, the computer industry grew rapidly. From 1982 to 1989, domestic minicomputer sales by such firms as IBM and Hewlett-Packard grew at an average rate of 9.3% per year, main frame computers at the rate of 92.9%, and microcomputers at 183.5%! Growth in exports was equally impressive. By 1989, IBM alone exported $380 million, up from $2.8 million in 1982—an annual increase of 102%! Nevertheless, it was clear that more flexibility would be required if growth was to continue.

The Computer Decree of 1990 provided this flexibility. Import permits were eliminated for all computer products other than used machines and multinational corporations were permitted to supply the Mexican market through exports to Mexico for the first time in 10 years. Computer manufacturers with production facilities in Mexico gained the flexibility to make adjustments in the facilities as warranted by market conditions.

NAFTA eliminates the Computer Decree of 1990. Provisions of the agreement include improved market access, rules of origin, intellectual property rights for electronics, and a common tariff for computers and computer parts.

The computer industry in Mexico has continued to grow rapidly. Even though Mexico is the 13th largest economy in the world, it has become the 6th largest personal computer market.

AGRICULTURE

Constitutional Protection

In the early part of the 20th century, land in Mexico was extremely concentrated with respect to ownership. In large part, the Mexican Revolution of 1910 was attributable to demands that the land be more equitably distributed. Agrarian reform was the single most urgent objective of Emiliano Zapata, who led an army of native Mexicans against the dictatorship of Porfirio Díaz.[5] Two of the most significant outcomes of the Mexican Revolution were the Agrarian Reform Act of 1915 and the Constitution of 1917. These two documents permit the Mexican government to expropriate large estates and to distribute land to peasants.

As a part of the Constitution of 1917, the concept of *ejido* was introduced into Mexican law. The term was used in medieval Spain to describe communal lands outside a village. Before the Spanish conquest of Mexico in the 16th century, communal property was common in Mexico. The Mexican Constitution stipulated that the government could confiscate large landholdings, assume ownership rights, and then distribute the land to *ejido* farmers, or *ejidatarios*, who had the right to use the land but would never own it. By law, *ejido* land could not be bought, sold, or rented.

Redistribution of Land

Actual land redistribution was limited, however. From 1917 to 1933 no more than 5% of Mexico's farmland (approximately 10.7 million hectares or 26.4 million acres) was redistributed. The first significant distribution began during the presidency of General Lázaro Cárdenas (1934-1940)—after the National Revolutionary Party, later renamed the Institutional Revolutionary Party or PRI, was established in 1929. During the Cárdenas administration, 20 million hectares was redistributed to *ejidatarios*. Also, various peasant groups were brought together to form the National Peasant Confederation (CNC), which still remains an element of the ruling PRI structure. The challenge to subsequent PRI administrations has been to reform agricultural policy without eroding the political support of CNC.

Immediately following the Cárdenas administration, redistribution of land was minimal. Despite the fact that the size of landholdings was limited by law, the accumulation of large landholdings was tolerated. Cattle farmers were even given assurances that their land would not be redistributed. Often the land was placed in the names of various family relatives or business associates. (This practice is still commonplace.)

In the 1960s and 1970s, during the administrations of Gustavo Díaz Ordaz and Luis Echeverría, a large amount of land was redistributed—more than one-third of the entire land area that had been redistributed up to that point. However, almost none of the land was irrigated and it has been estimated that no more than 10% of the land was arable. Since this time, only modest amounts of land have been redistributed.

The Agrarian Reform Law of 1971 stipulated that each *ejido* would have no less than 10 hectares (24.71 acres) if it is irrigated and no less than 20 hectares (49.42 acres) if it is not irrigated. However, *ejido* farms are usually much smaller. Approximately three-fifths of *ejido* and private farms are less than five hectares (12.4 acres) in area. Currently, more than half of Mexico is held by *ejidatarios* or as communal native Mexican lands.

Policy Reversal

Declines in production, investment, and infrastructure in the agricultural sector led to an evaluation by the Agriculture and Water Resources Secretariat during the administration of President Carlos Salinas de Gortari. After this evaluation, the Secretariat stressed the need for increased agricultural production and for higher standards of living for farmers. The major obstacles to the realization of these objectives were:

- Decline in investment and research and development.

- Legal constraints on the size of landholdings (causing land users to anticipate land seizure at some point).

- Small size of the *ejido* farms (preventing the realization of economies of scale).

- Too much government interference, including price supports and subsidies (distorting production patterns).

- Insufficient credit, insurance, seeds, water, fertilizers, maintenance, and roads.

To remedy these conditions, the Secretariat recommended:

- Greater certainty with respect to land tenure.

- Privatization of state-owned agricultural enterprises in processing and commercialization of agricultural products.

- Reduction of duties on certain imported agricultural production inputs.

- Revamping subsidy programs.

- Linkage of croplands, processing plants, and ports or roads through "agroindustrial corridors."

Beginning in 1990, Anderson-Clayton (a subsidiary of the British Unilever) was permitted to purchase certain state-owned facilities: a large vegetable oil refinery, a soybean processing plant, and a large-scale pasta plant. PepsiCo and Coca-Cola bought various state-run sugar mills. For all but the poorest farmers, the interest rate charged by Banrural (the agricultural development bank) was reset at the *cetes* rate plus 400 or 500 basis points instead of the previous concessionary rate of *cetes* minus 100 or 200 basis points. Import permits were eliminated for all agricultural products except grains, oilseeds, beans, and powdered milk.

A major restructuring of the legal and regulatory framework with respect to agriculture was instituted in February 1992. Under the new agrarian law:

- The redistribution of land officially has ended.

- *Ejidatarios* may (1) rent their land to or (2) enter into joint ventures or other contracts with private investors.

- Private companies may own land for the first time in Mexico since the Revolution in 1910.

These changes have encouraged more foreign investment in the Mexican agricultural sector.

Under the provisions of NAFTA, Mexican import licensing requirements on U.S. exports to Mexico are eliminated. The licensing requirements are replaced by either quotas or tariffs that are phased out over the transition period. Tariffs on some farm products are eliminated immediately, while others are phased out over a period of five, 10, or 15 years. The longest phase-out period is allowed for those products that are most sensitive to trade liberalization, including corn producers in Mexico and sugar, orange juice, and other horticultural crops in the United States.

Investment Opportunities

The key agricultural products that will benefit from all these reforms are sugar cane, mangos, strawberries, raspberries, pa-

paya, oranges, orange juice pulp, bananas, pineapples and other tropical fruits, avocados, frozen vegetables, asparagus, mushrooms, and carrots. Animal slaughtering and processed foods from poultry, pork, and beef are also promising agricultural sectors.

Investment by U.S. firms is already in place. Bird's Eye, Green Giant, and Campbell have Mexican operations for the production and processing of food for the U.S. market. For example, the Bird's Eye operation in Mexico imports seeds, fertilizers, and equipment from the United States. After the seeds have been developed into seedlings in greenhouses, they are turned over to Mexican farmers who plant, grow, and harvest them. Bird's Eye then freezes the produce in bulk and then ships it to the United States to be packaged into small quantities for sale.

The tropical fruit potential is especially attractive. Larger tracts of land are typically necessary for tropical fruits such as pineapples. Now that land allocation can be more certain, long-term leases of *ejido* land can make such investment possible.

In 1992, Carlos Cabal Peniche, formerly a banana and shrimp farmer from the Mexican state of Tabasco, led a group of investors to acquire Fresh Del Monte from the liquidators of Polly Peck International, a bankrupt British firm. The group bought the Florida-based Fresh Del Monte, world's largest producer and marketer of fresh pineapple and the third largest in bananas, for $536 million.[6] In mid-1994, Cabal also led the buyout of Del Monte Foods in San Francisco for $277 million in cash and the assumption of $700 million in debt. Del Monte had sustained large losses before the 1994 buyout—$63.6 million in 1992 and $58.4 million in 1993. However, bringing the two companies together appeared to be a good strategic move since Fresh Del Monte has such a presence in the tropical fruit market and Del Monte Foods has marketing and distribution networks in India and North and South America. Unfortunately, the Finance Ministry of Mexico seized control of Cabal's banking interests in September 1994 after alleging that Cabal illegally made loans to himself (for as much as $700 million) to finance his varied industrial interests. This has placed a dark cloud over what would have been a deal to form one of the largest food companies in the Americas.

Nevertheless, the fundamental attractions to investment in Mexican agriculture remain clear. Companies can take advantage of the (1) the high technology capabilities of the United States and Canada, (2) new laws that enable firms to establish long-term control of Mexican land, and (3) the potential in the area of non-grain fruits and vegetables. Clearly, such companies may be domiciled in the United States, Canada, or Mexico.

CONCLUSION

Commercial banks, securities firms, and other providers of financial services must understand the businesses in which their clients are engaged. This is particularly true with respect to international operations. In the Mexican market:

- The automobile industry is evolving into a full-service manufacturing infrastructure, complete with parts suppliers.

- The oil and gas industry offers less obvious, but equally promising, private-sector involvement in petrochemicals, drilling, and other services.

- The consumer goods market is growing, but a high level of competition demands astute market research concerning product mix, price point, and distribution.

- With the privatization of Telmex in a more competitive climate, joint ventures in long-distance, cellular, and data communications services will capture considerable market share.

- All facets of the computer industry—hardware, software, and other services—are in great demand in Mexico.

- In the agricultural industry, the relaxation of rules with respect to land control enable investors to enter into long-term contracts for the production of crops not easily grown in the United States or Canada.

Rapid change is occurring in these industries—all of which offer an opportunity for market expansion to the knowledgeable financier.

SELECTED REFERENCES

Barkema, Alan. "The North American Free Trade Agreement: What Is At Stake for U.S. Agriculture?" *Independent Banker*, February 1993, pp. 18-26.

"The Big One (Pemex)," *The Economist*, January 8, 1994, pp. 66-67.

Fink, Ronald. "Mañana? Gigante, Mexico's Most Ubiquitous Retailer, Is Betting on Free Markets to Produce a Consumption Boom," *Financial World*, September 1, 1992, pp. 60-63.

Mariscal, Jorge O. "Latin America Investment Strategy Highlights," Investment Research, Goldman Sachs, September 1993.

Messner, Stephen C. "Canada: NAFTA's Other Half," *Export Today*, October 1993, pp. 12-16.

Newman, Gray and Anna Szterenfeld. *Business International's Guide to Doing Business in Mexico*, New York: McGraw-Hill, 1993.

Ortega, Bob. "Wal-Mart Is Slowed by Problems of Price and Culture in Mexico," *Wall Street Journal*, July 19, 1994, pp. A1 & A5.

"A Peach or a Raspberry from Mexico," *The Economist*, July 2, 1994, p. 63.

Siegle, Candace. "Crap Shoot (Exporting to Mexico)," *World Trade*, November 1993, pp. 64- 66.

Smith, Geri. "The Remaking of an Oil Giant, 1993," *Business Week*, August 16, 1993, pp. 84-85.

Templin, Neal. "Mexican Industrial Belt is Beginning to Form As Car Makers Expand," *Wall Street Journal*, July 10, 1994, pp. A1 and A10.

Torres, Craig. "Mexico's Natural-Gas Reserves Remain Untapped, While Its Fuel Needs Grow," *Wall Street*, July 14, 1994, p. A6.

ENDNOTES

1. This is an increase over the 50% stipulated by the Canada-United States Free Trade Agreement.
2. Cifra is one of the stocks held in the Mexico Fund. See Chapter 5.
3. See also Chapter 3 for a description of the holding company controlled by Carlos Slim.
4. A Domos company representative confirmed that, as part of the transaction, Domos repaid $300 million of debt owed by Cuba to the Mexican government.
5. See also Chapter 1 for a discussion of the deposing of Porfirio Díaz.
6. Carlos Cabal also bought the Mexican bank Banco Union in 1991 for $300 million and merged it with Banco Cremi in June 1994.

7 Beyond NAFTA

INTRODUCTION

The North American Free Trade Agreement is one of a number of regional trade arrangements. The General Agreement on Tariffs and Trade (GATT) forms the basis for these various regional agreements, including NAFTA. The European Union (EU) has a longstanding history of attempts to coordinate trade and economic policies of its member countries. The EU is a group of strong countries with population and economic resources that rival the NAFTA zone. Interestingly, Japan, with the world's second-largest, single-country economy after the United States, has been slow to participate in such regional trade pacts. One notable exception is Japan's membership in the Asia-Pacific Economic Cooperation (APEC). As all of these agreements are seen as means to further economic development, they are also means through which banks and other financial institutions may expand product offerings and market share.

Less frequently discussed in this context are the regional trade pacts within Latin America and the Caribbean. The North American Free Trade Agreement makes it possible for financial institutions to more easily establish a presence in Mexico. Likewise, a presence in Mexico makes it possible to expand services into other growing regions of Latin America.

GATT: THE FOUNDATION FOR REGIONAL TRADE

The provisions of the General Agreement on Tariffs and Trade (GATT) are points of reference for virtually every trade agreement in force or in negotiation. GATT sets the worldwide standards for managing tariff and nontariff barriers to international trade.

The Motivation for GATT

In the nineteenth century, international trade was governed by two basic principles:

- The greater the economic differences between two countries, the greater their propensity to trade.

- The benefits of such trade are maximized under conditions of free trade.

In a sense, two countries with different economies could complement each other in a free trade environment. The two assumptions under which free trade yielded the greatest benefits were:

- Market imperfections, such as monopolies or restrictive tariffs, did not exist.

- No country could possibly improve its access to other markets by restricting its own imports from these markets.

The United Kingdom was the pioneer of free trade principles in 1846 when it unilaterally abolished its restrictions on the trading of corn. By the 1870s, this philosophy had resulted in the formation of a multitude of bilateral trade agreements in Europe. Each of these pacts had a common feature—the unconditional most-favored-nation (MFN) clause. This clause stipulated that each of the two countries in a bilateral agreement must offer the other any trade privilege that it granted to a third party. Because there were so many bilateral agreements in Europe, effectively they created a multilateral trade agreement. Under this system of liberalization, cross-border trade expanded rapidly.

However, this 19th-century spirit of trade liberalization was severely dampened by the protectionist legislation and practices that followed the Stock Market Crash of 1929. During the depression years of 1929 to 1932, the volume of world output declined by 20% and the volume of world trade fell at the even faster rate of 40%. The framers of GATT sought to reverse these effects.

The Basic Principles

During and after World War II (1939-1945), the British and the Americans led the initiative to restore to the world trade arena the principles of *comparative advantage, multilateralism,* and *nondiscrimination.* The theory of comparative advantage suggests that nations should (1) export those products that they can produce more efficiently than other nations and (2) import those products for which they are relative high-cost producers. Multilateralism is a policy that seeks to permit international trade without restrictive bilateral arrangements that may prevent trading partners from fully realizing their comparative advantage. Nondiscrimination prevents nations from applying treatment to either imports or exports that favors one nation at the expense of another.

On January 1, 1948, GATT was signed by over 80 fully participating countries and by almost 30 that signed special arrangements. GATT addressed reciprocal commercial rights and spelled out obligations of the signatories, explicitly including the concept of MFN treatment. Through GATT, common regulations and a framework for negotiating trade-liberalizing agreements were established. The GATT Dispute Settlement

System is a formal arrangement of regulations and action to be carried out by participants in the GATT agreements to reconcile any differences in matters involving mutual trade. Under this system, a GATT Panel is a panel of neutral representatives established by the GATT Secretariat to review facts in a dispute and to render findings and recommend action.

Because of GATT, world trade since the end of World War II has expanded faster than world output. The average worldwide tariff has declined from 40% in 1947 to approximately 5% today. This process has been facilitated by "rounds" of trade talks. For example:

- During the *Dillon Round* (1960-1962), the Common External Tariff was adopted in which the United States granted concessions for agricultural exports by other countries.

- The *Kennedy Round* (1964-1967) reduced tariffs by 35% to 40%, improved access to worldwide agricultural markets, and expanded the outlets for exports of less developed countries.

- The *Tokyo Round* (1973-1979) concentrated on a new set of tariff cuts and reducing other barriers to trade. The negotiators worked on GATT Codes of Conduct, that is, instruments that prescribe the standards of behavior by nations and govern the use of nontariff barriers to trade. Only signatories to each code are bound by its terms.[1] One of these codes of conduct involved government purchases, granting favored status to developing countries without seeking reciprocal arrangements. Another was the GATT Customs Valuation Code, that is, a formula (agreed to multilaterally) for appraising imported items for the purpose of setting the amount of duty payable by the importer in the importing country.

The most recent round, the Uruguay Round (1986-present) was most difficult to conclude. From the outset, there was an ambitious agenda that broached the most sensitive issues involving the trade of goods and services. In December 1990, the talks broke off when the United States and the European Community (now the European Union) remained deadlocked on the issue of EU farm subsidies. Altogether, there were unresolved matters in 15 broad areas including farming, patents, financial services, telecommunications, and textiles.

The *Montreal Round* was actually a meeting in December of 1988 among 96 nations for the purpose of expressing political urgency for successful conclusion of the Uruguay Round that had began in 1986. This meeting resulted in an agreement to:

- Liberalize trade in services.

- More swiftly settle trade disputes.

- Allow freer trade in tropical products, such as coffee, rubber, and bananas.

- Reduce tariffs by 30%.

- Ease nontariff barriers.

- Ease investment restrictions.

- Monitor an individual country's trade policies.

There were four areas in which the attendees of the meeting could not agree:

- Liberalizing trade in agriculture.

- Instituting protections for intellectual property.

- Implementing textile trade reforms.

- Establishing rules for protection against imports.

Early in 1994, the Uruguay Round was completed, including the resolution of some of the most difficult issues and the creation of a new trade organization. If the Uruguay Round is ratified in a timely fashion by the legislative bodies of the signatories, the

World Trade Organization (WTO) will begin operation in January 1995. This international group would rule on trade disputes between signatories of GATT. Critics of the new GATT cite the potential loss of national sovereignty that the WTO would represent, the loss of government revenues from tariffs, and the loss of jobs from competition from imports. However, proponents of the new GATT point to the benefits of the arrangement:

- The reduction of tariff and nontariff barriers that can increase worldwide output by more than $5 trillion (U.S. output by more than $1 trillion) over the next 10 years.

- The protection of intellectual property rights (patents and copyrights), which could prevent the loss from piracy and counterfeiting of an estimated $60 billion per year by U.S. businesses.

- New market opportunities for U.S. services firms, which export $163 billion per year, as international services trade is liberalized.

- Removal of significant barriers to overseas investment.

- Fair competition and open markets in agriculture, especially for U.S. farmers who lead the world in agricultural exports at $40 billion per year.

- Full participation of developing countries in global trade, which could significantly increase U.S. exports by as much as $200 billion over the next 10 years.

- Strengthened rules for dispute settlement that should reduce the uncertainty of foreign market participation and provide fairer competition from foreign competitors in the home market.

Regional Trade Agreements under GATT

Over time, and especially during the Uruguay Round of GATT, there has been some frustration with operating solely under the provisions of GATT. For example, preferential treatment is permitted by GATT for developing countries. However, as the developing countries have become "newly industrializing," there has been pressure on some of them to more fully adopt the free-trade principles of GATT. Also, some trade issues, such as intellectual property rights, have been difficult to manage under GATT. Finally, geographical proximities of countries to neighboring nations sometimes make it more efficient to address specific issues through bilateral or regional agreements. Thus, there has been a growing tendency for regional trade agreements such as the North American Free Trade Agreement.

Article XXIV of GATT allows the development of regional trade pacts by acknowledging the desirability of enhancing trade freedoms through the development of voluntary arrangements for the closer coordination of specific economies. However, in keeping with the basic principles of free trade, Article XXIV stipulates three conditions for such arrangements:

- Duties, tariffs, and other restrictions with respect to trade between the parties to the trade agreement must not be higher than before the agreement.

- Duties and other restrictive regulations must be eliminated on substantially all the trade between the parties to the agreement.

- Interim agreements must lead to a final, permanent arrangement within a reasonable length of time.

Thus, while GATT stresses the development of worldwide trading standards that embrace the principles of comparative advantage, multilateralism, and nondiscrimination, it also recognizes the inevitability of regional integration. Given the difficulty of concluding the Uruguay Round and the virtual mushrooming of regional trade agreements, it is safe to conclude that the force gaining momentum in international trade today is not multilateralism, but *regionalism*.

REGIONAL INTEGRATION IN LATIN AMERICA

The Stages of Regional Integration

The process of regional integration has been classified in five stages.[2] Each successive stage implies closer economic integration between the member countries than the preceding stage.

- Free Trade Area

- Customs Union

- Common Market

- Economic Union

- Complete Economic Integration

In a *free trade area*, tariffs and quantitative restrictions between the member countries are eliminated. However, trade policy of each member country vis-à-vis countries outside the free trade area is left to the discretion of each member country. A *customs union* is a free trade area in which the member countries also jointly determine the level of tariffs on goods from outside the free trade area. In a *common market*, not only tariffs and duties on goods are eliminated, but also factors of production (labor and capital) may flow freely between the member countries. When countries are part of an *economic union*, the common market member countries coordinate national economic policies (to a greater or lesser extent). When there is *complete economic integration* between the member countries, national economic policies are completely coordinated. The member countries virtually become one new country with the formation of supranational entities and a single monetary system.

The North American Free Trade Agreement represents the first stage of regional integration—a free trade area. On the other hand, the 12 member countries of the European Union have progressed from the stage of free trade area through common market and are now in the economic union stage. The ultimate goal of the EU is effectively to reach the 5th stage of complete economic integration with a European central bank and a single currency by the year 2000.

Exhibit 7-1 contains a comparison of the demographics of the members of NAFTA and the EU. The two regions are roughly comparable in terms of population, with 368 million residents in NAFTA and 347 million in the EU. Total 1992 GNP is also approximately the same at $6.7 trillion each, with NAFTA per capita GNP at $18,373 and that of the EU at $19,432. As a result, the two regions are well matched in terms of economic development and competitive capabilities. Of course, there are clearly differences in terms of the economic standing of individual countries within each region. The United States dominates in NAFTA while Germany, France, Italy, and the United Kingdom are by far the strongest economies in the EU. Despite similarities between the regions, however, the extent of economic integration is, and will likely continue to be, much greater within the EU than within NAFTA.

As compared to the European Union, the 15-member Asia-Pacific Economic Cooperation (APEC) Group is at the other end of the spectrum. APEC's modest goals to-date are to sustain regional growth and development, strengthen the multilateral trading system, and reduce investment and trade barriers without harm to other countries. Exhibit 7-2 shows that APEC controls a combined annual GNP of $11.7 trillion, with the United States and Japan as leading member countries. With China as the member country with the largest population, the residents of the region number almost 2 billion. Unlike EU members, members of APEC have per capita GNP that ranges from $379 (China) to $37,648 (Brunei) and averages $5,878, representing an extremely diverse set of economies.[3] Because of this diversity, a great deal of economic integration among these countries should not be expected to develop. In fact, the goals of the group do not qualify it for even the first stage of regional integration (free trade area).

On the other hand, the extent of regional integration throughout Latin America promises to be much greater. Exam-

EXHIBIT 7-1
NAFTA AND THE EUROPEAN UNION

Member Country	Population[1]	Gross National Product Total[2]	Per Capita
North American Free Trade Agreement			
United States	255,414	$5,904,822	$23,119
Canada	27,844	565,787	20,320
Mexico	84,967	294,831	3,470
	368,225	$6,765,440	$18,373
The European Union			
Belgium (1957)	10,039	$ 209,594	$20,878
France (1957)	57,338	1,278,652	22,300
Italy (1957)	57,844	1,186,568	20,513
Luxembourg (1957)	389	13,716	35,260
Germany (1957)	80,553	1,846,064	22,917
The Netherlands (1957)	15,167	312,340	20,593
Denmark (1973)	5,166	133,941	25,927
Ireland (1973)	3,536	42,798	12,104
The United Kingdom (1973)	57,701	1,024,769	17,760
Greece (1981)	10,454	75,106	7,184
Spain (1986)	39,077	547,947	14,022
Portugal (1986)	9,843	73,336	7,451
	347,107	$6,744,831	$19,432

[1] Represents 1992 population in thousands.
[2] Represents 1992 GNP in millions of U.S. dollars.

Note: The year noted in parentheses after the name of a country designates the year in which that country joined the European Union.

Sources: 1. *The World Bank Atlas 1994*, Washington, D.C.: The World Bank, 1994.
2. *Europe 1992: The Facts*, London: Department of Trade and Industry and the Central Office of Information, 1989.

EXHIBIT 7-2

NAFTA AND THE ASIA-PACIFIC ECONOMIC COOPERATION GROUP

Member Country	Population[1]	Gross National Product Total[2]	Per Capita
North American Free Trade Agreement			
United States	255,414	$5,904,822	$23,119
Canada	27,844	565,787	20,320
Mexico	84,967	294,831	3,470
	368,225	$6,765,440	$18,373
Asia-Pacific Economic Cooperation Group			
United States	255,414	$ 5,904,822	$23,119
Canada	27,844	565,787	20,320
Japan	124,318	3,507,841	28,217
China	1,166,144	442,346	379
Australia	17,540	299,323	17,065
New Zealand	3,415	41,186	12,060
Hong Kong	5,805	89,274	15,379
South Korea	43,663	296,349	6,787
Taiwan[3]	20,400	180,000	8,824
Singapore	2,814	44,315	15,748
Indonesia	184,274	122,825	667
Malaysia	18,610	51,917	2,790
The Philippines	64,187	49,462	771
Thailand	57,992	106,559	1,837
Brunei	273	10,278	37,648
	1,992,693	$11,712,284	$ 5,878

[1] Represents 1992 population in thousands.
[2] Represents 1992 GNP in millions of U.S. dollars.
[3] Data for Taiwan is for 1991. The World Bank does not report data for Taiwan, China—also known as Republic of China.

Sources: 1. *The World Bank Atlas 1994*, Washington, D.C.: The World Bank, 1994.
2. *Dictionary of International Trade*, New York: John Wiley & Sons, Inc., 1994.
3. Chai, Alan; Alta Campbell; and Patrick J. Spain. *Hoover's Handbook of World Business 1993*, Austin, Texas: The Reference Press, 1993.

ining trade agreements in this region is useful in analyzing potential market opportunities, with Mexico as a platform for expansion into other Latin American countries.

LATIN AMERICAN REGIONAL PACTS

Bankers who wish to fully capitalize on a presence in the North American Free Trade zone should understand the nature of trade agreements between Mexico and other Latin American countries, including the stage of regional integration of such pacts. Exhibit 7-3 lists the major agreements along with dates of formation and member countries. These agreements include:

- The Latin American Free Trade Area—LAFTA (replaced by the Latin American Integration Association—LAIA)

- The Central American Common Market—CACM

- The Caribbean Free Trade Association—CARIFTA (replaced by the Caribbean Community—CARICOM)

- The Andean Group

- Mercado Común del Sur—Mercosur

- The Group of Three.

As indicated by Exhibit 7-3, four of the six trade arrangements had their origins in the 1960s but were later relaunched or replaced by other arrangements. The results of these pacts has been mixed because of a past emphasis on import substitution that has been replaced by a definite orientation toward export expansion.

   Latin American Free Trade Area/Latin American Integration Association. The 10 member countries of LAFTA/LAIA are shown in Exhibit 7-4. In terms of 1992 GNP, Brazil has the largest economy ($425 billion), Mexico the second largest ($295 billion), and Argentina third largest ($200 billion). On a per capita basis,

EXHIBIT 7-3
LATIN AMERICAN TRADE AGREEMENTS

Year[1]	Member Countries

Latin American Free Trade Area (LAFTA)

1960   Argentina, Brazil, Chile, Ecuador, Mexico, Paraguay, Peru, Uruguay, Bolivia (1966), Venezuela (1967).

1980   Replaced by Latin American Integration Association (LAIA).

Central American Common Market (CACM)

1960   Guatemala, El Salvador, Honduras, Nicaragua.

1993   Relaunched, with Panama joining the group.

Caribbean Free Trade Association (CARIFTA)

1965   Antiqua, Barbados, Guyana, Jamaica (1968), Trinidad & Tobago (1968), Grenada (1968), Dominica (1968), St. Lucia (1968), St. Vincent (1968), Montserrat (1968), St. Kitts & Nevis (1968), Belize (1971).

1973   Replaced by Caribbean Community (CARICOM).

Andean Group

1969   Bolivia, Colombia, Chile, Ecuador, Peru, Venezuela (1973).

1976   Chile leaves group.

1990   Relaunched.

Mercado Común del Sur (Mercosur)

1991   Argentina, Brazil, Paraguay, Uruguay.

Group of Three

1991   Venezuela, Colombia, Mexico.

[1] Represents year of formation, replacement, or relaunch as applicable.

Note: The year noted in parentheses after the name of a country designates the year in which that country joined the applicable group.

Sources:
1. Edwards, Sebastian. "Latin American Economic Integration: A New Perspective on an Old Dream," *The World Economy*, July 1993, pp. 317-338.
2. "NAFTA is Not Alone," *The Economist*, June 18, 1994, pp 47-48.

however, Argentina tops the ranks with 1992 per capita GNP of $6,051. The population in the LAFTA/LAIA zone rivals that in NAFTA with 354 million residents, but the average per capita income is much lower at $3,022.

LAFTA originally had as its main objective in 1960 the gradual elimination of trade barriers and the progressive reduction of tariffs affecting trade flows. The goal was to accomplish this liberalization in a 12-year transition period of continuous multi-

---

EXHIBIT 7-4

LATIN AMERICAN FREE TRADE AREA (LAFTA)/
LATIN AMERICAN INTEGRATION ASSOCIATION (LAIA)

Member Country	Population[1]	Gross National Product Total[2]	Per Capita
Argentina	33,099	$200,282	$6,051
Brazil	153,850	425,412	2,765
Chile	13,599	37,064	2,725
Ecuador	11,028	11,843	1,074
Mexico	84,967	294,831	3,470
Paraguay	4,519	6,038	1,336
Peru	22,370	21,272	951
Uruguay	3,131	10,444	3,336
Bolivia (1966)	7,527	5,084	675
Venezuela (1967)	20,310	58,901	2,900
	354,400	$1,071,171	$3,022

[1] Represents 1992 population in thousands.
[2] Represents 1992 GNP in millions of U.S. dollars.

Notes: 1. The year noted in parentheses after the name of a country designates the year in which that country joined LAFTA (which was formed in 1960).
2. LAFTA was replaced by Latin American Integration Association (LAIA) in 1980.

Source: The World Bank Atlas 1994, Washington, D.C.: The World Bank, 1994.

lateral negotiations. The actual process was to follow a product-by-product strategy following GATT-type principles of MFN and reciprocity, while granting more favorable consideration for the least developed countries of Bolivia and Ecuador. Negotiations centered around two mechanisms:

- National lists—products for which each country individually agreed to reduce tariffs by at least 8% per year, with annual negotiations.

- Common lists—products for which *all* countries must have reduced tariffs to zero and must have eliminated all quantitative restrictions by the end of the transition period, with negotiations every three years. The ultimate objective was to have 75% of all trade covered by such provisions by the year 1972.

The products contained on the national lists more than doubled from 1962 to 1968, but progress stalled thereafter. Only one common list was ever approved (in 1964) and it never became effective.

The failure of LAFTA stems from a lack of diversity in the products traded intraregionally. Since most were basic primary products, the concept of comparative advantage was difficult to establish. In addition, there was relative macroeconomic instability in Argentina and Brazil, two of the major members of the group. The reactions to the lack of progress in the LAFTA were the formation of a subgroup (the Andean Group in 1969) and replacement of the organization by the LAIA in 1980.

LAIA did not seek to establish a free trade area within Latin America, but sought instead to facilitate the formation of bilateral commercial agreements that could later include other countries in the region. The basic approach of LAIA is bilateral tariff negotiations that later can be extended to other countries, with no predetermined schedule and no intent to establish a common external tariff for the region. That is, there is no stated intent to become a customs union.

Central American Common Market. In contrast to LAIA, the Central American Common Market is a much smaller group of five countries with a total population of only 27 million, as shown in Exhibit 7-5. The largest economy is Guatemala (1992 GNP of $9.6 billion). The highest per capita GNP is that of Panama at $2,440 and the average per capita GNP for the region is $980. This is clearly a much smaller region, with not as much in the way of economic activity as compared to LAIA.

The first steps to regional integration in Central America were bilateral trade agreements among the five countries of the region during the 1950s. By 1960 this arrangement had evolved into a full-fledged common market, the *CACM.* The treaty included an immediate adoption of free trade within the region for most manufacturing commodities and a regional payments mechanism administered by the Central American Clearing House. By 1966, more than 94% of the items of the CACM tariff

EXHIBIT 7-5

CENTRAL AMERICAN COMMON MARKET (CACM)

Member Country	Population[1]	Gross National Product Total[2]	Per Capita
Guatemala	9,746	$ 9,568	$ 982
El Salvador	5,387	6,283	1,166
Honduras	5,418	3,142	580
Nicaragua	3,916	1,325	338
Panama (1993)	2,514	6,133	2,440
	26,981	$26,451	$ 980

[1] Represents 1992 population in thousands.
[2] Represents 1992 GNP in millions of U.S. dollars.

Notes: 1. The year noted in parentheses after Panama designates the year in which that country joined CACM (which was formed in 1960).
2. CACM was relaunched in 1993.

Source: *The World Bank Atlas 1994*, Washington, D.C.: The World Bank, 1994.

classification were subject to free trade within the CACM and a common external tariff for goods from outside the CACM. These successes of the CACM have been attributed at least partially to relative inability of the small domestic import sectors to effectively resist the initiatives of the CACM.

Caribbean Free Trade Association/Caribbean Community. CARIFTA/CARICOM (Exhibit 7-6) is a group of countries with

---

EXHIBIT 7-6

CARIBBEAN FREE TRADE ASSOCIATION (CARIFTA)/ CARIBBEAN COMMUNITY (CARICOM)

Member Country	Population[1]	Gross National Product Total[2]	Per Capita
Antiqua	81	$ 395	$4,877
Barbados	259	1,693	6,537
Guyana	806	268	332
Jamaica (1968)	2,394	3,216	1,343
Trinidad & Tobago (1968)	1,268	4,995	3,939
Grenada (1968)	91	210	2,308
Dominica (1968)	72	181	2,514
St. Lucia (1968)	156	453	2,904
St. Vincent (1968)	109	217	1,991
St. Kitts & Nevis (1968)	42	181	4,310
Belize (1971)	200	442	2,210
	5,478	$12,251	$2,236

[1] Represents 1992 population in thousands.
[2] Represents 1992 GNP in millions of U.S. dollars.

Notes: 1. The year noted in parentheses after the name of a country designates the year in which that country joined CARIFTA (which was formed in 1965).
2. Montserrat, one of the Leeward Islands, also joined CARIFTA in 1968. The World Bank does not include this island in its database. However, its estimated population in 1980 was 12,000.
3. CARIFTA was replaced by Caribbean Community (CARICOM) in 1973.

Source: *The World Bank Atlas 1994*, Washington, D.C.: The World Bank, 1994.

an aggregate population of 5.5 million and average 1992 GNP of $2,236. The largest economy in the group is that of Trinidad & Tobago with a $5 billion GNP. The member country with the highest per capita GNP is Barbados—$6,537 in 1992. This is a group of extremely small countries with populations ranging from 12,000 (Montserrat) to 2.4 million (Jamaica).

In 1965, the year of its formation, the *CARIFTA* immediately freed imports and exports within the region from duties and non-tariff barriers. There was a 5-year transition period for those few products that the member countries previously had designated for import substitution treatment. Unlike the Central American agreement, CARIFTA did not establish a common external tariff for goods from outside the region. However, the benefits of the arrangement accrued primarily to the more economically advanced members of the group. The less developed members advocated changes that would be of more benefit to them.

In 1973, CARIFTA was replaced by *CARICOM*. The objectives of the new Caribbean group included the unification of monetary and fiscal policies, as well as commercial activity. Planning agencies for agricultural and industrial development were created. A common external tariff for goods from outside the region was instituted. The difficulties of integrating the economies of countries with different relative sizes remained, however, as did the problems associated with a lack of diversity of production capabilities among the members.

The Andean Group. The Andean Group represents a much larger population than either CACM or CARICOM. As Exhibit 7-7 shows, the five countries of the group have 95 million residents, compared to 27 million in CACM and 5.5 million in CARICOM. However, the economic status of the group is roughly the same. The 1992 average per capita GNP is $1,497, with a range of $675 (Bolivia) to $2,900 (Venezuela).

As a spinoff of LAFTA, the Andean Group was formed in 1969 with the expressed purpose of avoiding the problems experienced by the larger Latin American group, while pursuing import substitution and keeping out investment by foreign

EXHIBIT 7-7

THE ANDEAN GROUP

Member Country	Population[1]	Gross National Product Total[2]	Per Capita
Bolivia	7,527	$ 5,084	$ 675
Colombia	33,405	44,555	1,334
Ecuador	11,028	11,843	1,074
Peru	22,370	21,272	951
Venezuela (1973)	20,310	58,901	2,900
	94,640	$141,655	$1,497

[1] Represents 1992 population in thousands.
[2] Represents 1992 GNP in millions of U.S. dollars.

Notes: 1. The year noted in parentheses after the name of a country designates the year in which that country joined the Andean Group (which was formed in 1969).
2. Chile was one of the founding members of the Andean Group but left the Group in 1976.
3. The Andean Group was relaunched in 1990.

Source: *The World Bank Atlas 1994*, Washington, D.C.: The World Bank, 1994.

multinationals. It was felt that a comprehensive coordination of industrial planning would be necessary to accomplish these goals. The main objectives of the Andean Group were liberalization of regional trade, gradual achievement of a common external tariff, establishing strategic regional investment programs that would offset the costs of the integration process for specific members, and instituting a common code for foreign direct investment.

Despite the ambitious goals of the group, the results were not as dramatic as had been anticipated. As of 1980, over 25% of the items subject to tariff had not begun the liberalization process. By 1985, only three of the eight strategic regional investment programs had been approved. The reasons for the less-than-anticipated results were a large number of product exemptions from the tariff liberalization plan, no agreement on the common external tariff, and the inconsistency of regional industrial strategy vs. the strategies of individual member countries.

A Shift in Focus. It appears that early lackluster results of LAFTA, CARIFTA, and the Andean Group are tied directly to the common emphasis on regional import substitution in the face of individual economic systems that did not adequately complement each other. The debt crisis of the 1980s sharply underscored the fallacy of this inward focus. While Asian developing countries with a strong, outward, export-oriented focus grew rapidly, the Latin American economies suffered. These realities have pushed Latin American countries into a more aggressive stance in favor of export-oriented policies.

In 1990, the Andean Group was relaunched with all of its five members having begun individual trade and investment liberalization programs.[4] At a meeting in La Paz, Bolivia, the presidents of the five countries agreed to create an Andean common market by 1996. In a meeting in December 1991, the presidents agreed to more trade liberalization reforms in two days than had been agreed to in the previous 22 years of the Group's existence. The agreements in this historic meeting were:

- A free trade area between Venezuela, Colombia, and Bolivia effective in January 1992.

- The extension of the free trade area to Ecuador and Peru effective six months later in July 1992.

- A permitted list of exceptions to receive protection only until January 1993 (50 each for Venezuela, Colombia, and Bolivia; 100 each for Ecuador and Peru).

- Elimination of export subsidy programs for intra-Andean trade by January 1993.

- Lower external tariffs to become a common external tariff in the context of a customs union by the end of 1994.

- Provision for industrial, scientific, and technical cooperation between the member countries.

As a result of these measures, trade within the Group increased by 35% in both 1990 and 1991.

The debt crisis also had detrimental effects on the relatively successful CACM. As member countries erected non-tariff trade barriers to protect their foreign exchange positions, including multiple exchange rate schemes, the common external tariff ceased to be relevant. Then, in 1986, the Central American payments mechanism collapsed and each country was forced to individually undertake trade adjustments. The CACM was relaunched in 1993, this time including Panama, with objectives that were less geared to import substitution:

- Explicit export promotion arrangements.

- A common external tariff between 5% and 20%, much lower than the previous level.

These changes reflect a strong shift in focus—away from import substitution and protectionism, toward export-oriented policies.

Mercado Común del Sur. Not only have previous trade alliances been revamped, but new ones have materialized. As indicated in Exhibit 7-8, *Mercosur* is a combination of two of Latin America's three largest economies—Brazil (largest) and Argentina (third largest)—with two of its smallest—Paraguay and Uruguay.[5] It is the second largest Latin American trade affiliation after LAIA in terms of both population (195 million) and GNP ($642 billion in 1992).

Mercosur was created through the Southern Cone Common Market Treaty, also known as the Treaty of Asuncion. This treaty was modelled after the Treaty of Rome that led to the creation of the European Union. The group is dismantling trade barriers and encouraging cross-border investment and joint projects. Argentina and Brazil have agreed to reduce import duties to zero for trade within the group by the end of 1994, with Paraguay

EXHIBIT 7-8
MERCOSUR

Member Country	Population[1]	Gross National Product Total[2]	Per Capita
Argentina	33,099	$200,282	$6,051
Brazil	153,850	425,412	2,765
Paraguay	4,519	6,038	1,336
Uruguay	3,131	10,444	3,336
	194,599	$642,176	$3,300

[1] Represents 1992 population in thousands.
[2] Represents 1992 GNP in millions of U.S. dollars.

Note: Mercosur was formed in 1991.

Source: *The World Bank Atlas 1994*, Washington, D.C.: The World Bank, 1994.

and Uruguay agreeing to have done so by the end of 1995. The member countries have targeted a common external tariff of 35% and agreed to coordinate exchange rate and macroeconomic policy. Provisions exist for other countries to join as well.

There is early evidence that Mercosur will be a success by virtually any measure. Intra-regional trade has grown by a factor of 2.5 times since 1990. Those problems that have been noted are related to the disparity between the extent to which Argentina had controlled its economy and the less successful experience of Brazil. Now that Brazil has successfully contained its rate of inflation, the seeds of a European-Union type of arrangement among the member countries of Mercosur will no doubt take root.

Group of Three. Despite their geographic dispersion, Venezuela, Colombia, and Mexico have formed a trading alliance. Together, these countries represent 138 million people and a 1992 GNP of $398 billion (Exhibit 7-9). The *Group of Three* started with the less comprehensive goal of coordinating energy

EXHIBIT 7-9
GROUP OF THREE

Member Country	Population[1]	Gross National Product Total[2]	Per Capita
Venezuela	20,310	$ 58,901	$2,900
Colombia	33,405	44,555	1,334
Mexico	84,967	294,831	3,470
	138,682	$398,287	$2,872

[1] Represents 1992 population in thousands.
[2] Represents 1992 GNP in millions of U.S. dollars.

Note: The Group of Three was formed in 1991.

Source: *The World Bank Atlas 1994*, Washington, D.C.: The World Bank, 1994.

production activities and implementing a free trade zone through bilateral agreements among the member countries. However, by 1992, the three countries had announced negotiations for a full-fledged, trilateral free trade agreement.

THE SOUTH AMERICAN FREE TRADE AGREEMENT?

All too often, the attention of the business world is directed toward Europe and Asia because of historical trading patterns (in the first case) and high rates of economic growth (in the latter case). While clearly, there are opportunities in both these arenas, the potential for business development in Latin America should not be overlooked. Latin American countries are embracing market reforms at an unprecedented pace and it is likely that this trend will continue.

Chile has led the way in market reforms, moving so fast that the country has chosen thus far not to participate in bilateral and regional agreements in Latin America. The economy of Chile is the most admired in the region and is studied by developing countries throughout the world. Its outward focus on economic expansion has boosted the export share of GDP from 12% in the early 1970s to a 35% share today. The assets of the pension system, privatized since 1973, have grown to $12.5 billion or 35% of GDP. The average annual real rate of growth of per capita GNP in Chile was 6.1% between 1985 and 1992. This compares very favorably with the same rate of growth in Argentina (0.5%), Brazil (-0.7%), Peru (-4.3%), Mexico (1.1%), or even the United States (1.1%).

The reluctance of Chile to join Latin American trade arrangements appears to be a strategic choice that reflects its long-term objectives of being integrated with the largest economies of the world. Chile has expressed interest in being included in both APEC and NAFTA. It appears that it is only a matter of time before such membership is effected.

Other Latin American countries have seen this evolution in Chile and are following suit with similar reforms. Here too, apparent objectives are not difficult to identify. Mexico now has a free trade agreement with the United States (NAFTA), an ongoing trade relationship with nine other Latin American countries (LAIA), a commitment to pursue free trade with Venezuela and Colombia (Group of Three), and numerous bilateral trade agreements in Latin America. Other countries in the region are linked through one or more such arrangements. In October 1993, Brazil (Latin America's largest economy) proposed a South American Free Trade Agreement, linking all countries in the region in a free trade pact. In June 1994, Mercosur gave its official backing to the concept.

Market reforms in Latin America and the Caribbean will ultimately yield the same kind of results that have been seen in Chile. As industrial capacity is strengthened, trade increases, and incomes rise, the financial services industry will expand. Thus, a banking presence in the expanding Mexican market can pay ultimate dividends that extend far beyond the North American Free Trade zone.

SELECTED REFERENCES

Chai, Alan; Alta Campbell; and Patrick J. Spain. *Hoover's Handbook of World Business 1993*, Austin, Texas: The Reference Press, 1993.

Dictionary of International Trade, New York: John Wiley & Sons, Inc., 1994.

"A Disquieting New Agenda for Trade," *The Economist*, July 16, 1994, pp. 55-56.

Edwards, Sebastian. "Latin American Economic Integration: A New Perspective on an Old Dream," *The World Economy*, July 1993, pp. 317-338.

Europe 1992: The Facts, London: Department of Trade and Industry and the Central Office of Information, 1989.

Goto, Fumihiro; Kazutomo Irie; and Akihiko Soyama. *The Current Situation and Prospects for Regional Economic Integration: Asia-Pacific Free Trade Area Proposals and Japan's Choice*, Tokyo: Research Institute of International Trade and Industry, Ministry of International Trade and Industry, 1990.

Harbracht, Douglas; Owen Ullmann; Bill Javetski; and Geri Smith. "Finally, GATT May Fly," *Business Week*, December 20, 1993, pp. 36-37.

Jackson, John H. "Regional Trade Blocs and the GATT," *The World Economy*, March 1993, pp. 121-132.

"NAFTA is Not Alone," *The Economist*, June 18, 1994, pp 47-48.

Sapir, Andre. "Regionalism and the New Theory of International Trade: Do the Bells Toll for the GATT? A European Outlook," *The World Economy*, July 1993, pp. 423-438.

Seib, Gerald F. "Debate on GATT Recalls NAFTA Battle In Many Ways, but the Passion Is Gone," *Wall Street Journal*, July 14, 1994, p. A12.

The World Bank Atlas 1994, Washington, D.C.: The World Bank, 1994.

ENDNOTES

1. The phrase GATT Code of Conduct is synonymous with Multinational Trade Negotiations Code, or MTN Code.
2. These stages were developed by Bela Balassa and are the most frequently cited. (See Goto, Irie, and Soyama, *The Current Situation and Prospects for Regional Economic Integration.*)
3. The United States has requested that Mexico be permitted to join APEC, encouraging economic relations among Pacific and Asia countries and all members of NAFTA.
4. Chile elected not to participate in the relaunching of the Andean Group in 1990.
5. Mexico is Latin America's second largest economy.

BIBLIOGRAPHY

"A Disquieting New Agenda for Trade," *The Economist*, July 16, 1994, pp. 55–56.

"Agreement Brings Down Banking Barriers," *Euromoney* supplement, January 1993.

"Banks Act to Boost Their Capital Bases (Mexico)," *Euromoney supplement*, January 1994, pp. 22–24.

Barkema, Alan. "The North American Free Trade Agreement: What Is At Stake for U.S. Agriculture?" *Independent Banker*, February 1993, pp. 18–26.

"The Big One (Pemex)," *The Economist*, January 8, 1994, pp. 66–67.

Blanden, Michael. "Make Them Pay (Project Finance)," *The Banker*, January 1994, pp. 66–68.

"Booming Banks Must Stay Vigilant," *Mexico, Euromoney* supplement, January 1993, pp. 2–15.

Bradbury, Nicholas. "Playing Lean and Mean in Canada," *Euromoney*, November 1993, pp. 92–94.

"Calm After the Storm," *Mexico, Euromoney* supplement, January 1993, pp. 19–22.

Carroll, Paul B. "Mexico Family to Pay Ransom for Executive," *Wall Street Journal*, August 3, 1994, p. A5.

Chai, Alan, Alta Campbell, and Patrick J. Spain, editors. *Hoover's Handbook of World Business 1993*, Austin, Texas: The Reference Press, Inc., 1993.

"Debt and Equity Boom Brews as Mexico Awaits An Upgrade," *Mexico, Euromoney* supplement, January 1994, pp. 2–6.

Dunford, Campbell, editor. *The Handbook of International Trade Finance* New York: Woodhead–Faulkner/Simon & Schuster, 1991.

Dyer, Geoff. "Foreigners' Vote of Confidence in Mexican Bonds," *Euromoney*, September 1993, pp. 299–305.

Edwards, Sebastian. "Latin American Economic Integration: A New Perspective on an Old Dream," *The World Economy*, July 1993, pp. 317–338.

Emerging Markets Borrowers Guide, Euromoney supplement, September 1993.

"Emerging–Market Indicators," *The Economist*, March 26, 1994, p. 132.

Europe 1992: The Facts, London: Department of Trade and Industry and the Central Office of Information, 1989.

Exporting to Mexico, Hong King: Trade Media Ltd., 1992.

Exporting to Canada, Hong Kong: Trade Media Ltd., 1992.

Fink, Ronald. "Legions of the Lost Decade," *Financial World*, July 7, 1992, pp. 52–54.

Fink, Ronald. "Mañana? Gigante, Mexico's Most Ubiquitous Retailer, Is Betting on Free Markets to Produce a Consumption Boom," *Financial World*, September 1, 1992, pp. 60–63.

Fitch, Thomas. *Dictionary of Banking Terms*, New York: Barron's, 1990.

Foreign Trade Barriers, Washington, D.C.: Office of the United States Trade Representative, 1993.

Gandy, Tony. "The Best of Both Worlds (Technology)," *The Banker*, November 1993, pp. 88–92.

Globalization of Canada's Financial Markets, Ottawa, Canada: Canadian Government Publishing Centre, 1989.

Goto, Fumihiro; Kazutomo Irie; and Akihiko Soyama. *The Current Situation and Prospects for Regional Economic Integration: Asia–Pacific Free Trade Area Proposals and Japan's Choice*, Tokyo: Research Institute of International Trade and Industry, Ministry of International Trade and Industry, 1990.

Gramm, Phil. "Mexico Needs Trade, Not Aid," *North American International Business*, April 1991, p. 73.

Guide to Currencies," *Euromoney* supplements, 1993 and 1994.

Harbracht, Douglas; Owen Ullmann; Bill Javetski; and Geri Smith. "Finally, GATT May Fly," *Business Week*, December 20, 1993, pp. 36–37.

Jackson, John H. "Regional Trade Blocs and the GATT," *The World Economy*, March 1993, pp. 121–132.

Javetski, Bill, Stephen Baker and Ruth Pearson. "Can Mexico Embrace the U.S.—At Arm's Length?" *Business Week*, May 20, 1991, p. 63.

Johnson, Hazel. *Financial Institutions and Markets: A Global Perspective*, New York: McGraw–Hill, 1993.

Kensinger, John W. and John D. Martin. "Project Finance: Raising Money the Old–Fashioned Way," *New Developments in Commercial Banking*, Donald Chew, editor, Cambridge, Massachusetts: Blackwell Finance, 1991.

Kessler, Judd L. "How Mexican Laws Affect Foreign Business," *Export Today*, January/February 1993, pp. 42–45.

King, Paul. "New Law Enables EDC to Cultivate Fresh Assets," *Euromoney* supplement, September 1993, p. 31.

Kurtzman, Joel. *The Death of Money: How the Electronic Economy Has Destabilized the World's Markets and Created Financial Chaos*, New York: Simon & Schuster, 1993.

Laver, Ross. "Open for Business: Mexico Seeks Foreign Investors," *MaClean's*, March 26, 1990, p. 45.

Laver, Ross. "Mexico Fights Back," *MaClean's*, March 26, 1990, pp. 40–44.

Leuchter, Miriam. "NY Banks Rush to Expand in Mexico," *New York Times*, July 11, 1994.

Lipin, Steven. "Eight Banks Form Clearinghouse to Cut Cost of Foreign–Exchange Transactions," *Wall Street Journal*, August 1, 1994, pp. A2 & A4.

Maggs, John. "Pro–NAFTA Reception to Aim at New Members of Congress," *Journal of Commerce* (New York), February 24, 1993.

Mariscal, Jorge O. "Latin America Investment Strategy Highlights," Investment Research, Goldman Sachs, September 1993.

Marray, Michael. "The Best Brokers for Latin America," *Euromoney*, December 1993, pp. 93–100.

Marray, Michael. "Mexico Battles to Build Derivatives," *Euromoney*, July 1993, pp. 87–88.

Marray, Michael. "Mortgage–Backed Market Coming Next," *Euromoney*, November 1993, p. 22.

Martin, Gary. "Gonzalez Blasts Trade Pact, *San Antonio Express–News*, February 23, 1993.

Messner, Stephen C. "Canada: NAFTA's Other Half," *Export Today*, October 1993, pp. 12–16.

Messner, Stephen C. "South America: The Comeback Continent," *Export Today*, November/December 1993, pp. 40–44.

"Mexico," *Guide to Domestic Bond Markets, Euromoney* supplement, 1993, pp. 73–76.

"Mexico's Finamex Planning to Draw Investment in Japan," *Tokyo Business Today*, January/February 1993, pp. 50–51.

Moffett, Matt. "Mexico's New Peso May Look Like Less But It's Worth More," *Wall Street Journal*, January 8, 1993.

"NAFTA is Not Alone," *The Economist*, June 18, 1994, pp 47–48.

Newman, Gray and Anna Szterenfeld. *Business International's Guide to Doing Business in Mexico*, New York: McGraw–Hill, 1993.

"A Peach or a Raspberry from Mexico," *The Economist*, July 2, 1994, p. 63.

North American Free Trade Agreement," Chapters 11 and 14 and Annex VII, Washington: U.S. Printing Office, 1993.

"On Their Toes (Mexico)," *The Economist*, January 29, 1994, pp. 79–80.

Ortega, Bob. "Wal–Mart Is Slowed by Problems of Price and Culture in Mexico," *Wall Street Journal*, July 19, 1994, pp. A1 & A5.

Palmeri, Christopher. "Best of Times, Worst of Times," *Forbes*, June 20, 1994, pp. 198–199.

Peagam, Norman. "Appetite for Latin Deals Increases," *Latin American Trade Finance, Euromoney* supplement, May 1994, pp. 144–151.

Peagram, Norman. "Kimberly–Clark Creates a First for Mexico," *Euromoney*, March 1993, pp. 151–152.

Rehberg, Virginia. "Letters of Credit: Cracking the Code," *Export Today*, September 1991, pp. 21–23.

Robinson, Danielle. "Mexico's Big Two Fight for Dominance," *Euromoney*, March 1994, pp. 89–96.

Rosenberg, Jerry M. *Dictionary of International Trade*, New York: John Wiley & Sons, 1994.

Sapir, André. "Regionalism and the New Theory of International Trade: Do the Bells Toll for the GATT? A European Outlook," *The World Economy*, July 1993, pp. 423–438.

Sauvé, Pierre and Brenda Gonzalez–Hermosillo. "Implications of the NAFTA for Canadian Financial Institutions," *C.D. Howe Institute Commentary*, April 1993, pp. 1–21.

Sczudlo, Raymond S. "NAFTA: Opportunities Abound for U.S. and Canadian Financial Institutions," *The Bankers Magazine*, July/August 1993, pp. 28–33.

Seib, Gerald F. "Debate on GATT Recalls NAFTA Battle In Many Ways, but the Passion Is Gone," *Wall Street Journal*, July 14, 1994, p. A12.

Shepperd, Rosie. "Deregulation to Shake Up Mexico's Fund Managers," *International Bond Investor, Euromoney* supplement, September 1993, pp. 17–21.

Siegle, Candace. "Crap Shoot (Exporting to Mexico)," *World Trade,* November 1993, pp. 64–66.

Smith, Geri. "Mexico's No–Frills Mogul," *Business Week,* March 7, 1994, pp. 62–64.

Smith, Geri. "The Remaking of an Oil Giant, 1993," *Business Week,* August 16, 1993, pp. 84–85.

Smith, Geri, Stephen Baker, and William Glasgall. "Mexico: Will Economic Reform Survive the Turmoil?" *Business Week,* April 11, 1994, pp. 247–27.

Smith, Geri, Suzanne Woolley, and Chris Roush. "Why Insurers Are Splashing Across the Rio Grande," *Business Week,* August 9, 1993, p. 68.

Smith, Geri and Wendy Zellner. "The Gringo Banks are Drooling," *Business Week,* September 13, 1993, p. 84.

"The Spreading Maple Leaf," *The Economist,* January 15, 1994, pp. 68–69.

Talmor, Sharona. "After You (Technology)," *The Banker,* March 1994, pp. 74–76.

Talmor, Sharona. "Step–by–step (Technology)," *The Banker,* January 1994, pp. 71–75.

Talmor, Sharona. "Trade Partners Get Hooked Up (Technology)," *The Banker,* February 1994, pp. 65–67.

Templin, Neal. "Mexican Industrial Belt is Beginning to Form As Car Makers Expand," *Wall Street Journal,* July 10, 1994, pp. A1 and A10.

Texas Consortium Report on Free Trade: Final Report, Austin, Texas: Texas Department of Commerce, Business Development Division, October 1991.

Torres, Craig. "Mexico's Natural–Gas Reserves Remain Untapped, While Its Fuel Needs Grow," *Wall Street Journal,* July 14, 1994, p. A6.

Torres, Craig and Thomas T. Vogel, Jr. "Some Mutual Funds Wield Growing Clout in Developing Countries," *Wall Street Journal,* June 14, 1994, pp. A1 and A4.

Toulin, Alan. "Making Changes to Fabric of Canada," *The Financial Post* (Toronto), January 2, 1993.

Tugendhat, Eduardo. "The Changing Mexican Banking Scene," *Export Today*, July/August 1993, pp. 18–20.

U.S. Exports to Mexico: A State-by-State Overview 1987–1991, U.S. Department of Commerce, 1992.

Ullmann, Owen, Pete Engardio, Peter Galuszka, and Bill Hinchberger. "The Global Greenback," *Business Week*, August 9, 1993, pp. 40–44.

"Under Recession's Hammer: Auctioneer Clears Failed Businesses to the Wall," *The Hamilton Spectator*, January 2, 1993.

Verzariu, Pompiliu. *International Countertrade: A Guide for Managers and Executives*, Washington, D.C.: U.S. Department of Commerce, International Trade Administration, 1992.

Verzariu, Pompiliu and Paula Mitchell. *International Countertrade: Individual Country Practices*, Washington, D.C.: U.S. Department of Commerce, International Trade Administration, 1992.

"Viva NAFTA," *The Economist*, August 21, 1993, pp. 21–22.

Welch, John H. and William C. Gruben. "A Brief History of the Mexican Financial System," *Financial Industry Studies* (Federal Reserve Bank of Dallas), October 1993, pp. 1–10.

Wood, Nancy, "Reopening the Trade Winds," *MaClean's*, March 18, 1991, pp. 42–43.

World Bank Atlas 1994, Washington, D.C.: The World Bank, 1994.

Young, Leah R. "What Insurance Do You Need?" *Export Today*, February 1994, pp. 12–16.

Zecher, Joshua. "Banamex Cuts the Risk Designer–Style," *Wall Street Technology*, Vol. 11, No. 11 (April 1994), pp. 46–50.

Index

About the Author

Dr. Hazel J. Johnson is a Professor of Finance at the University of Louisville. She has worked as a C.P.A. and auditor for a Big Six accounting firm, as a bank financial analyst and as manager of internal audit for a national insurance company. She was formerly on the finance faculty of Georgetown University.

Her research has been published widely in the United States and abroad. She has acted as a consultant to more than 35 of the largest U.S. banks and as an advisor to the International Trade Subcommittee of the U.S. House of Representatives Banking Committee.

She has most recently published *The New Global Banker: What Every U.S. Bank Must Know to Complete Internationally* (Probus, 1993) *The Banking Keiretsu* (Probus, 1993), *The Bank Valuation Handbook: A Market-Based Approach to Valuing a Bank* (Probus, 1993), *Banking Regulation Today* (Probus, 1994), *Global Banking Today* (Probus, 1994), *Bank Asset/Liability Management (Probus, 1994).*